Instant Access 2000 Answers ...

W9-CDV-459

For Navigating in Access

To Do This	Select This	Or Click This	Or Press This
Create a new database	File | New		CTRL-N
Open an existing database	File | Open		CTRL-O
Print the selected object	File | Print		CTRL-P
Save the selected object	File | Save		CTRL-S
Save the selected object to a new name	File | Save As		F12
Save the selected object as a Web page	File | Export		
Send the selected object via e-mail	File | Send To		
Delete the selected object	Edit | Delete		DEL
Bring the Database window to the front	Window | database name: Database		F11
Exit from Access	File | Exit		ALT+F4

For Working in Design View

To Do This	Select This	Or Click This	Or Press This
Select a form	Edit | Select Form		CTRL-R
Select a report	Edit | Select Report		CTRL-R
Switch from Design to Form View	View | Form View		F5
Display the Field List	View | Field List		
Display the Toolbox	View | Toolbox		
Show properties for the selected object	View | Properties		

For Finding and Replacing Data

To Do This	Select This	Or Click This	Or Press This
Show the Find dialog box	Edit | Find		CTRL-F
Show the Replace dialog box	Edit | Replace		CTRL-H

For Creating and Designing Tables

To Do This	Do This
Create a table	Press F11, click the Tables button in the Database window, and click New.
Define a relationship	Close any open tables, press F11, and click the Relationships button on the Toolbar. To add tables to the Relationships window, use the Show Table dialog box that appears and drag the field you want to relate from one table to the related field in the other table.
Add or change indexes for a table	Press F11, right-click the desired table in the Database window, and choose Design View. Then, choose View | Indexes. In the Indexes dialog box that appears, enter a name for the index, choose a field, and choose Ascending or Descending (or make any desired changes to your existing indexes).

For Sorting Data

To Do This	Do This
Sort records within a datasheet	Click in the desired field of the datasheet, then click the Sort Ascending button (to sort in ascending order) or the Sort Descending button (to sort in descending order).
Sort records in a form	Click within the field of the form to be used for the sort, then click the Sort Ascending button (to sort in ascending order) or the Sort Descending button (to sort in descending order).

For Creating Forms and Reports

To Do This	Do This
Create a default form	Press F11, select a table or query in the Database window, then click the AutoForm button in the toolbar.
Create a form using the wizards	Press F11, select a table or query in the Database window, then click the arrow at the right of the AutoForm button in the toolbar, and choose Form from the menu. In the next dialog box, choose Form Wizard, and click OK.
Create a default report	Press F11, select a table or query in the Database window, then click the arrow at the right of the AutoForm button in the toolbar, and choose AutoReport from the menu.
Create a report using the wizards	Press F11, select a table or query in the Database window, then click the arrow at the right of the AutoForm button in the toolbar, and choose Report from the menu. In the next dialog box, choose Report Wizard, and click OK.

Access 2000 Answers!

About the Authors...

Edward Jones is a database applications development analyst and best-selling author whose books have sold over one million copies.

Jarel M. Jones is a Web designer, Visual Basic programmer, and coauthor of *Access 97 Answers! Certified Tech Support*.

Access 2000
Answers!

Edward Jones and Jarel M. Jones

Osborne/**McGraw-Hill**

Berkeley • New York • St. Louis • San Francisco
Auckland • Bogotá • Hamburg • London
Madrid • Mexico City • Milan • Montreal
New Delhi • Panama City • Paris • São Paulo
Singapore • Sydney • Tokyo • Toronto

Osborne/**McGraw-Hill**
2600 Tenth Street
Berkeley, California 94710
U.S.A.

For information on translations or book distributors outside the U.S.A., or to arrange bulk purchase discounts for sales promotions, premiums, or fund-raisers, please contact Osborne/**McGraw-Hill** at the above address.

Access 2000 Answers!

1234567890 DOC DOC 90198765432109

ISBN 0-07-211850-4

Publisher Brandon A. Nordin	**Proofreader** Carol Burbo
Associate Publisher and Editor-in-Chief Scott Rogers	**Indexer** David Heiret
Acquisitions Editor Joanne Cuthbertson	**Computer Designers** Roberta Steele Michelle Galicia
Project Editor Emily Rader	**Illustrators** Robert Hansen Beth Young Brian Wells
Editorial Assistant Stephane Thomas	
Technical Editor Mark Hall	**Series Design** Michelle Galicia
Copy Editor William F. McManus	

To Judie Jones and Nikki Jones, for just being there.

Jarel Jones

To all of my family at Inner Light, Washington, D.C.

Edward Jones-Mack

Contents @ a Glance

Contents

Acknowledgments

We would like to thank the staff at Stream International, who willingly committed much time and knowledge to this effort. Many of the support specialists spent untold hours searching the Stream data banks for the top questions and answers and reviewing manuscript and pages. Without all of their hard work, this book would not be the encompassing source of answers that it is. We would like to personally thank each of the following people for their assistance: Mike Blake, Joel Tanzi, Pat Alves, Howard Lotis, Paul Thobideau, Bob Pshefko, Bonnie Brown, and Jim Tiner.

The staff at Osborne was also a vital part of this book. Everyone worked hard to help us meet the important deadlines necessary in bringing this book to market. We would like to extend special thanks to Joanne Cuthbertson, Acquisitions Editor, for giving us the chance to take on this project and for those important suggestions that helped us refine the book's structure; Scott Rogers, Associate Publisher and Editor-In-Chief, for his work in bringing the overall series concept in cooperation with Stream International to reality; Emily Rader, Project Editor, who managed the editorial phases of the project; Stephane Thomas, Editorial Assistant, who helped organize all the components of the project; Mark Hall, Technical Reviewer, for an outstanding tech edit; and all of the Production staff, who contributed in ways too numerous to count toward the goal of making this book the best source of technical support available.

Introduction

There is no good time to have a problem with your computer or the software you are using. You are anxious to complete the task you started and do not have time to fumble through a manual looking for an answer that is probably not there anyway. You can forget about the option of a free support call, since most software vendors now charge as much as $30 or more to answer a single question.

Access 2000 Answers! can provide the solutions to all of your Access questions. It contains the most frequently asked Access questions, along with their solutions to get you back on track quickly. The questions and answers have been formulated with the assistance of Stream International, the world's largest provider of third-party technical support. Since Stream answers over one million calls a month from users just like you, odds are high that your problem has plagued others in the past and is already part of their data bank. This book is the next best thing to having a Stream International expert at the desk right next to you. The help you need is available seven days a week, any time you have a problem.

Access 2000 Answers! is organized into 16 chapters. Each chapter contains questions and answers on specific areas of Access. With this topical organization, you can read through questions and answers on particular topics to familiarize yourself with them before troubles actually occur. An excellent index makes it easy for you to find what you need even if you are uncertain which chapter would cover the solution.

Throughout the book you will also find elements that help you sail smoothly through Access tasks, whether you are a novice or a veteran user.

Chapter 1

Top 10 Frequently Asked Questions

Answer Topics!

Top 10 Frequently Asked Questions @ a Glance

This chapter presents solutions to the problems that have prompted the ten most frequently asked questions (FAQs) from users regarding Access 2000. Thousands of users have encountered these problems. They received expert help from Stream Corporation, and now you can, too!

You might never have to ask these questions if you review this chapter now, because if any of these problems arise later, you'll know what to do.

1. How does Access 2000 handle different version formats?

Access 2000's conversion lets you either convert the database to Access 2000 format or open and enable the database for use with the version of Access that created it. This allows environments running multiple versions of Access to continue using multiple versions. Access 2000 will convert a database into only one version prior to Access 2000, which is Access 97. To perform this conversion, choose Tools | Database Utilities | Convert Database | To Prior Access Database Version. You then are prompted for a filename and a location in which to save the converted database—you can't use the same name as the Access 2000 version of the database if you save it in the same file folder. You can use the same filename, however, if you change the location (the folder) where you save it.

Also, be aware that Access 97 doesn't support Data Access Pages, at least not in the same way that Access 2000 does. To support Data Access Pages (called Active Server Pages in Access 97), Access 97 requires that you install other software, such as Microsoft Personal Web Server or Microsoft Internet Information Server, as well as Active Server Pages (downloadable from Microsoft's Web site). The pages are not stored directly in the database, so you can't view or manipulate them in the same way as in Access 2000.

This technology was still new at the time Access 97 was released, and many of the bugs hadn't been worked out, so the process of creating these pages is both more complex and less stable than in Access 2000. Also, any code you have in your database might not function properly immediately after you convert it, because it refers to objects or files not stored on your system, such as functions that come from other databases or libraries. This can complicate the process of converting the database, and no easy way exists to work around it. You may need to fix the code as it breaks, line by line.

2. I've converted my Access 2000 database to an earlier version, but when I use it in Access 97, the code window opens and a message appears, saying "Can't find project or library." What's going on?

Access 2000, by default, installs the library files, called *dynamic link libraries (DLLs)*, in a different directory than the one used by default in Access 97. These DLLs are used by Visual Basic for Applications (VBA) when running code in your database. This installation can be a common problem when saving the database to the previous version of Access. To solve this problem, go into the Module window (either you will already be there when the code halts or you can open a module, new or existing, by clicking the Modules button in the Database window and then clicking New or highlighting an existing module and clicking Design) and choose Tools | References, which lists all the libraries Access can refer to when running code. Within that list, you will see an entry marked "MISSING:" followed by the library name (such as MISSING: Microsoft Data Access 3.5 Object Library). Uncheck the box beside this reference and click OK. This forces Access to look elsewhere for that library, and Access creates a new reference to the library after it locates it.

3. I see a new item on the Help menu called Detect and Repair. What does it do?

This option performs a check of the Office 2000 program files that is more thorough than the self-checking that each Office 2000 application normally does on startup. When you choose Help | Detect and Repair, Office scans the entire application for any possible problems. To repair any problems it finds, Office may ask you for the source you used to install Office, such as the CD-ROM, or ask you to close certain features or programs you have open.

4. The menus in Access 2000 applications are changing themselves on me! What's going on?

All Office 2000 programs use intelligent menu technology, a feature that Microsoft calls *personalized menus*. This feature causes the most recently used commands to move to the top of the menus. If you find this feature annoying, you can turn it off. In Access (or in any Office 2000 application), choose View | Toolbars | Customize. In the dialog box that appears, click the Options tab and then remove the check mark beside the Menus Show Recently Used Commands First option.

5. Can I import data from Outlook?

You can import data into an Access 2000 table from a number of MAPI (Messaging Application Programming Interface) files and address books in your Outlook profile, including your Personal Address Book folder and your Contacts folder. To do this, choose File | Get External Data | Import. When the Import dialog box appears, select Outlook under Files of Type at the bottom of the dialog box, and click Import. This launches the Import Exchange/Outlook Wizard, which asks from which MAPI file or address book you would like the data to be imported. After you select the address book you want to import, the Wizard shows you a preview of what the data will look like, and allows you to set some guidelines as to how it will be imported, such as which fields to skip and what data type to use. Access assigns field names based on the source you used in Outlook.

6. My Office applications are set to look and work the way that's best for me. Will installing Office 2000 overwrite all my settings?

The Office 2000 Setup program does its best to migrate your user settings. It compares the original default settings against your current settings, to analyze the differences and migrate them to Office 2000. Settings that it detects as unchanged from the original defaults are replaced with the new, Office 2000 defaults for those settings.

 7. My company gave me Office 2000 to install, but I can't find Access 2000 on my computer. What happened?

You may have been given the wrong edition of Office 2000. Office 2000 Premium Edition and Professional Edition include Access 2000. Office 2000 Standard Edition and Small Business Edition do not.

 8. I created a Data Access Page using the Page Wizard, but I can't add new records to it. Why?

Two reasons exist for why a Data Access Page might be read-only. The first is that you added grouping levels to the page. The wizard for creating Data Access Pages adds a grouping level by default, so it can be easy to breeze by this step and not even notice it. To prevent this, remove the default grouping level before you move to the next step in the wizard. A grouping level adds a filter of sorts to the page, and Data Access Pages with grouping are used more as a reporting tool than as a data entry tool.

The other reason is that the record source on which you based the Data Access Page is nonupdateable. This usually occurs when you base the Data Access Page on a nonupdateable query. Check to see whether the query is updateable; it likely isn't. You may need to modify the query to make it updateable if the join that you are using between tables does not allow you to add new records.

9. I turned on both my Standard and Formatting toolbars, but see only one toolbar. What's wrong?

Even though you may have selected to display both toolbars, by choosing View | Toolbars, a new Office 2000 default feature combines them to give you more space to display

objects on screen. To turn off this feature, choose View |
Toolbars | Customize. In the dialog box that appears, click
the Options tab and remove the check mark beside the
Standard and Formatting Toolbars Share One Row option.

10. How can I force Access to use a four-digit year format in my date/time values?

Access is fully Year 2000–compliant, which means that it can
properly recognize dates from 2000 onward. In earlier versions
of Access, you had to be careful about how you entered dates in
your records, because when you used two-digit year formats,
such as 2/4/88, Access read dates with years of 00 to 29 as 2000
to 2029. Thus, if you referred to dates prior to 1930, you had to
use a four-digit year format, to make Access know that you
meant 1900 to 1929. In other words, instead of using the
format 5/1/29 for May 1, 1929, you had to format it so that it
displayed 5/1/1929. Often, this was caught only after a lot of
data had already been entered, and fixing it involved using an
update query with a Format function, to format the dates into
a four-digit year, and then fixing them manually.

Fortunately, Access 2000 provides an easy way to force
users to make use of four-digit formatting: choose Tools |
Options, click the General tab, and then put a check mark in
the appropriate box under Use Four-Digit Year Formatting.
The boxes are for This Database and for All Databases. If you
want the change to be made only in the open database, select
This Database; otherwise, select All Databases.

Chapter 2

Access Basics

Answer Topics!

Access Basics @ a Glance

Although Access is a powerful database management program, it is designed to be easy to use. Many of the problems encountered with the package occur as a result of the vast array of features and the new ways Access provides to use all the graphical features Windows offers.

Even in simple tasks, such as installation and basic database creation, numerous potential problem areas exist. Some users experience difficulty installing Access on networks. Others find that a database becomes unmanageable with graphics. This chapter provides the answers to these and other basic questions, enabling you to overcome these problems and focus on more-advanced options.

The questions to which you'll find answers in this chapter pertain to the following topics:

Installation helps you with specifications and problems that arise when installing Access.

Opening and Converting Files provides information on opening and converting data between Access 2000 and other database software, including earlier versions of Access.

Managing the User Interface helps you control the overall appearance of Access as you work with different databases.

Security answers questions about Access security, the methods used to control rights to the data used by multiple users.

Troubleshooting provides information relating to error messages and other problems that may arise in regard to the general operation of Access.

The Basics of Access

One of the more challenging aspects of starting to use Access is learning the terms and concepts that refer to organizing your data. Whether you are upgrading from another database management program or using a database manager for the first time, you'll find that the following definitions will help you to work with the features of Access:

● **Database** A single file that contains the various Access objects—tables, queries, forms, reports, macros, and modules—that you work with on a regular basis. When you open a database, the Database window appears, as shown here, containing the objects in the database. You use the seven buttons at the left side of the window to choose which objects currently appear in the window.

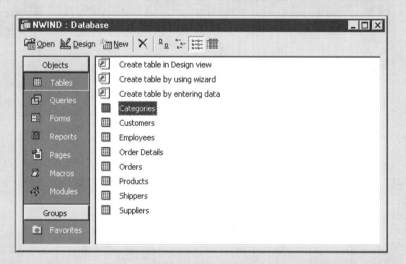

● **Tables** The containers that store your data. Tables are arranged in a row-and-column format, similar to that of spreadsheets. Each column, or *field*, holds a specific type of information, such as last names or phone numbers. Each row, or *record*, holds all the information related to a single entry, such as the last name, first name, address, city, state, ZIP code, and phone number for a particular customer. With relational database managers such as Access, a database often includes several different tables that contain related data. For example, a database designed to track videos rented from a small video rental store might have one table for customers and another table for the names of the tapes rented by those customers.

- **Queries**   Access objects that ask questions about the data in your database. Based on the way that a query is designed, it can retrieve and combine data from different tables in the database. For example, you might design a query to tell you how many customers have overdue accounts, or how many employees have been with the company for five years or more. Queries can also perform actions on groups of data, such as updating or deleting a certain group of records.

- **Forms**   Windows that provide an easy way to view existing records or add new records to the tables in your database. In Access, you can create forms that enable you to work with a single table or with multiple tables simultaneously, and you can print forms as well as display them.

- **Reports**   Access objects that are designed to show data, like forms, but are designed primarily to be printed, and can't be used for data entry.

- **Pages**   A special type of form that lets users view and edit Access tables using a Web browser.

- **Macros**   Stored sequences of actions in Access. They can be used to automate many everyday tasks and to simplify your work in Access.

- **Modules**   Procedures written in Visual Basic for Applications (VBA), the programming language underlying Access. By using VBA, you can write program code that accomplishes specialized tasks not otherwise possible with Access macros.

INSTALLATION

I reinstalled Access to fix corrupted program files, but I still have the same problems. What's wrong?

A reinstallation of Access won't fix corrupted files. Instead, you need to uninstall Access and then reinstall it. When you reinstall Access over an existing version of the program, the Setup routine detects the existing copy of Access and simply replaces any missing files. Hence, any corrupted program files are still there. To remove the existing Access program files completely, run Access Setup and choose Remove All. Then, reinstall Access by using the Setup program. If you know precisely which program files are corrupted, you can delete those files, start Access Setup, and choose Reinstall to replace them.

Caution: *If you are tempted to remove Access by dragging the folder from where the program is stored into the Recycle Bin (or by deleting the program's directory under DOS), don't. Many of the files used by Access aren't stored in the directory with the program files. Using Setup removes all the Access program files regardless of their location.*

What are the hardware requirements for installing Access 2000?

To run Access 2000, you need the following:

- A PC with a Pentium 75MHz or better processor, running Windows 95, Windows 98, or Windows NT Workstation 4 with Service Pack 3 or later.

- A PC with 16MB of memory if using Windows 95 or 98, or 32MB of memory if using NT Workstation.

- At least 100MB disk space. Hard disk space requirements vary widely, depending on how many components of Access (and of any other Office 2000 programs) you install. To avoid running short, at least this much disk space is advisable.

- A VGA or higher-resolution video adapter (Super VGA recommended), and a Microsoft mouse (or compatible) pointing device.

Although these are the "official" requirements stated by Microsoft, don't expect stellar performance from a 75MHz Pentium with just 16MB of RAM. If you plan to use multiple programs simultaneously, consider installing at least 32MB of RAM under Windows 95 or Windows 98. If you're using Windows NT, be aware that you can't run Access 2000 on versions of NT Workstation prior to version 4.

 Can I use a variety of language conventions for my database?

No, you cannot. The language conventions that Access uses for currency, list separators, date and time formats, and other settings are not controlled by Access. They are set by the options in the Windows Control Panel. These same settings are used by all Windows applications. Because you can select only one language setting at a time in Windows, you can use only one set of language conventions at a time in Access.

 What's the maximum size for an Access database?

In theory, an Access database is limited to 1GB in size. But, because tables in a database can be linked to tables stored in other Access databases or to tables stored as external files, the total amount of data is limited only by available disk space.

 How do I install Access 2000 on a network file server?

You want to run the Administrative installation of Access, which provides the various options for installation on a network. You do this by including the /A option after the word *Setup*. Insert the CD-ROM or Program Disk 1 in the drive. From the Windows desktop, choose <u>S</u>tart | <u>R</u>un. In the Run dialog box that appears, enter *x:***setup** /**A** (where *x* is the letter of your CD-ROM or diskette drive).

! ***Caution:*** *Network installations can be involved and potentially troublesome. If you are not the Network Administrator, you need to contact the Network Administrator before attempting this.*

 Can I install Access 2000 simultaneously on a machine that has an older version of Access installed?

You can install and run multiple versions of Access on the same computer, as long as each version of Access is installed in its own folder (directory). If you are going to run Access 2000 on a machine with an earlier version of Access installed and you want to keep the earlier version of Access, be sure to install Access 2000 in a separate folder. During the installation process, you must click the Customize icon that appears in the Setup dialog box. Then, when you reach the Removing Previous Versions screen, you must insert a check mark in the check box labeled Keep These Programs, to avoid the automatic removal of the older version of Access.

Remember, too, that Windows 95 associates (or "links") the .mdb extension used by all Access databases to the last version of Access you installed. So, double-clicking an MDB file in Windows Explorer or in My Computer launches the last version of Access that was installed. If you want to change the version of Access that's associated with MDB files, you need to change the file association under Windows; search Windows Help under Associating for details on how to do this.

I installed Access 2000 and now my old applications, written in the run-time version of Access, don't work. What happened?

When you run the Setup program for Access 2000, at some point you are asked whether you want to remove the components for older versions of Access. (If you installed Access as part of Office 2000, you are asked whether you want to remove components for earlier versions of Microsoft Office.) If you answer Yes to either of these questions, the Setup routine for Access 2000 deletes certain files that are used by applications written in the run-time versions of Access 2, Access 95, or Access 97. To resolve this problem, you have to reinstall your custom, run-time applications. Rerun Setup for your custom applications and click Reinstall in the Maintenance Program dialog box.

My Access 2000 installation didn't create a Workgroup Administrator icon for administrating workgroups on a network. Why not?

Unlike earlier versions of Access, Access 2000 does *not* automatically create a Workgroup Administrator icon for the Windows desktop. This behavior is intentional; Microsoft intends for you to manage workgroup security from within Access. But if you liked doing things the old way with a separate icon, you can still add one to your Programs menu on the Windows 95 taskbar, by following these steps:

1. Click the Start button, and choose Settings | Taskbar.
2. In the Taskbar Properties dialog box that appears, click the Start Menu Programs tab.
3. Click the Advanced button.
4. In the Explorer window that opens, double-click the Programs folder to show its contents.
5. Choose File | New | Shortcut.
6. In the Create Shortcut dialog box that appears, click Browse.
7. Find the file titled Wrkgadm.exe. If you accepted the default options during installation, the file is located in the Office/1033 folder.
8. Select Wrkgadm.exe and click Open.
9. Click Next.
10. Enter the name you want to assign to the shortcut, such as Access Workgroup Administrator, and then click Finish.
11. Close the Explorer window and the Taskbar Properties dialog box.
12. Click the Start button and choose Programs. You'll see the icon for the Workgroup Administrator added to your Programs menu.

OPENING AND CONVERTING FILES

 Can I open an Access 2000 database in an earlier version of Access?

You can't directly open an Access 2000 database in an earlier version of Access, because Access 2000 uses a file format that's different from the one used by all earlier versions. But you can save an Access 2000 database in Access 97 format, by opening the database and then choosing Tools | Database Utilities | Convert Database | To Prior Database Version. You can also use the File | Export option to export tables to a data format that can be imported by an earlier version of Access. If you are faced with a situation in which users of different versions of Access are on a network and must all use the same database, the following solution exists:

1. Store the tables in a database that's created in the earliest version of Access you are using on the network.

2. Create a "front-end" database in each version of Access that contains the queries, forms, and reports (but no tables) you need.

3. From within each of these "front-end" databases, attach to the tables that are stored in the database created in the earliest version of Access.

How many network users can have the same database open simultaneously?

On a network, up to 255 users can have the same database open at the same time.

Can I open or convert databases from earlier versions of Access?

When you want to work with databases created in earlier versions of Access, you have two choices:

 Open the database and work with the data it contains. This enables you to make changes to the data stored in the tables and use the other objects (the queries, forms, reports, and macros), but you can't make design changes to any of the objects in the database.

 Convert the database into the file format used by Access 2000. This enables you to make any changes you wish to the database. However, you can't open the converted database in an earlier version of Access.

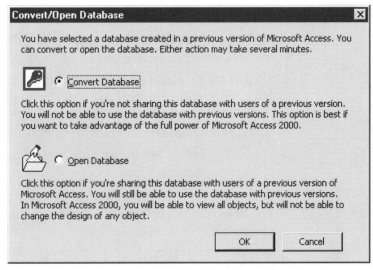

Figure 2-1 The Convert/Open Database dialog box

To open or convert a database from an earlier version, choose File | Open Database and select a database in the Open dialog box that appears. The next dialog box that appears, as shown in Figure 2-1, gives you a choice of converting or opening the database. If you click Convert Database and click OK, Access converts the older database into Access 2000 file format. If you click Open Database and click OK, Access opens the database while preserving it in the old file format.

Caution: *Before you convert a database, you may want to make a copy of the database, in case you aren't happy with the conversion for some reason.*

How can I import data from a data source other than Access?

You can use the following steps to import data from an external data source:

1. Open or create the database in which you want to store the data.

2. Choose <u>F</u>ile | Get External <u>D</u>ata | <u>I</u>mport.

3. In the Import dialog box, under the Files of <u>T</u>ype box, choose the type of file you want to import.

4. Enter a name and path for the file under File <u>N</u>ame. (Alternatively, you can use the Drive and Folder icons, located at the top of the dialog box, to navigate to a folder in which the file is stored, and then select it.)

5. Click I<u>m</u>port to bring the data into your Access database.

6. Depending on the type of data you are importing, Access may launch the Import Wizard to help you complete the process. If that happens, answer all the questions presented by the wizard.

MANAGING THE USER INTERFACE

 Whenever I delete an object, such as a table or a form, Access asks me for confirmation of the deletion. I find this annoying. Can I make Access stop asking for confirmation?

This could be dangerous, but yes, you can tell Access to stop asking for confirmation. Choose <u>T</u>ools | <u>O</u>ptions and click the Edit/Find tab in the Options dialog box that appears, as shown in Figure 2-2. In the Confirm portion of the dialog box, remove the check mark from the <u>D</u>ocument Deletions option and then click OK.

Is there a shortcut for entering the current date and time?

Yes, Access has shortcut keys for entering the current date and time. They can be used while entering data in tables, queries, or forms:

● Press CTRL-; (semicolon) to enter the current date.

● Press CTRL-: (colon) to enter the current time.

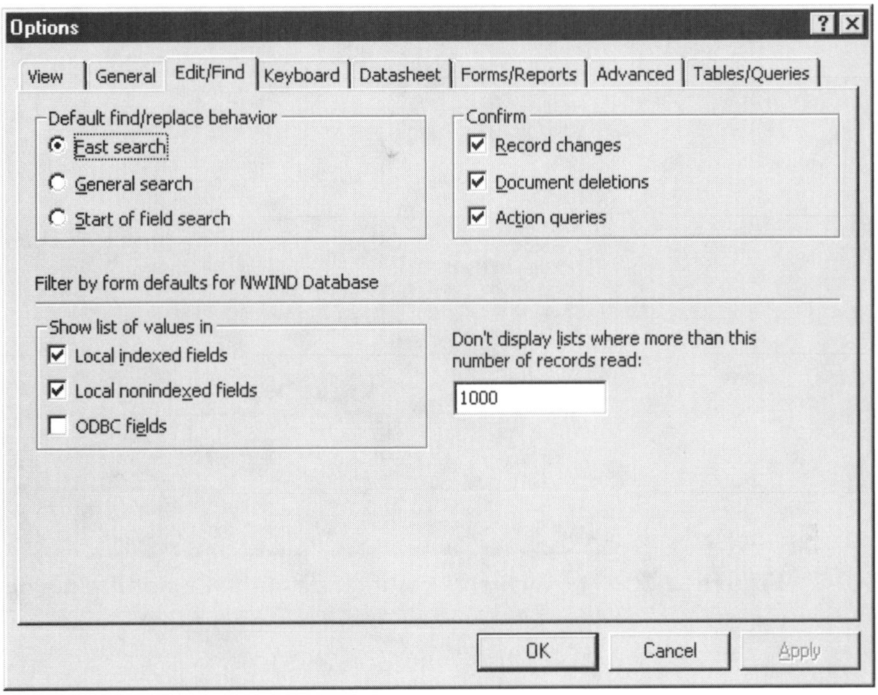

Options ? X

View | General | Edit/Find | Keyboard | Datasheet | Forms/Reports | Advanced | Tables/Queries |

Default find/replace behavior
- ● Fast search
- ○ General search
- ○ Start of field search

Confirm
- ☑ Record changes
- ☑ Document deletions
- ☑ Action queries

Filter by form defaults for NWIND Database

Show list of values in
- ☑ Local indexed fields
- ☑ Local nonindexed fields
- ☐ ODBC fields

Don't display lists where more than this number of records read:

1000

OK   Cancel   Apply

Figure 2-2 The Options dialog box

Can I create a custom menu that appears when I open a form or report?

You can change the Access menus you see when working on a form or report. (This can be helpful when you want to give users a form that doesn't have the standard Access menu options on it.) You add a custom menu to a form or report by attaching to the form or report's Menu Bar property a macro that creates a custom menu bar. (See Chapter 12 for more information about creating macros and about macros in general.)

How can I customize toolbars in Access?

You can add or remove buttons from the existing toolbars. Right-click any blank space in the toolbar you want to customize, and choose Customize from the shortcut menu

Figure 2-3 The available commands in the Customize dialog box

that appears. In the Customize dialog box, click the Commands tab to show the available commands, as shown in Figure 2-3.

Click your command category choice from the Categories list, and then click and drag any command button you want from the Commands list onto the toolbar. You can remove a button you've added to any toolbar simply by dragging it off the toolbar onto any blank portion of the dialog box.

How can I obtain a list of the definitions of objects in my database?

Access has a feature called the Database Documentor that produces a report that details the objects in your database. Using the Database Documentor, you can select any or all objects in your database and then produce a report documenting those objects. You can use the following steps to produce this report:

1. Open the database you want to document.

2. Choose Tools | Analyze | Documentor. In a moment, the Documentor window appears, as shown here. In appearance, this window resembles the Database window.

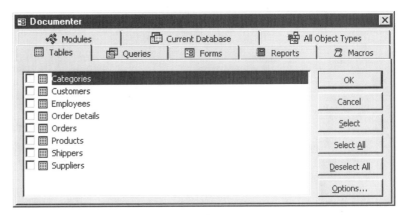

3. Click each tab (Tables, Queries, Forms, Reports, Macros, Modules, Current Database, or All Object Types) to select a different area, and in each area, click the check boxes beside the objects you want to print definitions for.

4. After you select all the objects for which you want printed definitions, click OK.

Access then produces a report containing the object definitions. An example of such a report is shown in Figure 2-4.

 ## Can I disable certain keys, such as F1?

Yes, you can disable keys so that other users cannot use them in your database. This can be useful in an application where you want to limit the users' options. To do this, create an AutoKeys macro that tells Access what to do when you press a certain key. The AutoKeys macro executes automatically each time a database is opened. You disable a key by telling Access to do nothing when the key is pressed. You can use these steps to create an AutoKeys macro:

1. Create a macro with the name **AutoKeys**.

2. Choose View | Macro Names to display the Macro Names column (if you don't already see it).

Microsoft Access - [Object Definition]

File   Edit   View   Tools   Window   Help   Show Me

100%   ▾   Close   W ▾   ...   ? .

Wednesday, April 07, 1999

Table: Customers   Page: 1

Properties

DatasheetGridlinesBehav	Both	Date Created:	9/13/95 10:51:32 AM
Description:	Customers' names, addresses, and phone numbers.	FilterOn:	False
GUID:	{guid {B92C1210-83C3-11D2-978D-00AA0060D5F9}}	Last Updated:	11/30/98 4:53:08 PM
NameMap:	{guid {550E CC0A-0000-0000-1012-2CB9C383D211}}	OrderByOn:	False
OrderOn:	True	Orientation:	0
RecordCount:	91	Updatable:	True

Columns

Name		Type	Size
CustomerID		Text	5
AllowZeroLength:	False		
Attributes:	Variable Length		
Caption:	Customer ID		
Collating Order:	General		
ColumnHidden:	False		
ColumnOrder:	1		
ColumnWidth:	1305		

Page: ◄◄ ◄   1   ► ►◄   ◄

Ready

Start | Paint Shop Pro | NWIND : Database | Object Definition | N 3:35 PM

Figure 2-4   A report containing object definitions from a database

3. Assign macro names by using the SendKeys code of the key you want to disable.

4. Add the SendKeys action and leave the Keystrokes argument empty.

5. Save and close the macro.

6. Save and close the database.

The next time you open the database, Access performs the AutoKeys macro. The effect of the AutoKeys macro remains as long as the database is open.

For example, you could create an AutoKeys macro to disable the F1 key. Type **{F1}** in the Macro Name column and choose SendKeys in the Action column. Leave the Keystrokes argument for the SendKeys action empty. The next time you open the database, Access will perform this macro every time you press F1. Because the Keystrokes argument is empty, no keystroke is sent to Access. Therefore, pressing F1 has no effect.

Can I hide a table so that it doesn't appear in the Database window?

If you want to hide a table in the Database window so that other users can't select it, a neat but little-known trick exists for doing this. Rename the table and give it any name that starts with the letters *Usys*. For example, if you want to hide a table named Salaries, you might rename it to Usyssalaries. (A quick way to rename the table is to right-click it in the Database window, choose Rename from the shortcut menu, and enter a new name in the dialog box that appears.) Access considers all tables with names that begin with the letters *Usys* to be system objects, and system objects are normally hidden in the Database window.

If you want to see this table again later, choose Tools | Options. When the Options dialog box appears, click the View tab and turn on the System Objects option. Click OK, and you'll be able to see the previously hidden table. (When done working with the hidden table, remember to turn off the option so that the appearance of system objects in the Database window doesn't confuse users.)

Caution: *If you are going to use the View tab of the Options dialog box to see the system objects in the Database window, be careful not to modify the actual system objects. These tables are used by Access for its internal operations, and you can cause major problems in the program's operation if you change or delete data stored in these tables.*

How do I get Access to maximize the Database window upon startup?

You can do this by creating an Autoexec macro that maximizes the active window. The Database window is the active window when Access starts, so it is the window that will be maximized by the macro. Use the following steps to create the macro.

1. Click the Macros button in the Database window.

2. Click <u>N</u>ew to open a new macro window.

3. In the Action column for the first row, click the drop-down arrow and choose Maximize from the list.

4. Choose <u>F</u>ile | <u>S</u>ave.

5. Enter **Autoexec** as the macro's name and click OK. Access automatically executes any macro named Autoexec when you open a database.

When you open the database after creating this macro, the Database window is maximized, as shown in Figure 2-5.

Tip: *You can prevent this or any Autoexec macro from running if you hold down the SHIFT key while opening the database.*

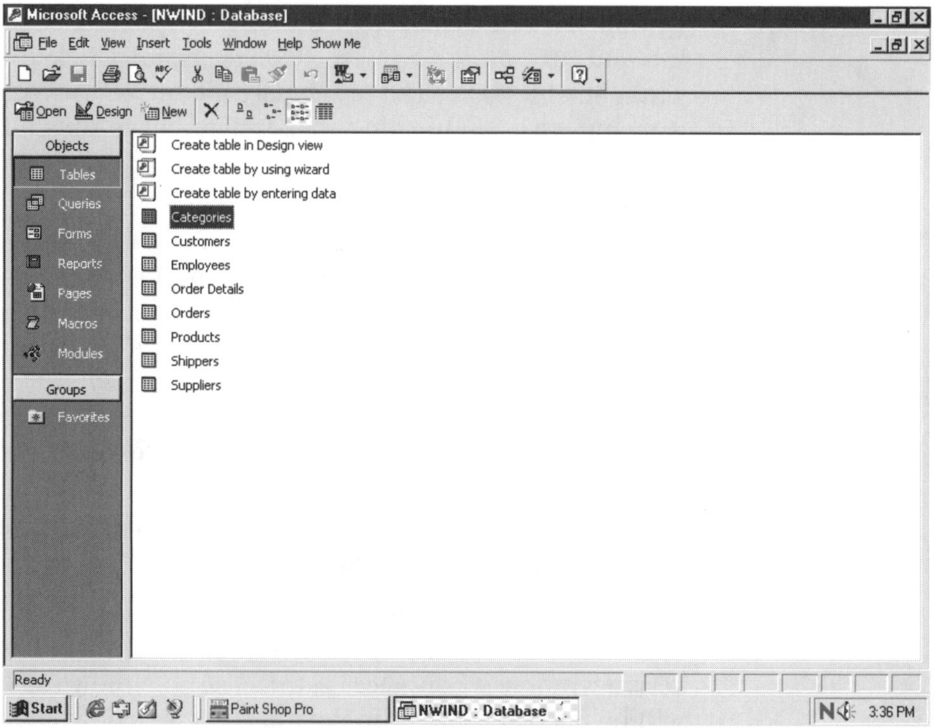

Figure 2-5   Maximizing the Database window

 ## Can I create a new toolbar with my favorite buttons?

Yes, you can create new toolbars containing any buttons you want to include. Use the following steps to create a custom toolbar:

1. Right-click any existing toolbar and choose Customize from the shortcut menu.

2. In the Customize dialog box that appears, click the Toolbars tab and then click New.

3. Enter a name for the custom toolbar in the New Toolbar dialog box, and click OK. The new toolbar appears, containing no buttons.

4. Drag the new toolbar to one side, so that you can see the new toolbar and the Customize dialog box at the same time.

5. In the Customize dialog box, click the Commands tab.

6. At the left side of the dialog box, click the category that contains the button you want to add to the new toolbar.

7. At the right side of the dialog box, find the button in the list, and click and drag it onto the new toolbar.

8. Repeat steps 6 and 7 for each toolbar button you want to add.

9. Click Close to close the Customize dialog box.

10. Drag the new toolbar to the location where you want it on the screen.

I find the Office Assistants annoying. How do I get rid of them?

Click the Office Assistant button in any toolbar to bring up the Office Assistant. Click the Assistant and then click Options to display the Office Assistant dialog box, shown in Figure 2-6. Click the Options tab, and turn off the Respond to F1 Key option, the Display Alerts option, and all the Show Tips About options. Click OK.

Some Office Assistants are more annoying than others. To change the character used for the Assistants, click the

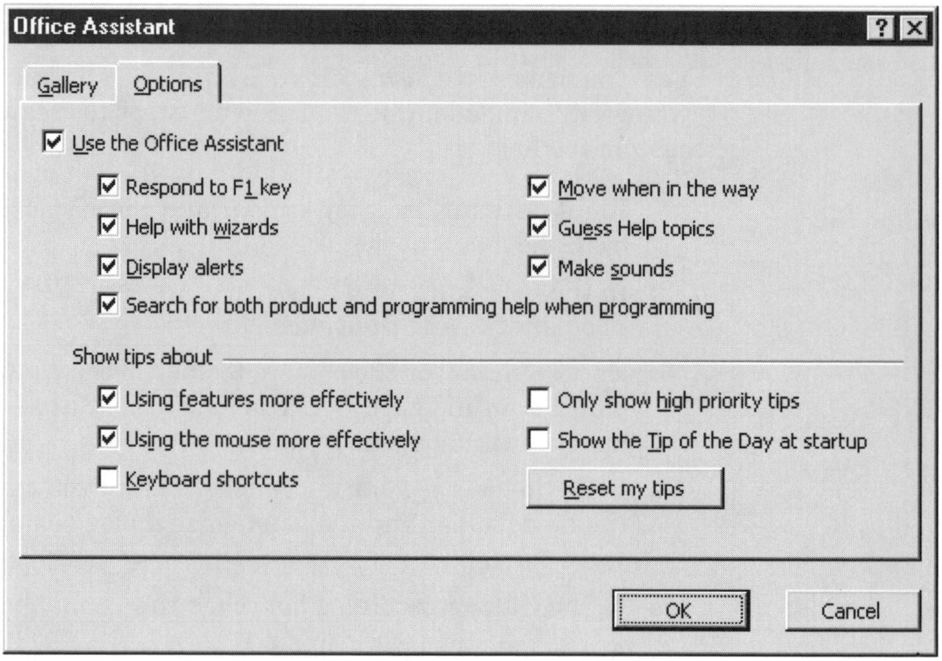

Figure **2-6** The Office Assistant dialog box

Gallery tab in the same dialog box and use the Next and Back
buttons to select a different Assistant. (If you change the
character used by the Office Assistant, you may be asked to
reinsert the installation CD-ROM, so that the new assistant
can be installed.)

What does the File | Send To command do, and why is it dimmed?

The File | Send To command saves the output of the selected
database object as a file and attaches that file to an e-mail
message. If the command is dimmed on your system, then
you don't have an e-mail system installed that's supported
by Access. To send objects from within Access, you must
either use an e-mail system that is Microsoft Office
97–compatible, or install Windows Dial-Up Networking. If
you installed your e-mail system after you installed Access,
you may need to reinstall Access so that the program
recognizes your e-mail provider.

 What does the <u>M</u>ake MDE File option under <u>T</u>ools | <u>D</u>atabase Utilities do to my database?

Saving a database as an MDE file results in a copy of the database that doesn't allow changes to forms, reports, or any VBA code stored in that database. (You can make changes to tables, queries, and macros in a database that has been saved as an MDE file.) If your database contains VBA code, saving it as an MDE file compiles all modules, removes all editable source code, and then compacts the destination database. Any VBA code will continue to run, but it can't be viewed or edited. In addition to preventing changes by unauthorized users, saving a database as an MDE file has performance benefits. The size of your database is reduced due to the removal of the code, and memory usage is optimized, improving performance.

! *Caution:* *If you save a database as an MDE file, be sure to maintain a copy of the original database (MDB) file in a secure location. You need it if you want to make any changes to the forms, reports, or code stored in the database.*

 My toolbars have disappeared. How do I get them back?

If another user (or an application written in Access) turns off a specific toolbar, it remains off until you turn it back on. Choose <u>T</u>oolbars | <u>V</u>iew. In the next menu that appears, select the toolbar that you want to turn back on.

SECURITY

I secured my database, but users can still get at the data by using Visual Basic or another front-end utility program. What do I have to do to prevent that?

Access security provides password protection, but it doesn't prevent others from reading your database with utilities or opening it in other software. To provide this level of protection, you need to *encrypt* the database, which saves

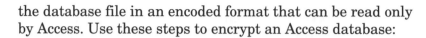

the database file in an encoded format that can be read only by Access. Use these steps to encrypt an Access database:

1. Close any database that is open.

2. Choose <u>T</u>ools | Security | <u>E</u>ncrypt/Decrypt Database.

3. In the dialog box that opens, specify the database you want to encrypt, and click OK.

4. Specify the name and location (drive and folder) for the encrypted database, and click OK.

Remember that Access's performance while working with encrypted databases is slower than with normal databases, because Access must translate the data as you retrieve it.

 Note: *You can save an encrypted version of the database to the same filename and folder as the previous (unencrypted) version. When you use the same filename and folder, and the database is encrypted successfully, Access then replaces the original database file with the encrypted version. If the encryption process fails for any reason, Access will not delete your original file.*

 I want to reassign permissions in a database, but someone else created it. How can I make myself the owner so that I can assign permissions?

You can, in effect, transfer ownership of an entire database to yourself (or to another user). To do this, you must create a new database and import all the objects in the other database into the new database. Here are the steps you need to follow to do this:

1. Start Access, using a workgroup containing the user account that should be the owner of the new database.

2. Create a new database by choosing <u>F</u>ile | <u>N</u>ew Database.

3. Choose <u>F</u>ile | <u>G</u>et External Data | <u>I</u>mport.

4. In the Import dialog box, make sure Microsoft Access is chosen as the file type, select from the list the database you want to import, and click OK.

5. In the next dialog box that appears, select each tab (Tables, Queries, Forms, Reports, Macros, and Modules) one at a time, and click the Select <u>A</u>ll button after clicking each tab.

6. Click <u>I</u>mport.

7. Click OK again after the Import process is complete.

 Note: *Before you can import a database that has security applied, you must have Open/Run permission for the database, Read/Design permission for its objects, and Read/Data permission for its tables. If you have permission for some (but not all) objects, Access will import only objects for which you have permissions.*

TROUBLESHOOTING

When I open my form or report, I see "#Name?" in some controls. What happened to my data?

"#Name?" is the error message that appears in a control when it can't find the data it is supposed to display. *Controls* are the elements of a form or report that can display data. Each control has many *properties* that define how it works. The Control Source property defines the source of the data that the control displays. If this property is set to a source that Access can't find or that doesn't exist, the "#Name?" error message appears instead of the missing data.

To change the Control Source property setting, open the form or report in Design view. (You can either select the form or report in the Database window and click the Design button, or right-click the form or report in the Database window and choose <u>D</u>esign from the shortcut menu that appears.) Right-click the problem control (the one that displayed the "#Name?" error message while in Form view) and choose <u>P</u>roperties from the shortcut menu, which opens the Properties window. Click the Data tab and examine the entry in the Control Source property. The current setting may be a mistyped field name, or it may refer to a field that you have removed from the underlying table or query. Set the

property to an existing source of data. After you fix the entry, your form or report should work correctly.

 ### I get the error message "Can't update. Database or object is read-only (Error 3027)." What does this mean?

Access reports this message when you try to make changes to objects in a database that has been marked as read-only by your network operating system. You may not have network rights to the file, or it may be stored on a read-only drive (such as a CD-ROM drive). You should contact your network administrator for help in getting full rights to the file.

How did my Access database become corrupted? Can I fix it?

Access database files can become corrupted on occasion, for the same reasons Word documents and other Windows files become corrupt: power surges, exiting Windows improperly, viruses, or network servers crashing. Any abnormality that affects the stability of your computer system can cause one of your database files to become corrupt. If Access shuts down unexpectedly for any reason, a database file can become corrupt.

Because file corruption can happen with databases, Access includes a repair utility as part of the program. To repair a database:

1. Close any open database.

2. Choose Tools | Database Utilities | Compact and Repair Database.

3. In the Database to Compact From dialog box, select the database that is to be repaired.

4. Click Compact.

You may lose some data when repairing a database. The best safeguard against serious data loss is to back up your database files on a regular basis.

Caution: *If you were editing data in a form or a datasheet when Access shut down unexpectedly, the last changes you made to the table will probably be lost, even after you repair the database. Return to the last records you were editing and verify whether your changes were saved.*

Why do I occasionally get the error message "Database locked by user 'Admin'" when I try to open a database?

When you see this message, it means someone else on your network has the file open in Exclusive mode. When Access security hasn't been enabled on a database, anyone who opens the database is called "Admin." If you're unsure who has the database open for exclusive use, check with your network administrator, who has commands available to determine who has the file open. After you discover the culprit, tell that user to choose Tools | Options, click the Advanced tab, and change the Default Open Mode option from Exclusive to Shared. When the user exits Access and then opens it again, the database will no longer be locked, and you and the other user can use it simultaneously.

I accidentally erased a database file. Can I get it back?

Assuming the database was stored on your hard drive, a chance exists that all is not lost. Files that you delete under Windows 95, Windows NT 4, or later are stored in the Recycle Bin. If you haven't emptied the Recycle Bin, you can get the file back by performing these steps:

1. Double-click the Recycle Bin icon on the Windows desktop.
2. Select the deleted file in the window that appears.
3. Choose File | Restore.

   If the file you erased was stored on a network drive, you should immediately contact your network administrator. Network operating systems provide utilities that can recover recently deleted files. (On a Novell network, the network administrator can run a utility called Salvage to recover the deleted database.)

 I have two filenames in my directory with the name I assigned to my database. Which one is my database?

The file with the .mdb extension is the database file. The file with the same name and the .ldb extension is a file that Access uses to store record-locking information for the tables in the database. When you are using a database on a network, Access uses the data in the LDB file to determine which records are locked and which users have locked the records. This enables Access to prevent file contention errors or corruption of the database by multiple users. In a multiuser environment, each user who opens the database has an entry in the LDB file.

The LDB file is created automatically when you open an Access database file. If you are working with Access on a stand-alone computer, where no one else can simultaneously open the database, you can delete this file to free up disk space.

Why does my file size increase so much when I embed or link graphics?

When you embed or link a graphic to an Access database, the database routinely increases by more than the size of the graphic, due to the way Access displays images in forms and reports. Access can store graphics in many different formats, but it can display only bitmaps (which are graphic images stored in Windows BMP format). When you paste a graphic into an OLE object field, and the graphic is not originally stored in bitmap format, Access creates a bitmap of the graphic and stores that bitmap along with the actual image data.

If you embed a bitmap image, the database increases by the size of the bitmap image. If you embed an image that's not a bitmap, the database increases by the size of the image plus the size of the bitmap that Access creates. If you link an image, Access stores both the bitmap and the data needed to establish the link.

This increase in size can be significant. In our testing, embedding an image stored in a JPG file of 63K resulted in an increase in database file size of 538K.

Why do I get the error message "Not enough memory on disk" when I'm working with a database on a network drive that has plenty of free disk space?

It's possible that your temporary drive is not on the network drive. Access uses a temporary directory to store temporary files as you work with data. If this temporary directory is on a disk that's short of free space, such as your local hard drive, you may see this error even though your network drive has sufficient free space. To check your temporary drive:

1. From within Access, choose Help | About Microsoft Access.

2. In the dialog box that appears, click System Info. The Microsoft System Information window appears, similar to the example shown here:

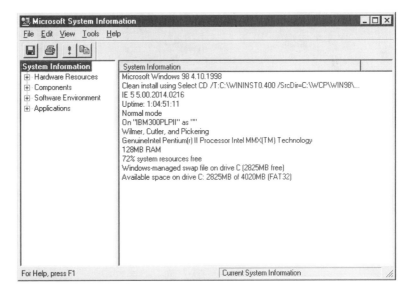

3. Look at the line that reads either "TEMP Directory" or "TMP Directory" (under Windows 95 or Windows NT), or "Windows-Managed Swap File on Drive *x*": (under Windows 98). This is your temporary directory. Check whether this is a valid directory and that free space for it exists. You may need to make more space available on the drive that contains this directory, to avoid getting these out-of-memory errors.

Tip: *Many other applications also use this temporary directory. Sometimes, not all of the temporary files are deleted when the applications are closed. Delete any BAK or TMP files in this directory to make space. Close all applications before doing this, because you don't want to delete a temporary file that is still in use.*

Chapter 3

Creating Tables

Answer Topics!

Creating Tables @ a Glance

Tables are the heart of your database—they are the Access objects that store all the data in your database. Before you can create and use forms, queries, or reports, you need to create tables and then store data in them.

During the process of designing tables, you can take several steps that will make the data entry process that follows a less tedious task. You can control the entry and the display of much of your data by means of settings that you establish while designing your tables. Also, effective database design requires the use of indexes and primary keys, when necessary, to speed searches and to make it possible to combine data from different tables in reports. These types of topics are detailed throughout this chapter.

The questions that you'll find in this chapter cover the following topics:

- **Defining Fields** discusses how to work with the different field types available in Access, and with their specifications.

- **Working with Primary Keys** provides answers to questions about primary keys in Access tables.

- **Working with Indexes** helps you decide when and how to use indexes as part of a table's design.

- **Controlling Data Entry and Data Display** answers questions that will help you design your tables in such a way that you can control how data is entered and displayed.

Designing Better Databases

If you're new to the intricacies of database design, you should spend some time learning about proper database design before you create your tables in Access. Any well-designed database involves careful planning of the necessary fields, and elimination of any unnecessary redundancies. (In the database world, this process is known as *normalization*.) This is an especially important process with relational databases, because it helps you to recognize when certain data should be stored in separate tables. Newcomers to database design often have a tendency to create single tables that contain all the data associated with a task. Such tables are hard to use and waste disk space. Carefully planning your tables helps you to avoid these kinds of problems.

When designing your tables, try to avoid duplicating information. For example, if you already decided to store the names and addresses of your customers in a table named Customers, don't duplicate those names and addresses in your Orders table. Instead, you can define a *relationship* between the two tables, so that when the Orders table needs a customer address to complete an order form, it simply obtains the address from the Customers table.

You should also avoid duplicating information within the same table. For example, when you record the number of hours that your employees work every week, you don't want to reenter the complete employee name and address each week. That's a waste of time. Instead, create an employee ID number and enter the ID number for the weekly time records. This employee ID can link to your table of employee information, so that the name and address are available without repeating them in each record.

After you arrange all of your tables and define any needed relationships, make sure that you check one last time with others who must use your database. You want to avoid editing the design of the tables after you enter data.

DEFINING FIELDS

How can I add new fields to an existing table?

You can add new fields to a table at any time. You can add them to the end of the table or put them at any desired location in the table. (Remember that the order of the fields in Design view initially determines the order of the fields in the table's datasheet.) To add a field to a table, follow these steps:

1. Open the table in Design view.

2. To insert the field within the table, select the row below where you want to add the field, by clicking the row selector button to the left of the field name. Press the INS key or choose Insert | Rows. A new blank row appears, as shown in the following figure, enabling you to fill in the required information. Or, to add the field to the end of the table, move the insertion point to the first blank row.

Clients : Table		
Field Name	Data Type	Description
ContactName	Text	
ContactTitle	Text	
Address	Text	

Field Properties

General | Lookup |

A field name can be up to 64 characters long, including spaces. Press F1 for help on field names.

3. Define the field by entering a field name, a data type, and an optional description.

4. Make any desired changes to the field properties.

 How can I change the initial value of an AutoNumber field to something other than 1?

Changing the starting value for an AutoNumber field is a bit complicated, but you can accomplish it by using these steps:

1. Create the table that contains the AutoNumber field that you want to change to start on a different number. Do not enter any records.

2. Create a second, temporary table with just one field. Make the field type Number, with the Field Size property set to Long Integer. Name the field by using the same name as the AutoNumber field that you want to change in the original table.

3. Enter one record in the new table. In the Number field, enter a number that is *one less than* the number that you want the AutoNumber field in the first table to start at. For example, if you want to start the AutoNumber field with 100, then enter 99 in the Number field of the temporary table.

4. Create an append query to append the one record in the second table to the first table. (For details on creating append queries, see "Action Queries" in Chapter 5.)

5. Run the append query. After appending the record from the second table to the first, you can delete the second (temporary) table and the query.

When you open the original table, you'll see the new record that you just appended, followed by a blank record. Enter any data in the existing record, and Access will continue numbering in the AutoNumber field with the next record. After you enter a record, you can delete the first record that you added with the append query.

 Can fields in my table be based on calculations involving other fields?

No, you cannot base fields in your table on the contents of other fields. In Access, tables hold raw data, not formulas or calculations. If you want to display the results of a formula by using other fields in the record, you need to create either a query with a calculated field or a form or report with a calculated control. (See "Calculations" in Chapter 5, or "Calculations and Controls" in Chapter 10, for more information on this subject.)

 ### If I change a field type in an existing table, will I lose all the data stored in that field?

Whenever you change a field type for a table that contains data, you risk losing data, depending on whether Access can handle the transfer of data. Access successfully keeps the data in an existing field if the change "makes sense"; for example, if you have a Text field that contains entries composed completely of numbers and change it to a Number field, Access keeps the data. If you change a Number field to a Yes/No field, entries with a value of 0 are converted to No values, and entries with any other numeric amount are converted to Yes values. If you change a Memo field to an OLE Object field, however, all the data in the Memo field is lost. If you reduce the size of a Text field, Access warns you that data may be truncated, and you must confirm the possible data loss before Access proceeds with the operation.

How do I create a table?

You can create a table by using these steps:

1. In the Database window, click the <u>T</u>ables tab.
2. Click <u>N</u>ew.
3. In the New Table dialog box that appears, click Design View, and then click OK. A Table window opens in Design view, as shown next. (If you select Table Wizard instead, Access starts the Table Wizard, which walks you through the process of creating a table. The Table Wizard provides sample tables to use as the basis of your own table.)

4. On each line in the top half of the Table window, enter the name of a field, its data type, and a longer description that will help you identify the field later. (The field name and data type are required entries, whereas the description is optional.) Try to keep field names short, to make them easier to work with in forms and reports.

5. As you define each field, the properties for that field appear in the bottom half of the Table window. (You can move between the top and bottom halves of the window by pressing F6 or by clicking anywhere inside the window to which you want to move.) Move to the box for the property you want to change, and enter the new setting.

6. If desired, create a primary key. (A *primary key* is a field or combination of fields that is unique for each record in the table.) Click the *selector* (the small box at the beginning of the row) for that field, or click and drag through multiple row selectors to select more than one field. Then click the Primary Key toolbar button or choose Edit | Primary Key.

7. When you finish defining the fields for the table, choose File | Save. Enter a name for the table and click OK. If you didn't create a primary key before, Access asks whether you want to create one now. Select Yes to have Access create an AutoNumber field and make it the primary key, or No to avoid creating a primary key.

What is a table?

Tables are the basis of your data. When you define a table, you define the *fields* that will be used to store the data. Each field contains a single type of information, such as an address, name, or phone number. Tables contain *records*, which are complete sets of information about a single entity. As an example, you might have a complete record for each customer, including entries in the Name, Address, and Phone Number fields. When displayed in Datasheet view, tables have a column and row layout, as shown here. Each column is a field, and each row is a record.

Customer ID	Company Name	Contact Name	Contact Title	
ALFKI	Alfreds Futterkiste	Maria Anders	Sales Representat	Obere Str. 57
ANATR	Ana Trujillo Emparedados	Ana Trujillo	Owner	Avda. de la Co
ANTON	Antonio Moreno Taquería	Antonio Moreno	Owner	Mataderos 23
AROUT	Around the Horn	Thomas Hardy	Sales Representat	120 Hanover S
BERGS	Berglunds snabbköp	Christina Berglund	Order Administratc	Berguvsvägen
BLAUS	Blauer See Delikatessen	Hanna Moos	Sales Representat	Forsterstr. 57
BLONP	Blondel père et fils	Frédérique Citeaux	Marketing Manage	24, place Klét
BOLID	Bólido Comidas preparada	Martín Sommer	Owner	C/ Araquil, 67
BONAP	Bon app'	Laurence Lebihan	Owner	12, rue des Bo
BOTTM	Bottom-Dollar Markets	Elizabeth Lincoln	Accounting Manag	23 Tsawasser
BSBEV	B's Beverages	Victoria Ashworth	Sales Representat	Fauntleroy Cir
CACTU	Cactus Comidas para lleva	Patricio Simpson	Sales Agent	Cerrito 333
CENTC	Centro comercial Moctezu	Francisco Chang	Marketing Manage	Sierras de Gra
CHOPS	Chop-suey Chinese	Yang Wang	Owner	Hauptstr. 29
COMMI	Comércio Mineiro	Pedro Afonso	Sales Associate	Av. dos Lusíac

Customers : Table

Record: 1 of 91

I'm creating a new table and I have an existing table with a similar structure. Can I duplicate an existing table somehow and then just modify the structure?

You can do this with the Edit | Copy and Edit | Paste operations, even if the table is in another database. In the Database window, click the existing table whose structure you want to use, and then choose Edit | Copy. (If you want to place the new table in a different database, close the current database and open the database in which you want to place the new table.) Next, select Edit | Paste. In the Paste Table

As dialog box that appears, enter a name for the new table, choose Structure Only, and click OK. The new table appears in the Database window. You now can open it in Design view and make the desired changes to the table structure.

What are field properties and how can I set them?

In a table, each field has *field properties* that let you decide how data is stored and displayed. When you click in a field in Design view, its field properties are displayed in the lower pane of the window, in the General tab, as shown here:

	Field Name	Data Type	Description	
	CustomerID	Text	Unique five-character code based on customer name.	
	CompanyName	Text		
	ContactName	Text		
	ContactTitle	Text		

Field Properties

General | Lookup |

Field Size	5
Format	
Input Mask	>LLLLL
Caption	Customer ID
Default Value	
Validation Rule	
Validation Text	
Required	No
Allow Zero Length	No
Indexed	Yes (No Duplicates)
Unicode Compression	Yes

A field name can be up to 64 characters long, including spaces. Press F1 for help on field names.

The following list describes the field properties, which differ depending on their data types:

- **Field Size** Use to define the maximum length for a Text field or to limit the number of values in a Number field.

- **Format** Use to specify a format for showing and printing text, numbers, dates, and times.

- **Decimal Places** Use with Number and Currency fields to specify how many decimal places appear to the right of the decimal point.

- **Input Mask**   Use to specify the pattern to be used when entering data such as telephone numbers or social security numbers.

- **Caption**   Use to change the default label for the field. The caption will appear instead of the field name in Datasheet view on forms and reports.

- **Default Value**   Use to cause a default value to appear automatically in a field.

- **Validation Rule**   Use to define rules for entering data.

- **Validation Text**   Use to cause a dialog box with a customized message to appear if invalid data is entered.

- **Required**   Use to specify whether an entry in the field is required for any new records.

- **Allow Zero Length**   Use with a Text field to determine whether records in that field are allowed to contain a zero-length, or empty, text string.

- **Indexed**   Use to indicate whether the field should be indexed.

- **Unicode Compression**   Use with a Text field to determine whether Unicode compression (a type of data compression that allows use of foreign character sets) is allowed for the field.

If you want to change the properties for the field, follow these steps:

1. In Design view, click the field whose properties you want to change.

2. Click the field property that you want to change, or press F6 and move the insertion point to that field property.

3. Enter the setting that you want for the property. In some cases, you can click the down arrow to see a list of available settings.

Which field types are available for tables?

Access has nine field types that can be used to store specific types of data:

- **Text** Use to store shorter text entries (up to 255 characters). The text can be any combination of letters, numbers, punctuation marks, blank spaces, and symbols.

- **Memo** Use to store longer text entries (such as multiple paragraphs of text). Memo fields can store up to 64,000 characters. (Note that you cannot add indexes based on Memo fields.)

- **Number** Use to store numeric values that aren't currency. Depending on the format that you apply, numbers can be whole or fractional values, and you can enter negative values by preceding the value with a minus sign.

- **Date/Time** Use to store dates, times, or both.

- **Currency** Use to store monetary values. (Access uses the unit of currency that is the Windows default. You can change the default unit of currency through the Regional Settings icon of the Windows Control Panel.)

- **AutoNumber** A special type of numeric field for which Access automatically provides a value each time a new record is added to the table. By default, the first record added in this field is assigned a value of 1, the second record added is assigned a value of 2, and so on. After a record is entered, the number in this field can't be changed. If a record is deleted, its value in the AutoNumber field will not be reassigned. (You can change the initial value of an AutoNumber field by following the directions provided earlier in this chapter in the question "How can I change the intital value of an AutoNumber field to something other than 1?")

- **Yes/No** Use to store logical (true or false, yes or no) values.

- **OLE Object** Use to store objects from other Windows applications that support OLE (Object Linking and Embedding). You can store graphics, spreadsheets, word processing documents, sound files, and other OLE objects in an OLE Object field. (You cannot index the contents of OLE Object fields.)

● **Hyperlink** Use to store a combination of text and numbers that are used as a *hyperlink address,* a path to a Web page or document file on your hard drive or on a local area network (LAN). Hyperlinks that identify Web pages are also known as URLs (an abbreviation for *Uniform Resource Locators*).

In addition to these field types, you can set the Field Size property, to specify how many characters a Text field can contain or the range of numbers that a Number field can contain. For example, if you know that a Text field is going to contain first names, you may want to set its Field Size property to 20, because you are unlikely to encounter a first name of more than 20 characters.

Tip: *By default, the Field Size property for a Text field is 50. If you anticipate longer entries, change this property to allow additional characters during data entry.*

How do I decide whether to use a Text field or a Memo field for storing moderate amounts of text?

This question often arises when you must store amounts of text that may run the length of an average sentence or two. If you know that you'll occasionally need to store more than 255 characters, the decision is automatic: you have to use Memo fields, because Text fields are limited to 255 characters. Although Memo fields can store up to 64,000 characters, they do have some limitations. You can't index a Memo field, and you can't use a Memo field to establish a relationship to records in another table. So, if you need to use the field as part of a relationship, or if you want to index the field, you need to use a Text field.

I need to store large amounts of text from word-processing documents. Should I use a Memo field or an OLE Object field?

If you're considering using Memo fields to store very large amounts of text that are stored in Windows word processing documents, consider using OLE Object fields instead. Memo fields are well suited for several sentences or a few paragraphs of text, but if you have multiple-page documents stored in a Windows word processor, OLE Object fields will probably serve your needs better. Keep in mind that if you use OLE Object fields and embed the data (rather than link it), the amount of disk space in your database will quickly be consumed as you add new documents. If you link documents to the database, you should exercise care not to delete them, because if you delete the linked document, users of the Access table will be unable to retrieve the data represented by the link.

How can I create a relationship to records in another table?

You can define a relationship between tables by doing the following:

1. Display the Database window, if it's not already visible.

2. Select Tools | Relationships. Access displays the Relationships window, with the Show Table dialog box over it. (If the Show Table dialog box doesn't appear, click the Show Table button on the toolbar.)

3. On the Tables tab, double-click the names of the two tables that you want to relate, and then click Close. This causes the two tables' Field list boxes to be added to the Relationships window.

4. In the Relationships window, drag the field that you want to relate from its table to the related field in the other table. When you do this, Access displays the Relationships dialog box.

5. Check the accuracy of the field names displayed in the two columns. Change them if needed. The fields used to relate the two tables don't need to have the same names, but they must be the same data type (with one exception) and contain the same kind of information. The exception is that you can relate an AutoNumber field to a Number field whose Field Size property is set to Long Integer.

6. Turn on the Enforce Referential Integrity option. (In most cases, you want to enforce referential integrity.

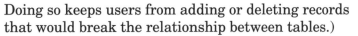

Doing so keeps users from adding or deleting records that would break the relationship between tables.)

7. Click the Create button to create the relationship. If you need to create any additional relationships, repeat these steps. (You can define only one relationship between any two tables.)

When you close the Relationships window, Access asks whether you want to save the layout (the arrangement of the window). The relationships are added to the database regardless of whether you save the layout.

 How can I establish a relationship between two AutoNumber fields?

You can't. Access will not let you establish a relationship between an AutoNumber field that is the primary key in one table and an AutoNumber field that is the foreign (or related) key in another table. However, because AutoNumber fields store data as numbers in Long Integer format, you can get around this obstacle by using as the foreign key field a Number field with the Size property set to Long Integer.

WORKING WITH PRIMARY KEYS

 Access always asks me to define a primary key. Do I need one?

A primary key is not always required, although primary keys are a recommended part of effective database design. If the table won't be the basis for a relationship with any other table, or you don't need to keep the records in the table in any specific order, then you don't need a primary key. If you do want to put the records in a specific order, however, you may want to use a primary key. A primary key gives Access a unique way to identify all the records in a table. Usually, primary keys are based on a single field, but they can be based on more than one field.

By default, the records in the table appear in ascending order based on the contents of the field or fields of the primary key, so the field of the primary key becomes the main index for the table. (You can change this either by sorting the table based on a specific field or by creating a query that sorts on a different field.)

Primary keys are used regularly in databases, although you may not realize it. Some identifiers that are widely used as primary keys in databases include patient ID numbers, employee numbers, and account numbers. Although you don't *have* to use primary keys, using them enables you to do the following:

● Create an index that will speed sorts, queries, and internal operations

● Establish relationships between tables

● Reduce the possibility of a duplicate record, because Access will not let you create two records with the same value in the primary key field

If you need a relationship between tables, or if you want to update two tables at the same time, you should use a primary key.

How do I delete a primary key designation?

One process that is not so obvious is how to delete a primary key that is no longer needed. To delete a primary key, follow these steps:

1. In the table's Design view, click the Indexes button on the toolbar. Access displays the Indexes window.

2. Select the row or rows containing the primary key index, and then press the DEL key.

3. Close the Indexes window.

Tip: *The primary key must not be a link relating this table to another table; otherwise, Access won't let you delete the primary key. You first have to delete the existing relationship in the Relationships window, and then you can delete the primary key.*

❓ How can I create a primary key based on multiple fields that aren't adjacent in the table structure?

You can do this without moving fields around in the table structure. Open the table in Design view and click the row selector button for the first field that you want to use as part of the primary key. Then, hold down the CTRL key as you click the row selector button for each additional field that you want to use as part of the primary key. After you select the needed fields, click the Primary Key button on the toolbar or select Edit | Primary Key.

WORKING WITH INDEXES

❓ Can I add an index to a table?

You can add indexes to tables to make searches faster when your tables contain thousands of records. You can add indexes to Text, Number, Date/Time, Currency, AutoNumber, and Yes/No fields. Indexes are used to sort through or search for data in a field quickly. You want to create indexes that order your records in the same way that you need to access your data. For example, if you often sort your table by department number, then creating an index for the Department Number field will speed up those sorts. Avoid creating too many indexes for a single table, however, because indexes slow down editing or entering new records.

To create an index based on a single field:

1. Open the table in Design view and select the field that you want to index.

2. Press F6 to move to the field's properties.

3. Set the Indexed property to Yes (Duplicates OK) if you want to allow duplicate entries in this field, or Yes (No Duplicates) if you want to keep this field unique for each record.

To create a multiple-field index:

1. Choose View | Indexes or click the Indexes toolbar button.
2. Enter the name for the index in the Index Name column.
3. Enter the name of the first field in the Field Name column next to the name of the index.
4. In the Field Name column below the first field, enter the name of the second field in the index. Continue this until you've added all the fields you want to index by.
5. Close the Indexes window.

How can I avoid duplicate values in a field that's not used for a primary key?

You can ensure that a particular field within a specific table never has two records with the same value, by adding an index with the No Duplicates property turned on to that particular field. (Primary keys use this type of index by default, because they do not allow duplicate values in the field.) For example, a table of insured cars at an automobile insurance agency might have a primary key field based on automobile ID numbers, and another field containing the license plate numbers of the automobiles. Allowing only unique entries in the License Plate field of this table makes sense, because no two automobiles have the same license plate number.

To add an index to a field and specify No Duplicates, open the table in Design view and click anywhere within the field. Then, in the Indexed property for the field, choose Yes (No Duplicates).

CONTROLLING DATA ENTRY AND DATA DISPLAY

 Can I specify a default value for a field?

Open the table in Design view, click the desired field, and then use the Default Value property to specify a default value for a field. The default value is added automatically when you add a new record. For example, in a table of names and addresses, you might set the default value of a City field to Pasadena. Pasadena then automatically appears in the City field when new records are entered. The user can leave that value unchanged or enter the name of a different city.

All field types can have default values, except for AutoNumber and OLE Object fields. For Text, Number, and Currency fields, default values typically are an arbitrary value that you choose, depending on the application. The default value for Yes/No fields usually is No, but you can change that to Yes if most of your records are likely to have a Yes value in a Yes/No field. You can also use expressions beginning with an equal sign as default values. Two common examples are =date, which provides the current date according to your PC's clock, and =now, which provides both the date and the time. You can use math calculations, as well. For example, the expression =date() + 30 produces a default value 30 days ahead of the current date.

 What's the difference between an input mask and a format?

Both input masks and formats affect the way that data appears in a table in Datasheet view. However, they serve very different purposes. The Format property setting affects the data in the field after it is entered. It changes how the data is displayed, and can make the data easier to read. For example, if you apply the Long Date format to a Date/Time field, a date of 11/24/98 appears as Tuesday, November 24, 1998.

An Input Mask property actually *restricts* the type of entry that you can make in the field. As you begin to make an entry, a template appears, indicating the entry that is needed. This template can also format the entry to make it easier to interpret. For example, if you start to make an entry in a Phone Number field with an input mask, it might look like this:

New Employees : Table

Address	City	Region	Postal Code	Country	Home Phone	Exter
230 Oak Park Lane	Pasadena	CA	92305	USA	(717) ▌ - ___	

Record: 14 4 [1] ▶ ▶I ▶* of 1

The underscores (_) are placeholders for entries. The hyphen and the parentheses make the phone number entries easier to read.

When you create an input mask, you use placeholder characters for entries. Some placeholder characters allow users to enter a character, digit, or text, whereas others require an entry. For example, you might use a placeholder character that requires an entry for each of the ten positions in the phone number.

Can negative numbers be displayed enclosed in parentheses, while positive numbers are displayed normally?

The way to accomplish this is to design a *custom format* that displays negative numbers in parentheses. Custom formats are created with special symbols that indicate what can appear in the field. You can enter this custom format as the setting for the field's Format property. Table 3-1 shows the symbols that you use to create particular custom formats.

Symbol	Effect
"xxx"	Displays the characters between the quotation marks without interpreting them as symbols, as in "N/A" to display N/A
\	Displays the character after the backslash without interpreting it as a symbol, as in \N/\A to display N/A
0	Displays a digit if one is entered, or a zero if one isn't
#	Displays a digit if one is entered; displays a blank if a digit isn't entered
@	Marks a required character
&	Marks an optional character
.	Marks the location of the decimal point
%	Multiplies the entry by 100 and displays a % after it
,	Inserts a thousands separator
E– or e–	Shows the number using scientific notation with a – for negative exponents and nothing in front of positive ones
E+ or e+	Shows the number using scientific format with a – for negative exponents and a + for positive ones
-	Displays the hyphen as a hyphen
+	Displays the plus sign as a plus sign
$	Displays the dollar sign as a dollar sign
()	Displays parentheses as parentheses
[color]	Displays the number using the color given. You can use black, blue, green, cyan, red, magenta, yellow, and white
*	Fills the field with the following characters

Table 3-1   Symbols Used to Create Custom Formats

A custom format can have up to four parts, with each part separated by a semicolon. The first part of the format controls how positive numbers display; the second part controls how negative numbers display; the third part controls how zeros display; and the fourth part controls how null fields display. You do not have to enter all four parts. If you enter only one part, all numbers use that format; if you enter two parts, zeros and nulls display using the setting for positive numbers. For example, to display numbers with a thousands separator and negative numbers in parentheses, you can enter **#,###;(#,###)** as the setting of the Format property of a Number field. This format displays numbers as shown here:

Expenses : Table				
Date	**Balance**	**Manager**	**Comments**	
4/14/99	(3,213)	M.Hernandez	Maria gave an office party to celebrate the Johnson
4/14/99	234	S. Williams	
4/18/99	1,231	J. Jameson	
4/21/99	(220)	L. Atkins	Larry took the accounting team to lunch.
4/22/99	535	R. Richards	

Record: 5 of 5

How can I cause a Phone Number field to display parentheses and a dash?

You can manage this task by changing the format specified in the Format property to add the parentheses and the dash. To create this format, you use a series of symbols that indicate how to display such data, as shown in Table 3-2. Text fields, such as your Phone Number field, have several unique symbols that are available to all types of fields.

Use	To
<	Display all characters as lowercase
>	Display all characters as uppercase
!	Fill the field from left to right rather than right to left
@	Display an entered character or space
&	Display an entered character or leave the position empty
[*color*]	Display the text in a specific color
\	Display the following character literally rather than symbolically
*	Fill the field with the following character
a space	Insert a space in the field
""	Enclose text to display it literally rather than symbolically

Table 3-2   Symbols Used by the Format Property

For example, to force a Phone Number field to display phone numbers entered in table fields with parentheses and a dash, use these steps:

1. Open the table in Design view and choose your Phone Number field.

2. Move to the Format property in the lower half of the window.

3. Enter **(&&&)&&&-&&&&**.

You could also use this format to enter social security numbers. For example, you could enter **&&&-&&-&&&&** in the Property field.

How can I enforce referential integrity?

With relationships, Access can enforce referential integrity to protect users from adding or deleting data that could break the relationship. For example, suppose that you have a table of customers that is related to a table of orders placed by those customers. The Orders table has several records associated with each customer. You don't want to delete a customer's record without deleting the records of the purchases made by that customer; otherwise, you would have numerous order records with no matching customers. When referential integrity is enforced, these kinds of accidental deletions aren't allowed to happen. Access can enforce referential integrity when the following conditions are met:

- The matching field of the primary table is a primary key, or is indexed with no duplicates.
- The related fields have the same data types.
- Both tables are in the same database.

If you want to enforce referential integrity, turn on the Enforce Referential Integrity option that appears in the Relationships window when you are establishing the relationship. After Enforce Referential Integrity is turned on, Access displays a dialog box that does not permit the change if it threatens to destroy the referential integrity of the database. For details on creating a relationship, see the question "How can I create a relationship to records in another table?" under the heading "Defining Fields," earlier in this chapter.

Can I display Text field entries in all uppercase letters, no matter how they are entered?

You can control the case table entries display in by setting the Format property for that field. In Design view, you need to select the field and then move to its Format property, displayed in the lower half of the window. Entering > for this property forces all entries to display in all uppercase; entering < forces all entries to display in all lowercase. If you use the > setting, the field might resemble the Customer ID field shown here:

Customer ID	Company Name	Contact Name	Contact Title	
ALFKI	Alfreds Futterkiste	Maria Anders	Sales Representat	Obere Str. 57
ANATR	Ana Trujillo Emparedados	Ana Trujillo	Owner	Avda. de la C
ANTON	Antonio Moreno Taquería	Antonio Moreno	Owner	Mataderos 2
AROUT	Around the Horn	Thomas Hardy	Sales Representat	120 Hanover
BERGS	Berglunds snabbköp	Christina Berglund	Order Administratc	Berguvsväger
BLAUS	Blauer See Delikatessen	Hanna Moos	Sales Representat	Forsterstr. 57
BLONP	Blondel père et fils	Frédérique Citeaux	Marketing Manage	24, place Klé
BOLID	Bólido Comidas preparada	Martín Sommer	Owner	C/ Araquil, 67

Record: 1 of 91

Can I display Yes/No fields as Affirmative and Negative, respectively, using different color fonts for each?

You can change how the values in the Yes/No field display by changing the Format property setting for the field. For example, you can enter **"Negative" [Red]; "Affirmative"**

[Black] to display Affirmative in black for Yes, and Negative in red for No. You enclose in quotation marks the text that you want to display in place of Yes and No. The colors appear in brackets, to indicate that they are the font colors rather than text to display. (You must also change the Display Control value in the Lookup tab of the Properties window to Text Box.)

How can I format a field to display a ZIP+4 code?

For this task, you can use either an input mask or a format. With an input mask, Access prompts you for the correct data by showing a template in Datasheet view. Whichever method you choose, you must make sure that the field to contain this extended ZIP code is a Text field. Select either method by switching to Design view, moving to the field, and changing one of the properties.

To add an input mask for the field, move to the Input Mask property. Then click the Build button (…) at the end of the line. Select the standard ZIP code input mask and then click Next twice. Select whether you want the data stored with the hyphen, and then select Next. Select Finish to add the input mask to the Input Mask property.

If you choose to use a format for the field, click the desired field while in Design view, and then move to the Format property and enter @@@@@-@@@@.

Chapter 4

Working with Access Data

Answer Topics!

Working with Access Data @ a Glance

Tables constitute the heart of your database, because they are the database objects used to store your data. In the last chapter, you learned about solutions for creating tables. In this chapter, your questions about working with tables are answered. When you have problems entering, editing, or sorting data, this chapter is where you can find the answers. Here is a breakdown of the topics covered in this chapter:

Displaying Your Data teaches you how to change the ways in which datasheets display the data in your tables.

Entering and Editing Data provides help on how to enter data faster and make changes to your data without problems.

Sorting and Filtering Data shows you how to best arrange your data, in terms of sort order and record selection.

Working with Relationships helps you understand relationships between tables, how you can best define them, and when and why you would want to.

Troubleshooting explains unexpected error messages and other general problems that can occur when running Access.

DISPLAYING YOUR DATA

 Can I change the column widths of multiple columns as a group?

You can change the width of any column by dragging its border in the column header area. You can do the same for a group of columns. First, click and drag across the field selector buttons of the desired columns, to select them as a group. (The field selector buttons are the buttons containing the field titles at the top of each column.) Then click and drag the right border of the field selector button for any one of the selected columns. As you do this, all the selected columns will resize as a group.

 Can I divide a name field into separate last name and first name fields?

One way you can split a full name field into its components is with a query. For example, assume that the field name that you want to split is called Full Name and that each entry in the Full Name field comprises a courtesy title (such as Mr. or Ms.), a first name, and a last name. Create a query to split it into three calculated fields. The following entries should appear in the Field row of the QBE grid:

```
Title: Left([Full Name], InStr([Full Name]," "))

First Name: Mid([Full Name], InStr([Full Name]," ")+1,
InStr(InStr([Full Name]," ")+1,[Full Name]," ")
-InStr([Full Name]," "))

Last Name: Trim(Right([Full Name],Len([Full Name])
-InStr(InStr([Full Name]," ")+1, [Full Name]," ")))
```

Next, run the query to make sure that the formulas are entered correctly. You can then change the query to a make-table query or an append query, depending on your specific situation. You can also change the query to an update query. Before you change the query, you need to add to the table the fields that will hold the parts of the name. Then change the query from a select query to an update query. Under the field names that hold the parts of the name, enter the same formulas that the calculated fields use. You can even copy the formulas from the calculated fields in the Field row to the Update To row. You can see how these formulas are placed under the field names in this QBE query:

After you design the query, run it. The formulas divide the full name into its parts and use the parts as the updated values for the fields. After the query runs, the Title field contains entries such as Mr., Mrs., and Ms., while the First Name and Last Name fields contain the first and last names. This example focuses on names, but you use similar calculated fields in a query for other fields that you want to divide. (See Chapter 5 for more specifics on designing and using queries.)

How can I find specific data in a large table?

A natural part of the editing process is finding what you want to edit. You can use the Find button on the toolbar or its equivalent—the Find command on the Edit menu—to search for data. You use these steps:

1. Open the desired table in Datasheet view.

2. Click anywhere within the field that you want to search, unless you want to search all the fields. (In a large table, searching a single field is faster than searching all the fields.)

3. Select Edit | Find to display the Find dialog box, shown next.

4. Enter in the Find What text box the text that you want to find.

5. If you want to search all the fields, change the Look In entry from the name of the current field to the table name.

6. Change the Match entry to Any Part of Field, unless you've entered the complete field contents as a search term.

7. Click Find Next. To search for additional entries with the same instructions, click the Find Next button again.

Can I change the fonts used to display my data in Datasheet view?

Yes, you can easily change the font and font size used to display your table in Datasheet view. You can change the font for a single table or change the default font used by all datasheets that do not have their own font setting. Open the table and choose Format | Font. In the Font dialog box that appears (shown here), select the font, font size, and font style that you want to use to display your table.

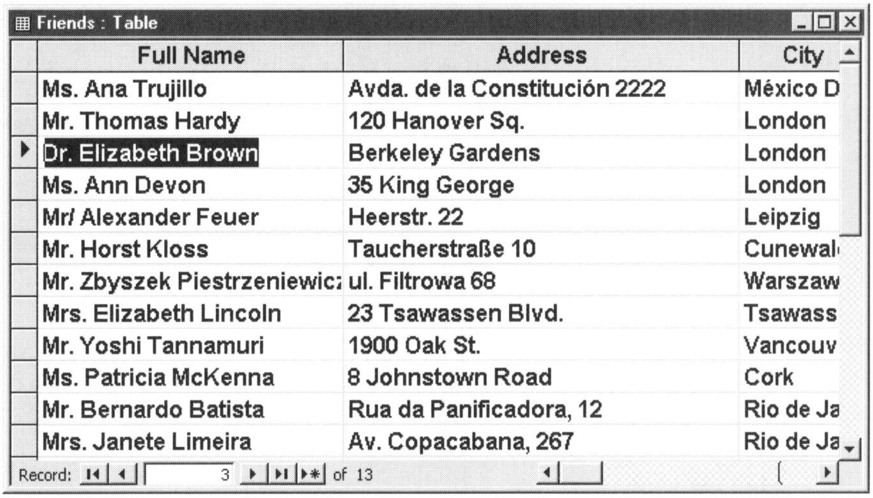
Friends : Table

Full Name	Address	City
Ms. Ana Trujillo	Avda. de la Constitución 2222	México D
Mr. Thomas Hardy	120 Hanover Sq.	London
Dr. Elizabeth Brown	Berkeley Gardens	London
Ms. Ann Devon	35 King George	London
Mr/ Alexander Feuer	Heerstr. 22	Leipzig
Mr. Horst Kloss	Taucherstraße 10	Cunewal
Mr. Zbyszek Piestrzeniewic:	ul. Filtrowa 68	Warszaw
Mrs. Elizabeth Lincoln	23 Tsawassen Blvd.	Tsawass
Mr. Yoshi Tannamuri	1900 Oak St.	Vancouv
Ms. Patricia McKenna	8 Johnstown Road	Cork
Mr. Bernardo Batista	Rua da Panificadora, 12	Rio de Ja
Mrs. Janete Limeira	Av. Copacabana, 267	Rio de Ja

Record: 3 of 13

Figure 4-1 A table with enlarged fonts

After making your selections, choose OK to close the Font dialog box. If you enlarge your font to make your table easier to read, the table might look similar to Figure 4-1.

You can also set the default font used by all tables and queries in Datasheet view. To do so, choose Options from the Tools menu.

Click the Datasheet tab in the dialog box that appears. In the Default Font portion of the dialog box, choose the font name, weight, and size, and the various font attributes, including italics. After setting the options, click OK. The options that you selected become the defaults for all tables and queries in Datasheet view, unless you use the Font command from the Format menu to change the settings for a specific datasheet.

How can I hide columns in a datasheet?

When you want to remove one or more columns from view, you can do so with the Hide Columns command on the Format menu. You hide columns with the following steps:

1. Select the field that you want to hide, by clicking its field selector at the top of the column in the datasheet. (You can select multiple adjacent columns by holding the SHIFT key and clicking each field selector.)

2. Select Format | Hide Columns.

To reveal columns that you've hidden previously, select Format | Unhide Columns to display the Unhide Columns dialog box, shown here. Click the hidden columns that you want to redisplay, and then click Close.

Unhide Columns	? X
Column:	Close

☐ Customer ID
☑ Company Name
☑ Contact Name
☑ Contact Title
☑ Address
☑ City
☑ Region
☑ Postal Code
☑ Country
☑ Phone
☑ Fax

Tip: *The ability of Access to hide one or more columns can be a valuable aid in getting a quick report of the precise data that you want. You can hide unwanted columns to omit fields that you don't want to see, use the filter techniques to omit records that you don't want to include, and then print a report by choosing Print from the File menu. For specifics on filtering data, see "Sorting and Filtering Data," later in this chapter.*

How can I view long entries that I make in Memo fields while working on a datasheet?

Data entry into memo fields is usually done through a form, but an easy way exists to add data to Memo fields without opening the form. You can use the Zoom box to open a window into the Memo field. To enter the data using the Zoom box, move to the Memo field in which you want to enter the data and press SHIFT-F2. When you do this, a Zoom dialog box opens, as shown next. Type the desired data of the memo and then click OK to store the data.

 Tip: *The Zoom box can be used in any location designed to accept text (not just Memo fields), such as criteria cells, field property cells, and the like.*

 ## How can I automatically open tables that I work with?

If you use the same tables every day, you might prefer to open them automatically when you open a database. You can accomplish this task by means of a macro. To create a macro that opens a table automatically at the same time that you open a database, follow these steps:

1. In the Database window, click the Macros button, and then click New.

2. Move and size the Macro window that appears (see Figure 4-2) so that you can see both it and the Database window at the same time.

3. In the Database window, click the Tables tab.

4. From the list of tables, click and drag the first table that you want to open automatically to the first row of the Macro window's Action column.

5. Click and drag the next table that you want to open automatically to the next row of the Macro window's Action column.

6. Repeat step 5 for all remaining tables that you want to open automatically.

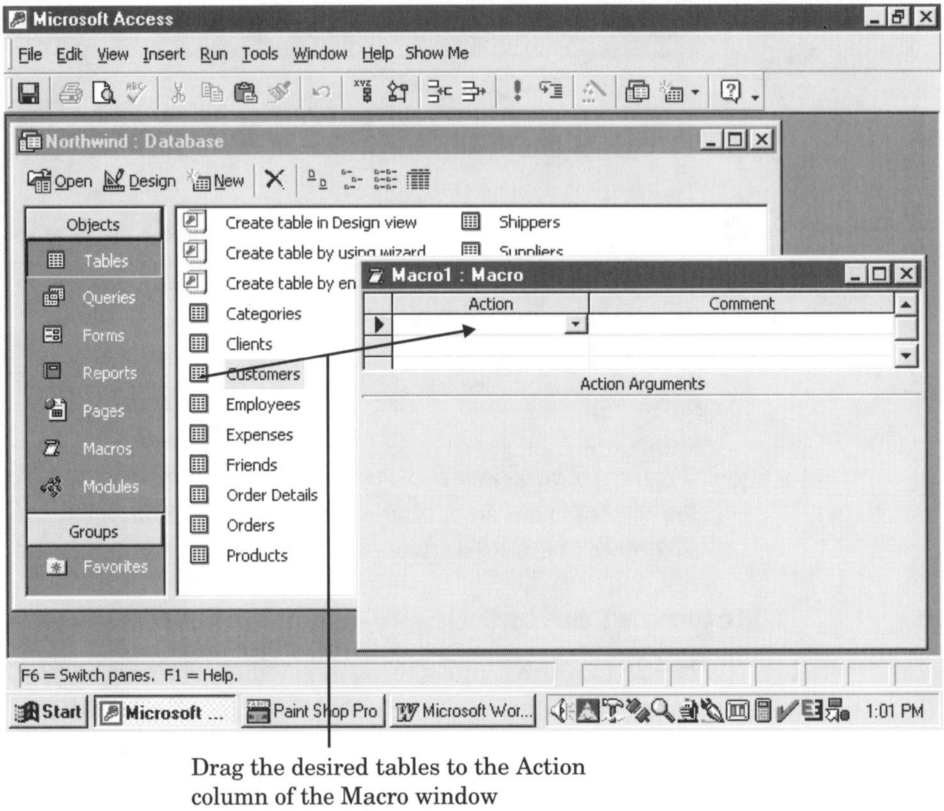

Drag the desired tables to the Action
column of the Macro window

Figure 4-2   The Macro window

7. With the Macro window still active (click anywhere within
    it if it isn't active), choose File | Close. Click Yes in the
    Save Changes dialog box that appears. When prompted
    for a name, enter **Autoexec**, and then click OK.

After performing these steps, you can close the database
(while the Database window is still active, choose File |
Close). Afterward, whenever you open the database, the
tables you added to the macro will open automatically. In
Access, any macro saved under the name Autoexec runs
whenever the database containing the macro is opened. (You
can prevent the macro from running by holding down the
SHIFT key as you open the database.)

 ## How do I change the order of fields in a datasheet?

The original display of fields will match the order in which the fields were laid out in the table's design. Your preferred method of data entry may involve a different arrangement of fields, or you may want to move them around so that you can sort them easier. In Access, rearranging fields is done by a drag-and-drop operation with the mouse. To rearrange a table's fields, perform these steps:

1. Open the desired table in Datasheet view, if it is not already open.

2. Click the field selector for the field that you want to move. When you do so, the field becomes selected, as shown in Figure 4-3.

3. Place the mouse pointer over the field selector and click and hold the left-mouse button. (The rectangular drag-and-drop symbol will be added to the mouse pointer.) As you drag the mouse pointer to the left or right of the selected field, a heavy vertical bar appears, indicating the new position of the field.

Title	Lastname	Firstname	Address
Ms.	Trujillo	Ana	Avda. de la Constitución 2222
Mr.	Hardy	Thomas	120 Hanover Sq.
Dr.	Brown	Elizabeth	Berkeley Gardens
Ms.	Devon	Ann	35 King George
Mr.	Feuer	Alexander	Heerstr. 22
Mr.	Kloss	Horst	Taucherstraße 10
Mr.	Piestrzeniewicz	Zbyszek	ul. Filtrowa 68
Mrs.	Lincoln	Elizabeth	23 Tsawassen Blvd.
Mr.	Tannamuri	Yoshi	1900 Oak St.
Ms.	McKenna	Patricia	8 Johnstown Road
Mr.	Batista	Bernardo	Rua da Panificadora, 12

Friends : Table

Record: 1 of 13

The selected field is shown in reverse video

Figure 4-3 The selected field within a datasheet

4. Drag the mouse pointer (and the vertical bar along with it) to the desired location for the column, and then release the mouse button. In the example shown in Figure 4-4, the Firstname field has been placed in front of the Lastname field.

Tip: *You can move more than one column at a time if the columns are adjacent to each other; just hold down* SHIFT *while clicking additional columns. Then, with all the columns selected, click in the field selector of any of the desired columns and drag the columns to a new location.*

How can I find all of my overdue accounts?

To find all of your overdue accounts, add a filter that compares the due date in the table with today's date. The filter's criterion is **<Date( )**, entered under the date field used to indicate your due date. You can use the following steps:

1. Select <u>R</u>ecords | <u>F</u>ilter | <u>A</u>dvanced Filter/Sort.

2. Drag the date field used as your due date from the Field List to the Field row of the first column.

	Title	Firstname	Lastname	Address	
▶	Ms.	Ana	Trujillo	Avda. de la Constitución 2222	
	Mr.	Thomas	Hardy	120 Hanover Sq.	
	Dr.	Elizabeth	Brown	Berkeley Gardens	
	Ms.	Ann	Devon	35 King George	
	Mr.	Alexander	Feuer	Heerstr. 22	
	Mr.	Horst	Kloss	Taucherstraße 10	
	Mr.	Zbyszek	Piestrzeniewicz	ul. Filtrowa 68	
	Mrs.	Elizabeth	Lincoln	23 Tsawassen Blvd.	
	Mr.	Yoshi	Tannamuri	1900 Oak St.	
	Ms.	Patricia	McKenna	8 Johnstown Road	
	Mr.	Bernardo	Batista	Rua da Panificadora, 12	

Friends : Table

Record: 14 ◄ | 1 | ► | ►I | ►* | of 13

Figure 4-4 The Firstname field relocated ahead of the Lastname field

3. In the Criteria row for that column, enter **<Date( )** as the desired expression.

4. Select <u>R</u>ecords | Appl<u>y</u> Filter/Sort.

How can I right-align entries in a text field?

Right-aligning text and Memo fields is as simple as changing the field's Format property. Display the table's design and move to the field that you want to right-align. Switch to the bottom half of the window and type * for the Format property. This change fills the entry's display with spaces. It also right-aligns the entry. When you save the table's design changes, you will see that your modified fields are right-aligned.

How do I change the row heights in a datasheet?

You can change the height of a datasheet's rows by dragging the bottom edge of any record selector button. At the far left side of the datasheet, move the mouse pointer near the bottom of any record selector button until the pointer changes shape to a double-headed arrow. Then drag to the desired new row height. As an alternative, you can choose F<u>o</u>rmat | <u>R</u>ow Height and enter a desired value for the row height.

ENTERING AND EDITING DATA

I'm attached to tables outside of Access. I can open and view the data, but why can't I make changes to attached tables?

When you're working with tables attached from SQL servers, normally you can't edit the data in the tables unless that table has a unique index on the server. If you want to edit a table that does not have a unique index, you can create an index in Access via a data definition query by using the CREATE INDEX statement in SQL. The index must be based on a field containing unique values. If any of the field's values in the table are duplicates, all attempts to update the table will be unsuccessful.

How can I carry data forward from one record to the next?

You may find that you use the same entry repeatedly in one field of your table. For example, if your employees all live in one state, you don't want to enter the state in each record of the Employees table. To copy the entry made for the same field in the previous record, just press CTRL-' (apostrophe). Access copies the same field's entry from the previous record to the new record.

I enter 01/01/32 in a date field and Access assumes the date to be in the 1900s, while I want it to be in the 21st century. When I enter a date of 01/01/28, I get the desired results. What's going on?

What you are seeing is Access's automatic protection against "Y2K" (Year 2000) problems. Access assumes that any two-digit year between 30 and 99 belongs to the 1900s, but that any two-digit year between 00 and 29 comes after 1999. The easiest way to get around this behavior is to provide room for the user to enter the full year when entering dates. You could choose the Long Date Format in the field's design, but that makes dates take up a lot of space on the screen. A better solution is to use a custom format that uses the full year in the table's design. Open the table in Design view. In the Format property for the date field, enter **mm/dd/yyyy** as the desired format. This displays the date in the short date format, but with all four digits shown for the year. The user must do a little more typing when entering dates, but at least you're sure you'll get the correct year.

How can I delete all records in a table?

Before proceeding, remember that deletions are *not* undoable; once you delete all the records in a table, there's no way to get them back (short of restoring from a backup disk or reentering them). With this in mind, you can use the following steps to delete all the records in a table:

1. Open the table in Datasheet view.
2. At the upper-left corner of the Datasheet, click the table selector button (the unmarked button located at the

intersection of the row of field selector buttons and the column of record selector buttons). When you do this, the entire table will be selected.

3. Press DEL.

4. Answer Yes in the confirmation dialog box that appears.

If you are relatively sure that you want to delete all the records, but you want to keep a copy of the data as a backup, an alternative method of accomplishing the same task is to create a new copy of your table without any data in it. You can use these steps to do this:

1. In the Database window, select the table that you want to copy.

2. Choose Copy from the Edit menu.

3. Choose Paste from the Edit menu.

4. Enter the name for the new table in the Table Name text box.

5. Select the Structure Only button and click OK.

The table that you create has all the same attributes and settings as the original table, but contains none of the data.

How can I delete duplicate records?

You can use the Find Duplicates Query Wizard to create a query that lists duplicate records. However, the dynaset that results from this query is read-only, so you won't be able to delete the entries directly; consequently, your only option is to examine or print the list and go back into the original table to find and delete the duplicates. An alternative method to using the wizard is to create a new table without the duplicate records, delete the old table, and then give the new table its name. You can use these steps to do this:

1. Create a make-table query based on only the table containing the duplicate records. Make sure that all the fields in the table are included in the QBE grid.

2. Click any blank area of the query, and open the query's property sheet by selecting View | Properties.

3. Set the Unique Values property to Yes.

4. Run the make-table query. The query selects all the records that have unique values and creates a new table that has no duplicate records. You can now delete the old table and give the new table its name.

✚ *Tip:* *Make sure that you include all the fields from the table in the QBE grid and display them. Otherwise, your new table might not have all the same fields as your original table.*

Why can't I edit certain fields in my table?

Certain types of fields can't be edited in Access. These fields look like other fields in a datasheet, but Access won't allow you to edit them when you try. The following list includes the types of fields that can't be edited and the possible reasons:

● **Calculated fields** These fields contain results of calculations based on one or more other fields. Because they do not contain actual table data, they can't be edited.

● **AutoNumber fields** Access automatically maintains the entries in these fields, even after they have been added to the table, thus preventing you from editing them.

● **Fields in a locked record** Access will not let you make any changes to data in records on a network that have been locked by others. If the record that you are trying to edit displays a circle with a diagonal slash in the record selector area, the record is being changed by another network user. You must wait until the other user is done before you can make any changes.

● **Fields in a locked database** If the database was opened in read-only mode, or if it was locked by the network operating system software, you can't make any changes to its records or any other objects in the database.

Also, if you have set validation rules, and the data that you want to enter doesn't meet the validation criteria, Access rejects the data that you attempt to enter.

 Why can't I insert records between rows, as I could with dBASE or FoxPro?

Unlike dBASE and FoxPro, Access has no insertion capability. In other words, there is no simple way to insert a new record between existing records. The new records must be added to the end of the table. But this capability really isn't needed in Access. Unlike older products, in which insertions were used mostly to keep databases in order, Access enables you to maintain order in a table at any time by sorting the table. Also, Access queries, forms, and reports can easily be designed so that they automatically sort the data before producing a result.

 How can I enter data into an OLE Object field?

You use Windows cut-and-paste techniques to enter OLE data into OLE Object fields of an Access table. You can do this with the following steps:

1. Use normal Windows techniques (such as pressing ALT-TAB or clicking the appropriate Windows taskbar icon) to switch to the application that contains the OLE data you want to place in the Access table.

2. Using normal Windows selection techniques, select the desired data.

3. In the other Windows application, select Edit | Copy.

4. Switch back to Access and locate in the datasheet the record in which you want to place the OLE data.

5. Click the OLE Object field.

6. If you want to embed the OLE data, select Edit | Paste. If you want to link to the data, select Edit | Paste Special. Then, turn on the Paste Link option in the dialog box that appears and click OK.

How can I update records in my table with the values from another table?

If the updated table is simply an updated version of the table in your database, you might delete the old table and give the imported table the deleted table's name. However, you may find that the imported table contains data for only some of your fields and that you need to use an update query.

For example, suppose that your company just installed a new phone system, so that all of its employees have new phone numbers. The department in charge of installing the phone system just sent you an Access table containing Employee IDs and the new phone numbers assigned to each employee. You don't want to delete your old Employees table, which contains additional data such as benefits, home addresses, phone numbers, and payroll data. To update only the field containing the employees' work phone numbers, do the following:

1. Create a new query, adding both the original table and the table with the new phone numbers.

2. Create a join between the tables by using the primary key, which should be the Employee ID field.

3. Add the fields that you want to update from the original table, in this case the Work Number fields from the Employees table, to the QBE grid.

4. Make this query an update query either by choosing Update Query from the Query menu, or by clicking the down arrow beside the Query Type toolbar button and choosing Update Query from the drop-down menu.

5. In the Update To row of the QBE grid under each field that you want to update, enter the name of the table, a period, and the field from the table with the new data you want to use to update the original table. For example, to update the work phone numbers of your employees, you would enter the expression **[New Numbers].[Numbers]** in the Update To row in the column below the field from the original table that the query will update.

6. Run your update query.

SORTING AND FILTERING DATA

Is there a way to filter data shown in a datasheet?

You can filter a datasheet so that only certain records appear. You do so through the following steps:

1. Open the table in Datasheet view.

2. Find a record that contains data similar to the data that you want to filter. (Figure 4-5 shows an example; in the first row of the figure, Spain is shown in the Country field.)

3. Click the field that you want to use as a filter.

4. In the toolbar, click the Filter By Selection button.

	Company Name	Contact Name	Contact Title	Country	Phone
+	Romero y tomillo	Alejandra Camino	Accounting Manag	Spain	(91) 745 620C
+	Santé Gourmet	Jonas Bergulfsen	Owner	Norway	07-98 92 35
+	Save-a-lot Markets	Jose Pavarotti	Sales Representat	USA	(208) 555-80S
+	Seven Seas Imports	Hari Kumar	Sales Manager	UK	(171) 555-17'
+	Simons bistro	Jytte Petersen	Owner	Denmark	31 12 34 56
+	Spécialités du monde	Dominique Perrier	Marketing Manage	France	(1) 47.55.60.
+	Split Rail Beer & Ale	Art Braunschweiger	Sales Manager	USA	(307) 555-46£
+	Suprêmes délices	Pascale Cartrain	Accounting Manag	Belgium	(071) 23 67 2
+	The Big Cheese	Liz Nixon	Marketing Manage	USA	(503) 555-36'
+	The Cracker Box	Liu Wong	Marketing Assista	USA	(406) 555-58C
+	Toms Spezialitäten	Karin Josephs	Marketing Manage	Germany	0251-031259
+	Tortuga Restaurante	Miguel Angel Paolir	Owner	Mexico	(5) 555-2933
+	Tradição Hipermercados	Anabela Dominques	Sales Representat	Brazil	(11) 555-216i

Customers : Table

Record: |◄ ◄ | 1 | ► ►| ►* | of 91

Figure 4-5   Data in a particular field of a record serves as the basis for a filter

When you do this, a filtered datasheet appears, like the one shown in Figure 4-6. (In the figure, note the presence of the word "Filtered" in the Status bar of the datasheet.) To cancel the effects of the filter when you are done using it, select Records | Remove Filter/Sort, or click the Remove Filter button.

If you want to filter the datasheet on more than one field or add sorting criteria, you can create an *advanced filter* for the datasheet. This process is similar to designing a query— you fill in a filter form that resembles the QBE grid used in queries, and you add the desired sorting and selection criteria. You use these steps to create an advanced filter:

1. Open the table in Datasheet view.

2. Select Records | Filter, and then choose Advanced Filter/Sort from the next menu that appears.

3. In the Filter Design View window that opens, choose a desired sort order and enter criteria to limit the records that appear.

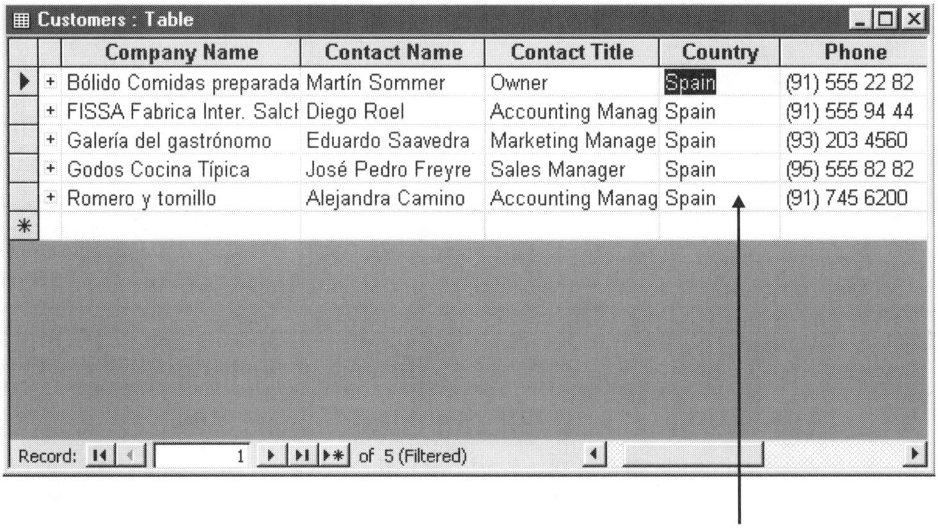

		Company Name	Contact Name	Contact Title	Country	Phone
▶	+	Bólido Comidas preparada	Martín Sommer	Owner	Spain	(91) 555 22 82
	+	FISSA Fabrica Inter. Salcl	Diego Roel	Accounting Manag	Spain	(91) 555 94 44
	+	Galería del gastrónomo	Eduardo Saavedra	Marketing Manage	Spain	(93) 203 4560
	+	Godos Cocina Típica	José Pedro Freyre	Sales Manager	Spain	(95) 555 82 82
	+	Romero y tomillo	Alejandra Camino	Accounting Manag	Spain	(91) 745 6200
*						

⊞ Customers : Table

Record: ◄◄ ◄ 1 ► ►◄ ►* of 5 (Filtered)

A filtered datasheet shows only those records with "Spain" in the Country field

Figure 4-6 A filtered datasheet after using the Filter By Selection button

To use an advanced filter after you create it, either select Filte_r_ | Appl_y_ Filter/Sort or click the Apply Filter button in the toolbar. To cancel the effects of the filter, either select _R_ecords | _R_emove Filter/Sort or click the Remove Filter button in the toolbar.

Caution: *Be aware that filters exist on a temporary basis. Once you close a table or exit Access, the filter is lost. If you plan to use the same filter conditions repeatedly, you should either create and save a query that provides the same results or save the filter as a query. To do this, while the Filter Design View window is open, choose _File_ | Save _A_s Query.*

Can I sort data that's in a datasheet without creating a query?

Access provides two ways to sort the records in your table without using a query. You can either use the sorting toolbar buttons or create an advanced filter that sorts the records in a datasheet (see the previous question).

When you sort using the toolbar buttons, you have to select the fields you want to use to sort the records. In Datasheet view, you can select multiple fields for sorting. The first field selected sorts all records. The second field selected sorts only the records with the same first field value. In a form, you can sort on a single field only. Select the field or fields by which you want to sort, and then click the Sort Ascending or Sort Descending button.

Note: *The Sort Ascending and Sort Descending buttons are equivalent to choosing _S_ort from the _R_ecords menu and then selecting Sort _A_scending or Sort Des_c_ending.*

Note: *Because Access sorts the fields from left to right, you may need to change the order of the fields to obtain the desired sort order.*

WORKING WITH RELATIONSHIPS

How can I create a relationship when one field is an AutoNumber field?

As a rule, the fields that you use to create a relationship must be the same type. However, if you are trying to create a relationship using an AutoNumber field, the second field must be a Number field with the Field Size property set to Long Integer.

What are cascading updates and deletes?

Cascading updates and deletes affect what Access does with data when you update or delete a record in one table that relates to records in other tables. If you have a cascading update, all records in related tables are updated when you change data in a primary table. For example, if you change a customer number in the Customers table, all related tables that contain the customer number update their records to use the new customer number. With a cascading delete, when you delete a record in a primary table, all related data is deleted. This means that when you delete a customer in your Customers table, Access deletes all records for that customer in related tables.

Cascading updates and deletes can be useful, because they can speed data entry and make sure that all related records are updated at the same time. On the other hand, they can also change or delete data without you realizing it. Cascading updates and deletes are not set automatically. You have the opportunity to create them as you create the relationships. In the Relationships dialog box, after you select the Enforce Referential Integrity check box, the additional options in the dialog box are enabled. You can then select the Cascade Update Related Fields and Cascade Delete Related Records check boxes before selecting Create to create the relationship. Unless you select one of these check boxes, you don't have cascading updates or deletes.

How do I create a relationship?

You can create a relationship between two tables by using the following steps:

1. Click the Tables button in the Database window.

2. Select Tools | Relationships to display the Relationships window. If this is the first time that you're establishing this relationship, the Show Table dialog box, shown here, appears in front of the Relationships window:

3. Choose the table or query that you want to use as part of the relationship, and then click Add to add it to the Database window.

4. Repeat step 3 for each additional table or query needed as part of the relationship, and then click Close.

5. To establish the desired relationships, choose from one table the field or fields that you want to use for the link and drag them to the related field or fields in the other table. (Usually, the primary key in one table is related to a field containing similar data in another table.) When you drag and drop the field, the Edit Relationships dialog box appears, as shown next.

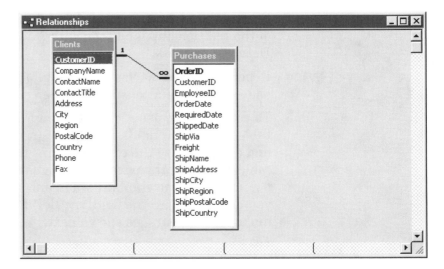

6. Check that the fields being used are the correct fields for a relationship. (Access makes a fairly accurate guess as to which fields it should use, but you may prefer a different set of fields than Access chooses by default.)

7. Select the Enforce Referential Integrity check box to maintain the relationship between the tables. When you enforce referential integrity, Access keeps you from entering records that don't fit the type of relationship between the tables.

8. Click Create to create the relationship. Relationships are shown in the Relationships window by using lines, as you can see here:

Note: *When you create a relationship between two tables by using an AutoNumber field, the other field must be a Long Integer Number field.*

How do I delete a relationship?

You can delete a relationship in Access by opening the Relationships window and removing the join line between the tables. Use these steps:

1. Select <u>T</u>ools | <u>R</u>elationships to open the Relationships window.

2. Select the line between the tables that indicates the relationship.

3. Press DEL.

4. Select <u>Y</u>es when Access prompts you to confirm that you want to delete the relationship.

How do I modify the join type used in a relationship?

In Access, joins used in relationships can be equi-joins, left outer joins, or right outer joins. With *equi-joins*, Access includes only the rows in which the joined fields from both tables are equal. With *left outer joins*, Access includes all records from the table on the right side of the join line (in the Relationships window) and only those records from the table on the left side of the join line in which the joined fields are equal. With *right outer joins*, Access includes all records in the table on the left side of the join line and only those records from the table on the right side of the join line in which the joined fields are equal.

By default, when you create a relationship, Access uses an equi-join for the join type, unless you specify otherwise. To change an existing join type, open the Relationships window by choosing <u>T</u>ools | <u>R</u>elationships. Right-click the join line for the relationship that you want to change, and choose Edit <u>R</u>elationship from the menu that appears. This causes the Edit Relationships dialog box (shown earlier, under "How do I create a relationship?") to appear.

In the Edit Relationships dialog box, click Join Type. This causes the Join Properties dialog box, shown here, to appear. In the dialog box, choose the first option to specify an equi-join, the second option to specify a left outer join, or the third option to specify a right outer join. Click OK, and then click OK again to close the Edit Relationships dialog box.

Join Properties   ? ☒

  ⦿ 1: Only include rows where the joined fields from both
     tables are equal.

  ○ 2: Include ALL records from 'Clients' and only those records
     from 'Purchases' where the joined fields are equal.

  ○ 3: Include ALL records from 'Purchases' and only those
     records from 'Clients' where the joined fields are equal.

        [OK]   [Cancel]

Can I remove tables from my Relationships window?

Yes, you can remove the tables from your Relationships window without deleting the tables themselves from your database. Select the table in the Relationships window and select Relationships | Hide Table. You can also right-click the table's title bar and select Hide Table. Access removes the table from the Relationships window. Removing the table does not change the relationships the table has. You can always put back the table later either by choosing Relationships | Show Table or by clicking the Show Table button.

How can I view related data?

One way to view related data is by means of relational forms, which are covered in Chapter 8. However, with Access 2000, you can also view related data directly in Table view, by opening a *subdatasheet* for any desired record. When you open a table in Datasheet view and that table is related to another table, small plus symbols appear at the left edge of the table, as shown in Figure 4-7.

To view the related data, click the plus symbol for the desired record. When you do this, a subdatasheet opens for that record, displaying the related data, as shown in Figure 4-8.

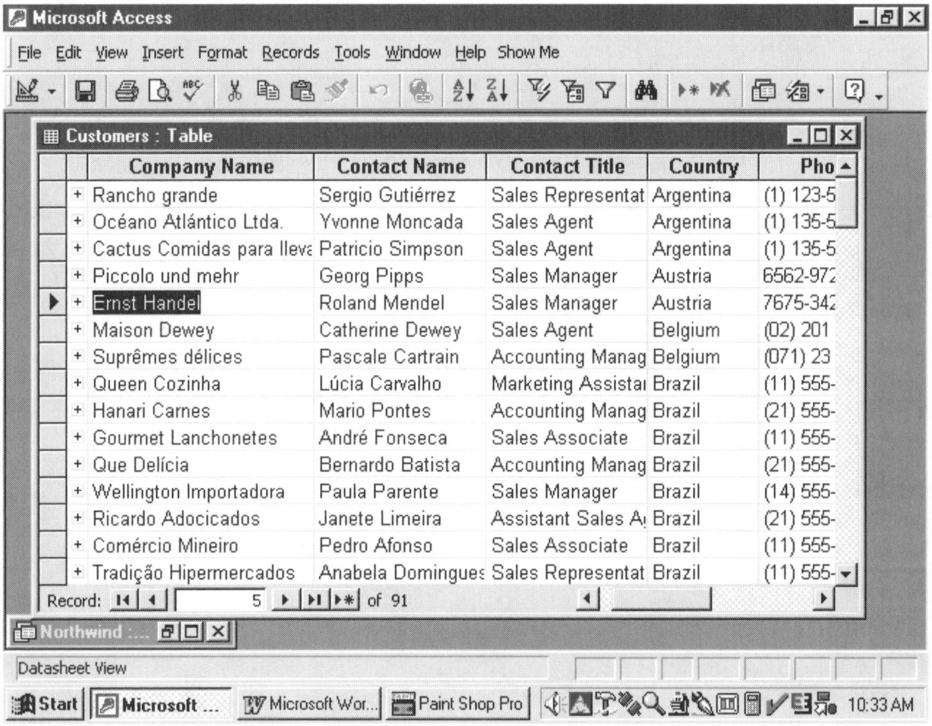

Figure 4-7 Data from a table having related records

What is a relationship?

In Access, a *relationship* is a link between two tables that indicates how the data in those two tables is related. When you create a relationship, you tell Access which fields in the two tables contain the same data. For example, you might create a relationship between your Employees table and your Payroll table by using the Employee ID field in each table. Usually, one of the fields used to create the relationship is the primary key for its table. Both fields must have the same data type; for example, you can't create a relationship using a Number field in one table and a Text field in the second table, because they contain different types of data.

The tables can have a one-to-one relationship or a one-to-many relationship. In a one-to-one relationship, each record in table A (the primary table) matches exactly one record in table B (the related table) and vice versa. Therefore, you can

Figure 4-8 A subdatasheet for a record in a table

enter a record in table B only if the related record already exists in table A and no other record in table B is related to the record in table A. In most one-to-one relationships, you want to redesign your tables to combine the information in the two tables. However, sometimes the one-to-one relationship is intentional.

In a one-to-many relationship, each record in table A (the primary table) matches many records in table B (the related table), but each record in table B relates to only one record in table A. Therefore, you can enter records in table B, the related table, only when the related record already exists in table A. Unlike a one-to-one relationship, you can add records in table B when table B already has records that are related to the same record in table A. For example, you might have one record in your Employees table with many related records in your Projects table.

The ABCs of Relationships

With relational databases, there are three ways in which you can establish relationships between tables. Tables can have a one-to-one, one-to-many, or many-to-many relationship. Access directly supports the first two, and you can indirectly accomplish the third by redesigning many-to-many relationships into multiple one-to-many relationships.

The first step is understanding which table is primary and which tables are related to it. As an example, you could create a relationship between a Customers table and an Orders table. The relationship would indicate which items have been ordered by a specific customer. In this case, the Customers table is the primary table, and the Orders table is the related table (also known as the *foreign* table). By relating the two tables, you eliminate any need to store a customer name and address in the Orders table. Instead, you store just the Customer ID for each order that's stored in the Orders table. Other data needed on invoices or sales reports, such as the customer name and address, can be obtained from the Customers table.

A *one-to-one* relationship exists when each record in the related table corresponds to only one record in the primary table. One-to-one relationships are usually a bad idea, because the duplicated fields in the two tables waste disk space. In most cases, you can add the fields in the related table to the primary table and make one larger table. However, situations do arise when one-to-one relationships are needed. As an example, an employee database might use separate tables for employee home addresses and employee medical data. If different security levels were desired for the different tables, it would make sense to store them separately and establish a one-to-one relationship between the two.

A *one-to-many* relationship is the most common type of relationship used in a database. In a one-to-many relationship, each record in the primary table corresponds to one or more records in the related table. The relationship described in the previous example of customers and their orders is a one-to-many relationship. Any one customer may have placed several orders, but each order belongs to only one customer. One-to-many relationships like this one avoid unnecessary and repetitive data entry.

A *many-to-many* relationship exists when many records in one table are related to many records in another table. Access (along with most PC-based database managers) does not directly support many-to-many relationships. However, you can indirectly support this type of relationship by joining together two one-to-many relationships via a query. A common example of a many-to-many relationship involves an inventory of parts and the suppliers of those parts. The Inventory table contains various parts that have come from one or more suppliers, and each supplier in the Suppliers table provides one or more parts. The Inventory table might contain the description, cost, and quantity for each item in the inventory, along with a unique item number for the item. The Suppliers table might contain the name and address of each supplier, along with a unique Supplier ID number. To relate the tables and provide data on the many-to-many relationship, you would need another table containing just two fields: Item Number and Supplier ID. The third table would serve as an intermediate table linking the other two tables, which contain the "many" data.

Regardless of the types of relationships you use, you will need key fields containing unique data, so that the relationships can be easily established. This is why Access is so insistent about suggesting that you use primary keys when you create new tables.

TROUBLESHOOTING

I get a "duplicate key" error when I try to enter a record. What does this mean?

Whenever you get an error that says "Can't have a duplicate key," the record that you entered is the same as another record in the table. When the Indexed property of a field is set to Yes (No Duplicates), you cannot have two values in that field that are the same. One of the values must be changed.

Why do I see tables starting with "Msys" in the Database window?

The tables that you see with strange names are system tables, and they are used by Access to keep track of its internal operation. Attributes for various objects, file locking information, and custom toolbar designs are just a few of the types of information stored within the system tables. You should *not* modify or delete data in any of these tables. If you change these tables, you can cause major problems with the operation of Access. By default, the tables are hidden. You can hide them again by performing the following steps:

1. Select Tools | Options.
2. In the dialog box that appears, click the View tab (if it isn't already selected).
3. Turn off the System Objects option.
4. Click OK.

Chapter 5

Basic Queries

Answer Topics!

Basic Queries @ a Glance

In Access, a *query* is basically a question that you ask Access about the data that's stored in your tables. When you query Access, it processes the data and displays the records that answer your question. Its response is in the form of a temporary table, called a *dynaset*. This chapter answers questions about the two general types of queries: the basic *select query*, which responds to your questions, and the *action query*, which updates or deletes existing data. Chapter 6 answers your questions about the more advanced query types in Access, such as relational queries and queries that produce crosstabs of your data.

The questions that this chapter answers deal with the following areas:

Query Basics explains the terms associated with queries, the types of queries you can work with, and the specifications and limitations of queries.

- **Managing Fields** helps you to ensure that your queries' fields appear where and when you want them to.

- **Query Criteria** helps you to structure criteria in your queries so that you get the data you need.

- **Action Queries** provides answers to questions about action queries, which enable you to update or delete tables, based on the design of the query.

- **Sorting Data** helps you to control the order in which the data is presented that's retrieved by your queries.

- **Calculations** tells you how to obtain the kinds of calculations you want, and what to do when a type of calculation doesn't give you the results you expect.

- **Troubleshooting** helps you to deal with unexpected error messages and other general problems when running Access.

Query Design in a Nutshell

A significant part of the effective use of queries in Access revolves around the use of the QBE (query by example) grid, the lower pane of the query window, shown here:

Field:	Address	City	Region	PostalCode	Cou
Table:	Employees	Employees	Employees	Employees	Emp
Sort:					
Show:	☑	☑	☑	☑	
Criteria:		"Seattle"			
or:					

You fill in the various rows of the QBE grid to tell Access what conditions to use when retrieving your data. The various rows of the QBE grid enable you to select fields to include in the query results, choose a sort order, show or hide fields from the results, and specify criteria that determine which records appear in the results. The following are the rows of the QBE grid:

- **Field**   Contains the names of the fields. You can add field names either by dragging fields from field lists above the QBE grid or by choosing field names from a drop-down list box that appears when you click inside the row. The Field row can also contain *calculated fields*, which are expressions that provide values based on a calculation involving one or more fields.

- **Table**   Contains the name of the table (or existing query) that supplies the fields used by the query.

- **Sort**   Determines whether the field sorts the records in the dynaset.

- **Show**   Determines whether the field appears in the resulting dynaset or is hidden.

- **Criteria**   Contains the criteria that select which records appear in the dynaset.

Three basic steps are involved in designing a query in Access. First, you tell Access from which tables or other queries the data should be retrieved. (In Access, a query can be based on tables, other queries, or a combination of both.) Next, you tell Access which fields you want included in the results of the query. Finally, you describe any sorting and selection criteria that should apply to the results. The following sections provide a more-detailed description of the three steps that you need to perform to create a basic query in Access.

Identifying the Source of the Data

1. In the Database window, click the Queries button.
2. Click New. Access displays the New Query dialog box:

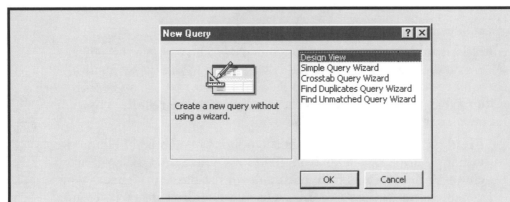

3. Click Design View and then click OK. (The remaining choices are used for the special-purpose queries listed.) In a moment, Access opens a new Query Design View window and displays a Show Table dialog box above it:

4. Click the table that you want to inquire about, and then click Add.

5. Repeat step 4 for each additional table that you want to add to the query. (You can also add existing queries to the design of a new query, by clicking the Queries tab and choosing an existing query as a data source for the new query.)

6. Click Close to close the Show Table dialog box. The Query Design View window shows a grid for the query itself (in the lower half of the window) and field lists for the tables or existing queries that are supplying the data (in the upper half):

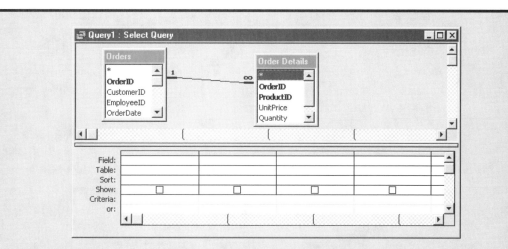

Choosing the Fields Returned by the Query

After you identify the source of the data for the query, you need to tell Access which fields should be included in the query results. Follow these steps to do this:

1. In the field lists in the upper half of the window, choose the field that you want to see listed first in the query results. Click and drag that field to the first empty column in the Field row.

2. Repeat step 1 for each field that you want to add to the query results.

Specifying Sorting and Selection Criteria

The final step in designing a query is to tell Access how you want the data sorted, and what *criteria,* or selection rules, should apply to the data. You can use these steps to choose a sort order for the data retrieved by the query:

1. Choose the field that you want Access to use first when ordering the records. For example, if you are querying a Customers table, you might want to retrieve the records in alphabetical order, by last name.

2. Click the Sort row for the field that you want Access to use first, and then, from the drop-down list, choose the desired sort order (Ascending or Descending).

3. To sort based on multiple columns, repeat steps 1 and 2 for each additional column to be sorted. Note that when you are sorting based on more than one column, the column of most importance in the sort order must be the leftmost column. (You can click and drag columns around in the query grid, as needed.)

You can specify your selection criteria by performing these steps:

1. Click the Criteria row within the field that Access should use to retrieve the desired information.

2. Enter the selection criteria in the column. If you're searching for records in which a field contains a specific value (such as a numeric amount or a date), enter that value. If you want to retrieve records with a specific text entry—such as a City field equal to San José—enter that text. For example, entering **USA** in a Criteria row under a Country column, as shown here, would retrieve all records in which USA appears in the Country field of a table:

Query1 : Select Query

Clients
Address
City
Region
PostalCode
Country

Field:	PostalCode	Country	Phone	Fax	
Table:	Clients	Clients	Clients	Clients	
Sort:					
Show:	☑	☑	☑	☑	
Criteria:		"USA"			
or:					

3. Repeat step 2 for additional fields for which you want to specify selection criteria.

After you perform these steps, to run the query to retrieve the desired data, click the Run toolbar button or choose Query | Run. The

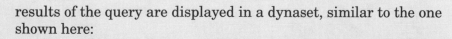

results of the query are displayed in a dynaset, similar to the one shown here:

Company Name	Address	City	Region	Postal Code	Cou
Great Lakes Food Market	2732 Baker Blvd.	Eugene	OR	97403	USA
Hungry Coyote Import Sto	City Center Plaza	Elgin	OR	97827	USA
Lazy K Kountry Store	12 Orchestra Terrace	Walla Walla	WA	99362	USA
Let's Stop N Shop	87 Polk St.	San Francisco	CA	94117	USA
Lonesome Pine Restaurar	89 Chiaroscuro Rd.	Portland	OR	97219	USA
Old World Delicatessen	2743 Bering St.	Anchorage	AK	99508	USA
Rattlesnake Canyon Groc	2817 Milton Dr.	Albuquerque	NM	87110	USA
Save-a-lot Markets	187 Suffolk Ln.	Boise	ID	83720	USA
Split Rail Beer & Ale	P.O. Box 555	Lander	WY	82520	USA
The Big Cheese	89 Jefferson Way	Portland	OR	97201	USA
The Cracker Box	55 Grizzly Peak Rd.	Butte	MT	59801	USA
Trail's Head Gourmet Prov	722 DaVinci Blvd.	Kirkland	WA	98034	USA
White Clover Markets	305 - 14th Ave. S.	Seattle	WA	98128	USA

Query1 : Select Query

Record: 1 of 13

Much of the power behind Access queries depends on how you structure the criteria used by your query. For more specifics on using criteria to your best advantage, see the section titled "Query Criteria," later in this chapter.

QUERY BASICS

 ### What is an action query?

An *action query* performs an action, such as deleting records or changing your data. As opposed to *select queries*, which just let you view your data, action queries actually do something to the data in your tables. You typically use action queries to handle mass updates to your data. For example, you could use an action query to increase every value in a Cost field of an Inventory table by four percent. Access provides four types of action queries:

- **Append queries**   To add data to an existing table
- **Delete queries**   To delete records that meet certain criteria specified by the query

- **Update queries** To change the data in existing tables for all records that meet certain criteria specified by the query
- **Make-table queries** To create new tables by using data extracted from existing tables

What is a dynaset?

A *dynaset* is a temporary table that Access creates when a query runs. The term *dynaset* is an abbreviation for *dynamic set of records*. The word *dynamic* refers to the fact that when Access displays a dynaset, it displays live data from the tables included in the query. In other words, what you see in a dynaset is the real data, and not some static representation of it. You can make changes to the data in a dynaset, and when you do so, you change the underlying data in the table. You can even add new records to a table by entering new records into a dynaset. Likewise, if you change the data in the tables that are used as data sources for the dynaset, the data in the dynaset changes accordingly.

Tip: *Because Access uses the same view for a dynaset and for a table's datasheet, you can apply the same changes to properties that you could for a datasheet. You can increase or decrease the width of columns, change row heights, move columns around, and hide columns, just as you might do with a datasheet.*

How large can a query's resulting dynaset be?

The maximum size of a resulting dynaset is actually a limitation of disk space. Dynasets created by your queries are limited to 1GB in size.

How many characters can I have in a cell of the QBE grid?

You can have up to 1,024 characters in any single cell of the QBE grid. (You may need a large number of characters when entering complex expressions for criteria or for calculated fields.)

 How many fields can I sort by in my query?

You can sort by up to 255 characters, which can be contained in one or more fields. To sort by a field in your query, you choose Ascending or Descending from the Sort row underneath the field's name. Access starts sorting by the leftmost field and works its way right. Note that the maximum differs from early versions of Access, which limited you to ten fields. You can sort on more than ten fields as long as the total number of characters involved in the sort doesn't exceed 255 characters.

 How many tables can I include in a query?

You can use up to 32 tables in a query. The fields can either appear in the query's dynaset or select which records from another table will appear in the dynaset.

Why can't I name a query with the same name as an existing table?

For the purposes of holding data, Access considers tables and queries to be the same type of objects. This enables Access to display both tables and queries as data sources for other objects, such as forms and reports. If you try to give a query the same name as an existing table, Access displays a dialog box asking whether you want to replace the existing table with the query. If you click Yes, the existing table is overwritten by the query.

✚ *Tip: Many professional Access developers use three-character identifiers in object names to specify the object type. Thus, if you had an Employees table and an Employees query, their names would not conflict, because they would be something like tbl Employees and qry Employees.*

What does QBE stand for?

QBE stands for *query by example*, which describes a method of obtaining data that was pioneered by IBM in the 1970s. Access uses *graphical QBE* (or *graphical query by example*) to

describe the data that you're looking for and to obtain results quickly. With graphical QBE, you can perform most of the aspects of designing the query by dragging objects around on a query form. Using QBE lets you retrieve the information that you want without programming.

Access converts the query design in the QBE grid into a Structured Query Language (SQL) statement. SQL (pronounced "sequel") is a standard language used by many database management applications. You can create a SQL statement directly, without using the QBE grid, but this isn't necessary, unless you are already comfortable using SQL.

What is a select query?

In Access, the most commonly used type of query is the *select query*, which asks a question and selects information in response, based on how you structure the query. For example, you might create a query to find out which employees worked over 50 hours last week, or to determine which clients had overdue invoices.

When your tables become large, you need to find the data you want quickly. That's what select queries do. Without select queries, your tables are nothing more than long lists of data. When run, select queries display *dynasets*, showing temporary tables that display the exact information that you need.

Figure 5-1 shows a select query, both in its Design view and as a dynaset (after the query has been run). The upper portion of the window shows the query's design. You can see that the QBE grid selects the fields that will appear in the resulting dynaset. The query also selects which records will appear, by including only those records whose Unit Price is greater than $30.00. The query's dynaset, in the lower half of the window, shows the records that match the criteria.

Tip: *Switch to the dynaset from a Query window by clicking the View toolbar button, shown here, or by choosing View | Datasheet View. The View button, which alternates between Datasheet and Design views, is just like the button that you use to switch between Datasheet and Design views for a table.*

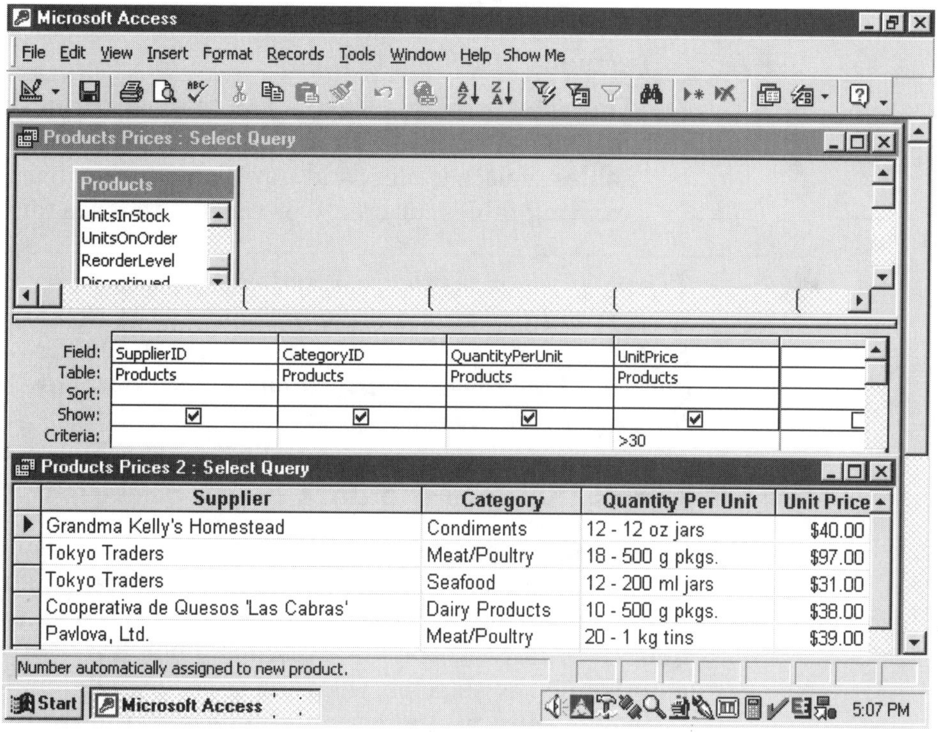

Figure 5-1   A select query and its resulting dynaset

What is a SQL-specific query?

A *SQL-specific query* is any query that you can't create by
using only the QBE grid. Instead, you create the query by
typing an appropriate SQL statement directly into the SQL
view window. The following types of SQL-specific queries are
common to Access:

● **Union**   Combine data from multiple tables into a single
table. The resultant table is called a *snapshot,* because
unlike a dynaset, it is *not* updateable.

● **Pass-through**   Enable you to send SQL statements
("pass them through") directly to a database server on a
network, using the syntax of SQL that's appropriate to
your database server. You use pass-through queries to

work with tables stored on a database server, without actually attaching to them.

● **Data-definition** Enable you to create or modify tables and their indexes. You can use these queries to create tables, delete tables, add new fields to the design of existing tables, or create or remove indexes for a table.

Tip: *If you want to use a SQL-specific query, search Access's online help for more information on SQL and SQL-reserved words. Also, if you are creating pass-through queries, check the documentation for your database server for the proper SQL syntax.*

Why can't I update the data in my query?

In Access, some types of queries and certain fields in queries can't be updated. An easy way to tell whether a query is updateable is to look at the last record in the resulting query's dynaset. If the last record is a blank record with an asterisk on the selector, then the query *is* updateable (although some of the individual fields within the query might not be updateable). The following types of queries aren't updateable in Access:

● Crosstab, pass-through, or union queries

● Queries that calculate a sum, average, count, or other type of total on the values in a field

● Queries that include attached tables lacking indexes or primary keys

● Queries for which permission to update or delete records is not available

● Queries with the Unique Values property set to Yes

● Queries based on three or more tables in which a many-to-one-to-many relationship exists

● Queries that include more than one table or query, and the tables or queries aren't joined by a join line in Design view

Some queries let you update some, but not other, fields in the queries. Fields that cannot be updated include:

- Some fields in a query based on tables with a one-to-many relationship
- Calculated fields
- Fields from databases that were opened as read-only
- Fields deleted or locked by another user
- A Memo or OLE Object field in a *snapshot*, which is an unchanging dynaset created by SQL-specific queries

Tip: *Another way to check whether a query is updateable is to see whether the Records | Data Entry command is dimmed. If it is dimmed, you can't update the records in the query.*

What's the difference between View | Datasheet and Query | Run?

When you are in Design view for a query, you can see the dynaset containing the results of the query if you do either of the following:

- Choose View | Datasheet View (or click the toolbar's View button)
- Choose Query | Run (or click the toolbar's Run button)

So, the obvious question arises: What's the difference between the two? For select queries, no difference exists: running a query or changing from Design view to Datasheet view provides the same result. However, an important difference does exist with action queries, which change existing data or create new tables. When you have an action query open in Design view, switching to Datasheet view displays a dynaset that shows how the data will be affected, but the changes specified by the action query aren't performed. On the other hand, if you run the action query, the changes specified by the design of the action query (adding or updating records, deleting records, or creating new tables) are carried out.

MANAGING FIELDS

How can I hide fields in the resulting dynaset?

You can hide fields from the dynaset that results from your queries. For example, you might want to display only those customers based in Canada, but you do not want the data from the Country field of the table included in the results of the query. To omit a field from the results, click the Show check box to remove the check mark in the box. (By default, a check mark appears in the Show check box for any field included in the query, indicating that the field will be shown in the results.) As an example, in the query shown here, the Country field contains a criteria limiting the records to Canada, but the check mark has been removed from the Show box in the field column; hence, the dynaset that results from the query will not include the data from the Country field.

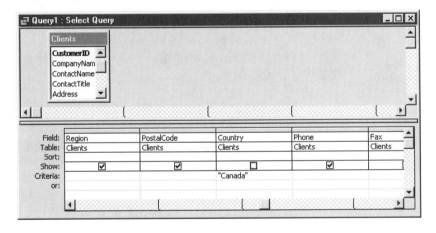

Caution: You can't omit any fields that you plan to use in forms or reports based on the query.

 How can I change the order of the fields in a query's dynaset?

You can rearrange the fields in a dynaset with the same methods used to move fields in a datasheet. Use these steps to move the fields in a query dynaset:

1. Select the field that you want to move by clicking the field selector button at the top of the column.

2. Click and hold down the left mouse button as you point to the field selector button. The shape of the mouse pointer changes to a small square.

3. While keeping the mouse button depressed, drag the field to the desired location. As you drag the field, a solid bar appears, showing where the relocated field will appear when you release the mouse button, as shown here:

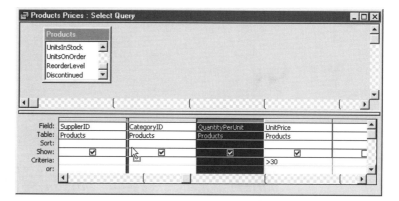

 Can I rename a column to make its title different from the field name?

As part of your query design, you can specify a different name for the column titles in a dynaset. In the Field row for the desired field, click the start of the field name, and type the new name, followed by a colon. For example, if a field is named 99 Sales and you want the column in the resulting dynaset to be titled "Sales for 1999," your entry in the Field row would be as follows:

```
Sales for 1999:[99 Sales]
```

 ### How can I easily view a long expression in the QBE grid?

Access offers a way to easily see lengthy entries in the QBE grid. Click the desired cell of the grid and press SHIFT-F2. Access opens the Zoom box, displaying the entry, as shown here:

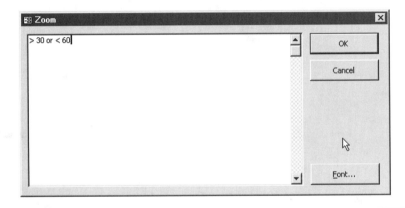

Tip: The Zoom box can also display long entries in other parts of a query, such as an entry in a Field row. You can use this Zoom box in other areas of Access, such as when entering data in Memo fields of a table or when entering expressions into controls used in forms and reports.

QUERY CRITERIA

I want to search for text that includes the word and within the text, but Access thinks I'm trying to use the And operator. How can I change this?

Access considers the words *and*, *or*, and *not* to be operators. So, if you use these words as part of a query string, Access assumes the words are being used as operators rather than as literal

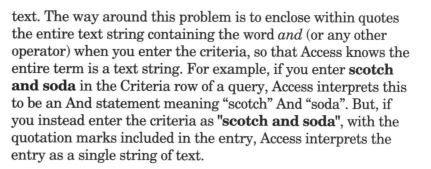

text. The way around this problem is to enclose within quotes the entire text string containing the word *and* (or any other operator) when you enter the criteria, so that Access knows the entire term is a text string. For example, if you enter **scotch and soda** in the Criteria row of a query, Access interprets this to be an And statement meaning "scotch" And "soda". But, if you instead enter the criteria as **"scotch and soda"**, with the quotation marks included in the entry, Access interprets the entry as a single string of text.

How can I structure my query criteria to search for dates based on today's date?

You can include the Date() function to create queries that retrieve data relative to the current date, according to your PC's clock. For example, you could enter a criterion **<=Date()-30** in a query field called Hire Date, to tell Access to retrieve the names of any employees hired 30 or more days ago. An expression such as =Date() retrieves records with today's date in the Date field.

How can I search for records that don't match a value?

You can use the Not operator to select records that don't meet a specific condition. For example, you could enter an expression such as **Not Atlanta** in the City field of a query to retrieve all records with anything other than *Atlanta* in the City field. You could enter an expression such as **Not 4/15/2000** in a Date Sold field to find all records with a sales date other than 4/15/2000.

Can I design my query criteria to select records based on only one word in a Memo or Text field?

Yes, you can have your query search for a single word in a longer entry. For example, to search for the word *Blue* in a field, open the query in Design view. Move to the Criteria row beneath the field and enter **Like "*Blue*"**. Run the query either by clicking the Datasheet View button or by choosing View | Datasheet View.

How can I structure my query criteria to find all records in a table that were entered this month?

Assuming that the table has a field containing the date that records have been entered, you can create a query that chooses only the records that you entered this month. To do this, create your query as normal. Then, assuming the field that contains the date of entry is named Entry Date, add the Entry Date field to the QBE grid. Move to the Criteria row for this column and enter **Year([OrderDate])=Year(Now())** **And Month([OrderDate])=Month(Now())**. When you run this query, the dynaset shows only the records entered during the current month.

How can I search for records that contain no value?

You can use the Is Null operator to retrieve records that are missing data in a particular field. For example, suppose that you want to see a list of all clients who don't have a fax number. You can do this by entering the criterion Is Null in the Criteria cell underneath the Fax Number field of the query. The opposite of this expression is Is Not Null; you can enter **Is Not Null** in a Criteria cell to find all records that contain a value of any kind in the field.

How can I query a table for a large range of values, such as all sales between January 1 and June 31?

The *comparison operators,* including > (greater than), < (less than), and = (equal to), can be used to select records that fall within a certain range of values. Database users often think only of numeric and currency values as falling within certain ranges, but you also can use the comparison operators with text and date values. The comparison operators can be used to construct these types of queries. The following are some examples:

- In a Date field, you could use **>= 1/1/99 and <=6/30/99** to retrieve records with entries that fall between January and June of 1999.

- In a Cost field containing currency amounts, you could enter the criterion **>10 and < 50** to specify a range between 10.00 and 50.00.

- In a query field containing last names, you could enter **> "M" and < "Zz"** in the QBE grid to retrieve all last names beginning with the letters *M* through *Z*. The addition of the second letter *z* is important in this case, because without it, Access would retrieve all names up to *Z*, but none following the letter *Z* alone. This would have the effect of omitting all last names that begin with *Z* that contain more than one character.

Tip: *You can also use the Between...And operator to specify ranges. For example, you could enter* **Between 10 And 50** *as a criterion value in a query.*

 ## How can I specify my criteria when the query runs?

You can provide different criteria each time that a query runs by creating a *parameter query,* a query that automatically asks you for the needed criteria each time the query runs. You can use the same select queries that you have already created as the basis for parameter queries. Instead of having to open the query window and type the new criteria into the query grid, Access will display dialog boxes with prompts, asking you for the criteria. You can create a parameter query with the following steps:

1. Create a query with the tables and the fields that you want.

2. In the Criteria cells underneath the fields that you want to use as parameters, enter your parameter text, enclosed in square brackets. (This text will be used as a prompt in the dialog box that Access displays when the query runs.) For example, if you want a parameter in a Country field to ask for the name of the country to include in the search when the query runs, you can enter an expression such as **[Enter the desired country name:]** in the Country field, as shown here:

![Query1 : Select Query window showing the Clients table with fields CustomerID, CompanyNam, ContactName, ContactTitle, Address, and a query grid below with Field row: PostalCode, Country, Phone, Fax; Table row: Clients for each; Show checkboxes checked for PostalCode, Phone, Fax; Criteria row: [Enter the desired country name:] under Country]

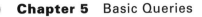

3. Save the query (choose <u>F</u>ile | <u>S</u>ave or press CTRL-F4 and answer Yes to the prompt that appears).

When you run the query, Access displays a dialog box that asks for the parameter value:

Enter Parameter Value	✕
Enter the desired country name:	
OK	Cancel

When you type the data and click OK, the query runs and provides the data according to your criteria.

Tip: *Although this example uses a parameter with a single value, you're not limited to a single value in a parameter. One common use of multiple values in the same parameter is to prompt for a range of values, usually done with numbers or dates. For example, consider a query based on a table that contains a Date field for the date of hire of employees. If you want a parameter query that prompts for all employees hired between two dates, you could enter an expression such as* **Between [Enter the starting date:] And [Enter the ending date:]** *in the criteria cell for the Date field. When you run the query, Access asks for the starting date and then asks for the ending date. The resulting records shown in the query would contain only those records falling between the two dates.*

Tip: *Parameter queries are useful as a data source for forms and reports, because they provide an easy way to ask users of the database for the necessary information to obtain selective data. You can create parameter queries and then change the Record Source properties of your forms and reports to draw data from the parameter queries. For example, if your application has a sales report that needs to be run on a weekly basis, you can base the report on a parameter query that asks for the starting date and the ending date of sales. That way, each time the report runs, the user enters the appropriate dates for that week, and the resulting report contains records from the desired week's sales.*

How can I use wildcards in my query criteria?

You can use wildcard characters to find groups of records in which the entries match a specific pattern. The valid wildcards are the question mark (?), which represents any single character in the same position as the question mark, and the asterisk (*), which represents any number of characters in the same position as the asterisk. You can use these wildcard characters in text-based or date-based expressions. For example, the expression "M*s" could be used in a Criteria cell underneath a Last Name field to find names such as Morris, Masters, and Miller-Peters. The expression Like "6/*/2000" in the Criteria cell for a Date field could be used to retrieve all records in which that date falls in June 2000.

ACTION QUERIES

 ### How can I add records from one table to another?

For this task, you should create an *append query,* an action query that adds the results of the query to other tables. Use the following steps to create an append query:

1. Design a select query that produces a dynaset containing the records that you want to add to the other table.

2. Run the query to make sure that the results provide the data that you want to add to the other table.

3. Switch to Design view either by clicking the View toolbar button or by choosing View | Design View.

4. Choose Query | Append Query. Access displays the Append dialog box, shown here:

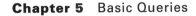

5. In the Table Name drop-down list box, choose the table to which you want to add the records, and then click OK.

6. Run the query by clicking the Run toolbar button or by choosing Query | Run.

7. Access displays a confirmation dialog box, indicating how many records will be appended to the destination table. Click the Yes button.

 ### How can I use a query to delete a batch of records?

You can do this with a *delete query*, a type of action query that deletes all records found by the query's criteria. Use these steps to create a delete query:

1. Design a select query that produces a dynaset containing the records that you want to delete from the table.

2. Run the query to make sure that the results provide the data that you want to delete from the table.

3. Switch to Design view by clicking the View toolbar button (or by choosing View | Design View).

4. Choose Query | Delete Query. The title of the Query window changes to Delete Query, indicating that when you run the query, it will delete all the specified records.

5. Run the query by clicking the Run toolbar button (or by choosing Query | Run). Access displays a confirmation dialog box, telling you how many records will be deleted from the table.

6. If you do not want to delete the records, click No. Otherwise, click Yes to run the query and delete the records.

 Before I run an action query, can I make sure that it will affect the correct records?

You can check which records your action query will affect before you run it. In fact, doing so is a good idea, to avoid accidental and unwanted modifications or deletions of data. After you design an action query, but before you run it, choose View | Datasheet View to check which records it will affect. The dynaset that appears displays the records that will be affected by your action query.

If the query selects the correct records, you can switch back to the query's Design view and run the query. (Click the Design View toolbar button or choose View | Design View.) Click the Run toolbar button (or choose Query | Run) to run the action query.

Can I use a query to find duplicate values in a table?

The easiest way to locate duplicate values in a table is to use the Find Duplicates Query Wizard. This wizard prompts you for information about how you want to search for duplicates, and then creates the query based on your answers. In the

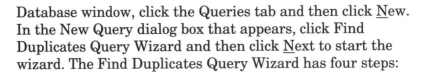

Database window, click the Queries tab and then click <u>N</u>ew. In the New Query dialog box that appears, click Find Duplicates Query Wizard and then click <u>N</u>ext to start the wizard. The Find Duplicates Query Wizard has four steps:

1. Select the table in which you want to find duplicate records.

2. Select the fields you want to search for duplicates. The query considers to be duplicates any records that are the same in all the fields that you select here, even if they are different in other fields.

3. Select any other fields that you want displayed in the query's dynaset. These fields won't be checked for duplicates.

4. Enter a name for the query, and choose whether you want to open it in Datasheet view or Design view.

 I get a "Key violations" error message when I try to run an append query. What does this mean?

This message appears when your append query is attempting to add records to an existing table, and the new records have values in key fields that are the same as values that already exist in the key fields of the table. Access will not allow an append query to cause changes that would create duplicate values in the key fields of records, nor will Access permit any changes that attempt to create null (or empty) values in key fields. When update or append queries attempt to create records that violate these guidelines, the results are *key violations*. You must change the values in the incoming records or in some other manner omit the new records or the changes that are causing the problem.

How can I update the values in a table, based on the results of a query?

For this task, you need to use an *update query*, an action query that updates (or makes specific changes to) all records meeting certain criteria. Update queries are a very handy tool to have when you need to change data in a global fashion. For example, suppose that you need to assign a new telephone area code to the records of all residents living in a particular city. Or, in an Employees table, suppose that you want to increase all salaries of a given type of worker by $.50 an hour. You can use the following steps to create an update query:

1. Design and test a select query that retrieves the records that you want to update.

2. Choose Query | Update Query or click the Update Query toolbar button. Access adds the Update To row to the query grid, as shown here:

3. In the Update To cell for the field that you want to update, enter an expression or a value that will change the data. For example, you could increase salaries by $.50 in a Salary field by entering **[Salary] + .50**. Or, if you want to change all area codes for residents of Stafford, Virginia, from 703 to 540, you enter **Stafford** in the Criteria cell of the City field, **VA** in the Criteria cell of the State field, and **540** in the Update To cell for the Area Code field. For the example shown in the preceding illustration, the update query will increase the UnitPrice field for all products costing $30.00 or more by the amount of $3.00.

4. Run the query by choosing Query | Run or by clicking the Run toolbar button. Access displays a confirmation dialog box, telling you how many records will be updated. Click Yes to run the query and update the records.

SORTING DATA

 How can I sort records if I used the asterisk to drag all the fields to the query?

To sort based on a field, that field must be included individually in the QBE grid. However, you can avoid dragging all the fields individually. Just drag into the QBE grid, in the column beside the one containing the asterisk, the field on which you want to base the sort. This means the field is in the query twice: once as part of the asterisk selection of all fields, and once in the column that you just added. Turn off the Show box for the field (so that it doesn't appear in the resulting dynaset twice) and choose the desired sort order from the Sort row.

I'm sorting based on a combination of fields, and I want the first field used for the sort to appear in a different column of the query's dynaset than at the left of the other fields used for the sort. How can I do this?

Fields that you use for a primary sort order must be the leftmost fields. However, because nothing prevents you from placing the same field in the QBE grid twice, you can work around this problem, as follows:

1. Add the field for the sort at the left side of the QBE grid.
2. Turn off the Show check box for that field.
3. Add the same field again at the desired position in the QBE grid, but leave on the Show check box in that column.

 The records in my dynaset aren't being sorted properly. What's wrong?

Incorrect sorts in queries virtually always are caused by an improper arrangement within the QBE grid of the fields used for the sort. When you are sorting based on more than one field, the fields must be arranged from left to right *in order of precedence*, because Access sorts multiple columns according to this left-to-right order of precedence. Among a group of

sorted fields, the leftmost field gets the highest priority in a sort, followed by the field to its right, followed by the next field to the right, and so on. Suppose that you want to sort a group of records in a mailing list first by state, and then by city for records with the same state, and then by last name for records with the same city. In such a case, the State field must be to the left of the City field, and the City field must be to the left of the Last Name field, as shown here:

Query1 : Select Query				

My People
Title
Firstname
Lastname
Address
City

Field:	State	City	Lastname	Firstname	Zip
Table:	My People	My People	My People	My People	My People
Sort:	Ascending	Ascending	Ascending		
Show:	☑	☑	☑	☑	
Criteria:					
or:					

You can drag fields around within the QBE grid to achieve the desired order of precedence when sorting based on multiple fields.

 Note: *Another common sorting problem is caused by poor data entry training. If the person who entered the data learned to type on a typewriter, the record may contain the letter l instead of the number 1, or the letter O instead of the number 0.*

CALCULATIONS

What are calculated fields, and how can I add one to a query?

Besides having fields that are a normal part of a table's design, you can also include calculated fields in an Access query. *Calculated fields* contain data that is the result of calculations involving other fields, and usually are based on Number or Date fields that are in the same table. You can create a calculated

field in a query by entering an expression in an empty cell in the Field row of the QBE grid. The expression that you enter is what performs the calculation. You can precede the expression with a name and a colon: if you do so, that name will be used for the field name in the resulting dynaset. If you omit a name and a colon, Access names the field Expr*N*, where *N* is a numeric value, starting with 1 for the first calculated field used, and incrementing by 1 for each calculated field in the query.

For example, if a query contains fields for Sale Price and Quantity Sold, you could create a calculated field named Total Cost by entering an expression such as the following in an empty cell of the Field row:

```
Total Cost:[Sale Price] * [Quantity Sold]
```

When the query runs, Access multiplies each of the values in the Sale Price field by the corresponding values in the Quantity Sold field to produce the new values, which are stored in the field named Total Cost. The following table shows examples of expressions that could be used to create calculations:

Calculation Type	Result
Sum	Total of values in a field
Avg	Average of values in a field
Min	Lowest value in a field
Max	Highest value in a field
Count	Number of values in a field (null values are not counted)
StDev	Standard deviation of values in a field
Var	Statistical variance of values in a field
First	Value from the first record in the underlying table or query
Last	Value from the last record in the underlying table or query

Tip: *Calculated fields can also be used to concatenate, or combine, text strings. To concatenate text strings, use the concatenation operator (&) as part of the expression. For example, you could use an expression such as **[First name]** & " "& **[Last name]** to create a calculated field in a query that combines the Last name and First name fields into a single name. When you enter long expressions to perform calculations, you can see the entire expression, without scrolling, by pressing SHIFT-F2 to show the expression within the Zoom box.*

How can I include calculations in my queries?

Often, you may want to perform calculations on groups of records. Although you can obtain totals in reports, you can also do this in your queries. You can obtain the following types of calculations in your queries:

- Totals
- Averages
- Maximum or minimum values
- A count of the numbers of values
- Standard deviation
- Variance (the square of standard deviation)
- First value in a field
- Last value in a field

Because you obtain calculations based on groups of records, you first need to decide how you want to group the records in your query. Then, you must include the fields that are necessary to group the records in the manner that you have chosen. To perform calculations in the query, open the

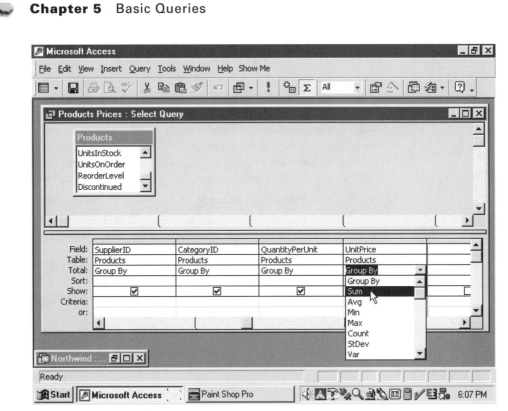

Figure 5-2 A QBE grid containing calculations

query in Design view and choose <u>V</u>iew | <u>T</u>otals (or click the Totals toolbar button). The Totals row appears in the QBE grid, and the designation Group By appears in every field of the query. Click within the Group By row in any field to open a list box of available calculation types, as shown in Figure 5-2, and choose the type that you want to use. After you choose the type of calculation, run the query, and the calculation appears as a result.

Can I use a calculation to convert text in a Text field to all uppercase or to all lowercase?

You can convert the case of text in a query's resulting dynaset by using the Ucase() and Lcase() functions within the query criteria. The Ucase() function converts text to all uppercase, whereas the Lcase() function converts text to all lowercase. You enter **Ucase**(*fieldname*) or **Lcase**(*fieldname*), where *fieldname*

is the name of the existing field. Because this use of an expression results in the column of the dynaset being named Expr: followed by your expression, you may want to give the column a new name. To do so, you add the new name, followed by a colon, and then the function. For example, if you want to capitalize all the text in a field named First Name, you could enter an expression such as the following in the Criteria row of the QBE grid:

```
Firstname:Ucase([First Name])
```

Note that if you use the trick shown here of providing an alternative name followed by a colon, you can't use a name that's the same as the existing field. If you do so, Access displays an error message that warns you of a circular reference in the expression.

 My query includes a calculated field that subtracts two Date/Time fields. However, the calculated field displays fractional numbers instead of times. How can I see the times?

The fractional number that you see in the field is the *serial value* that Access uses to represent a date or time. As you enter dates and times into Date/Time fields, Access stores the values internally as serial numbers, which can then be used in calculations. The integer part of the value that you see in the calculation represents the number of days between the two dates, and the fractional value represents the portion of the day that passed between the two times entered.

If the values that you are subtracting result in a difference that is *always less than one day in length*, an easy solution to the problem is simply to change the format for the calculated field to display the value in Date/Time format, as follows:

1. Click in the calculated field in the QBE grid.

2. Click the Properties toolbar button (or choose View | Properties) to display the field properties for the calculated field.

3. Click the Format property and type **hh:mm:ss** into the property. Although this isn't one of the choices in the

drop-down list, Access accepts and applies the value, thus producing correct times.

If the calculated value may be more than one day in length, the solution gets considerably more involved. You need to create a function in Visual Basic for Applications (VBA) and use that function in the expression for the calculated field. The function creates a string out of the time information stored as a fractional number. Use these steps to create this procedure:

1. Click the Modules tab in the Database window.

2. Click New.

3. Type the following code into the Module window that appears:

```
Function HrsMinsSecs(TimeVar As Double)
Dim Hrs As Long, Mins As String, Secs As String
If IsNull(TimeVar) Then
        HrsMinsSecs = Null
        Else
Mins = Format(DatePart("n", TimeVar), "00")
Secs = Format(DatePart("s", TimeVar), "00")
Hrs = (Fix(TimeVar) * 24) + DatePart("h", TimeVar)
HrsMinsSecs = Hrs & ":" & Mins & ":" & Secs
End If
End Function
```

4. Close the Module window. When asked whether you want to save the module, answer Yes and enter any name that you want for the module.

5. Open the query in Design view, click the Field cell for the calculated cell, and type:

```
=HrsMinsSecs(value to convert)
```

For this example, you might enter the following:

```
=HrsMinsSecs([Last Date]-[First Date])
```

6. Click the Datasheet View button to display the query's dynaset. The calculated field should now display as a

time, in the format HH:MM:SS. For example, if Last Date equals 12/25/98 22:30 and First Date equals 12/24/98 18:00, this function displays the result as 28:30:00 instead of 1.1875.

I created a calculated field that divides two numbers, but the results don't show any decimal places, although they should. What's wrong?

Two possible reasons exist for why your calculated field may not show any digits to the right of the decimal place: you are using either the wrong operator or the wrong Decimal Places property setting.

To find the cause of this problem, switch back to Design view for the query. Make sure that you used the forward slash (/) as the division operator in your formula, instead of the backslash (\). Among the Access operators, the backslash is the symbol for *integer division*. This operator divides two integers and returns an integer result. If the values that you divide with the backslash have decimal values, Access rounds them and then performs the division. Hence, 234.56\21.34 is the same as 235\21. If this is the cause of your problem, simply change the backslash to a forward slash, and the formula should work correctly.

If the problem isn't an incorrect operator, you may have set the Decimal Places property to zero. To check this, click in the calculated field in Design view and choose View | Properties. If the Decimal Places property is set to 0, change the entry to the number of decimal places that you want returned.

Can I designate the number of values that a query should return for the highest or lowest values in a field?

You can do this by changing the Top Values property for the query. (Doing so also can make your queries appear to run much faster if you are querying large amounts of data.) You can use the Top Values property to create a query that returns a specific number of the highest or lowest values in a field. For

example, you could create a query that returns the records of your top five salespeople. Use the following steps to do this:

1. Create the query to select the records that you want included.

2. Sort the query by the field from which you want to select the top or bottom records. If you want to select the largest values in that field, sort in descending order. If you want to select the smallest values, sort the field in ascending order.

3. Open the Query Properties sheet by clicking the Properties toolbar button (or by selecting View | Properties). If you see Field Properties at the top of the window, click an empty area of the query design.

4. Click in the Top Values property and choose the desired option from the list, as shown here. For example, choose 5 to have the query return the top five values, or choose 25% to have the query return the top 25 percent of the values. You can also enter a different specific value, either as a number of records or as a percentage.

Query Properties		×
General		
Description		
Output All Fields	No	
Top Values	All	▼
Unique Values	5	
Unique Records	25	
Run Permissions	100	
Source Database	5%	
Source Connect Str	25%	
Record Locks	All	
Recordset Type	Dynaset	
ODBC Timeout	60	
Filter		
Order By		
Max Records		
Subdatasheet Name . . .		
Link Child Fields		
Link Master Fields		
Subdatasheet Height . . .	0"	
Subdatasheet Expanded	No	

5. Click the Datasheet View toolbar button (or choose View | Datasheet View) to display the query's dynaset.

 My query's calculated field displays too many places to the right of the decimal. How can I limit the decimal places it shows?

You can control the number of decimal places displayed in a Number field of a query by changing the properties for that field. Use these steps:

1. Click the Design View toolbar button (or choose View | Design View) to switch to Design view for the query.

2. Move to the calculated field whose decimal places you want to limit.

3. Choose View | Properties or click the Properties toolbar button.

4. Click the Format property and choose one of the formats from the drop-down list.

5. Enter the number of decimal places that you want displayed.

6. Click the Datasheet View toolbar button (or choose View | Datasheet View) to return to the query dynaset. You now will see only the selected number of digits after the decimal point.

 How can I round the results of a calculation from four decimal places to two, so that I can use the rounded results in another expression?

If you needed to control only how many decimal places appear in the Datasheet view, you could change the Decimal Places property. However, because you want to use the calculation again later, you need to control the actual number. To do this, combine the Val and Format functions. For example, type this:

Val(Format(*expression*, "#.00"))

The Format property extracts the number by using only two decimal places. However, in the process, the Format property converts the number into text. The Val() function converts the text back into a number.

 ## Why do I get rounding errors when I create a calculated field by using fields with the Currency format?

The calculated field is not inheriting the Format property of the Table field. Therefore, the results of the calculated field often round improperly. You can correct this by changing the calculation that you are using, as follows (assuming that you want to round to two decimal places):

1. Multiply the result of your calculated field by 100.
2. Use the Int function to truncate the number (removing the decimal places).
3. Divide the number by 100, which gives the correct result.
4. Use the Ccur() function on the resultant value to convert it back into a currency amount. In doing this, you nest the formula for the calculated field within another formula.

To make the final formula easier to read, you may want to create two calculated fields: your original field and the field that does this. For example, if your calculated field is called Profits1, the new field's entry might be the following:

```
Profits:Ccur(Int(Profits1*100)/100)
```

A calculated field in my query is based on a Number field that has a Scientific Format property. Why does the field in the resulting dynaset appear using a General format?

Access does support *property inheritance* from the existing fields of underlying table to queries. Hence, the properties set for the fields in a table are automatically applied to those same fields used in queries. When a Number field uses a Scientific Format property in a table, it uses the same format in a query.

The problem with calculated fields is that they are not real fields, so they cannot support property inheritance from tables to queries. To format a calculated field correctly in the query, you need to set its Format property directly. To change this property, click in the calculated field in the QBE grid. Click the Properties toolbar button (or choose <u>V</u>iew | <u>P</u>roperties) to display the field properties for the calculated field. Click in the Format property, open the drop-down list, and select Scientific.

TROUBLESHOOTING

When I try to run my query, I get a message saying "Can't group on fields selected with '*'." What can I do?

Here are some of the reasons you might get this message:

- The Output All Fields property is set to Yes. You need to go into the properties for the queries and make sure that the Output All Fields property is set to No.

- The QBE grid for a crosstab query includes an * in the Field row. Remove the * from the QBE grid.

- You tried to change a select query into a crosstab query, and the QBE grid already has an * in the Field row. Remove the * before you change the query into a crosstab query.

- You are trying to execute a SQL statement that has an aggregate function or Group By clause as well as an asterisk (*). Change the SQL statement to remove the asterisk, aggregate function, or Group By clause.

I deleted the Format property settings for a field in my query, but it still uses the same format instead of the one assigned in the table. What can I do?

If the dynaset does not display data by using the current property settings, Access has failed to refresh the display type for the query. To force Access to display the data properly, save the query, close it, and reopen it. When you reopen the query and run it again, Access displays the data according to the current property settings for the query.

? Why do I get an "Out of memory" error when I run my query, even though my computer has plenty of memory?

If you get this error while trying to run a complex query, Access isn't complaining about any limitation of installed memory in your PC. The message actually refers to a shortage of memory in an internal amount of program space that Access sets aside to compose all the expressions used in your queries. In earlier versions of Access, this space was limited to 64K. In all versions of Access since Access 95, the old 64K limit has been replaced with a dynamic limit that provides more room, but it's still possible to build a query that is too complex to run. You can reduce the complexity of queries by using these steps:

- Remove any unneeded fields from the query.
- Shorten table names and column names.
- Minimize the expressions used in underlying queries.
- Avoid *stacked queries*, situations in which query 1 and table 1 provide data to query 2, and query 2 and tables 2 and 3 provide data to query 3, and so on. Where possible, replace stacked queries with a single query that performs the operation.

Chapter 6

Advanced Queries

Answer Topics!

Advanced Queries @ a Glance

Chapter 5 discussed general questions about queries, basic select queries, action queries, and parameter queries. This chapter covers the more advanced areas of using Access queries, including SQL-specific queries, such as the pass-through query.

Select queries are fairly straightforward, because they simply select the records to display in response to a question that you pose. The more advanced queries discussed in this chapter provide new options and new challenges. The questions for which you'll find answers in this chapter deal with the following areas:

Displaying Data in Queries discusses unusual methods to control the ways in which data is displayed or edited in your queries.

Parameter Queries helps you to structure queries that enable you to obtain more specific results, by using such tools as partial-string searches.

Relational Queries provides you answers regarding the queries that enable you to retrieve data from more than one table at a time.

Crosstab Queries provides assistance regarding queries that are used to provide a cross-tabulation of numeric data.

SQL and Programming explores the advanced query topics of using SQL statements to manipulate data directly on a database server, and using Visual Basic for Applications (VBA) code to manipulate queries.

Working with Calculations details how to use calculations within queries to obtain more-varied and unusual results.

Troubleshooting helps you to deal with unexpected error messages and other general problems when using queries.

DISPLAYING DATA IN QUERIES

Is there a way to display all fields from a query's underlying tables without adding all the fields to the QBE grid?

You can display all the fields without manually adding them, by setting the query's Output All Fields property to Yes. Use these steps:

1. Open the query in Design view.
2. Click any blank area of the query, outside the QBE grid.
3. Select View | Properties to display the Properties window for the query.
4. Set the Output All Fields property to Yes.

I want to display my query's dynaset, but I also want to prevent edits. Can I do this without setting security on the query object?

You can accomplish the same result by creating a form that displays your query as a datasheet, with the form's editing capabilities disabled. Use these steps:

1. In the Database window, select the query and then choose AutoForm from the New Object toolbar button, to create a form that includes all the fields from the query.
2. Switch to the form's Design view.
3. Display the Property list for the form (select View | Properties).
4. Set the Default View property to Datasheet.
5. Set the Views Allowed property to Datasheet.
6. Set the Allow Edits, Allow Deletions, and Allow Additions properties to No.
7. Save the form.
8. Now, when you look at data through the form, you will see a datasheet containing data from the query. You cannot edit the datasheet.

Tip: *If you are worried that users will open the query and not the form, you can copy the SQL statement from the query and paste it into the form's Record Source property. Then you can delete the query, and the form still shows the correct data in its datasheet.*

PARAMETER QUERIES

 I want to create a parameter query in which users have to enter only part of a Text field's entry. Can I do this?

Presumably, you want to create a parameter query in which users don't have to enter the complete entry to have Access find matches. For example, you can enter part of a name when responding to the prompt for the parameter, but have the query return all records that include your response, even when it's only part of the name. You can do this by concatenating the * wildcard and the parameter value.

For example, suppose that you want to find matching entries in your First Name field. You might enter the following criterion in the Criteria row:

```
Like [Enter first name:] & "*" Or Is Null
```

This criterion matches any entries with either the complete parameter value or the complete parameter value and trailing text. For example, if the user enters the value **Jo** in response to the parameter, Access searches the First Name field and returns all records containing "Jo" alone, or "Jo" combined with all other text (such as John, Joan, and Joseph).

Specifying Or Is Null allows you to enter no parameter value and retrieve all records, including ones that have no entry for that field.

I want my parameter query to select all records when a user doesn't specify parameters. How can I do this?

In parameter queries, users are prompted to supply entries each time you run the query. The entries often provide criteria, enabling you to create a query with criteria that change every time. For example, your parameter query could present the invoices for a single week. The dates the user enters determine which week's invoices are included in the dynaset.

To produce a parameter query that displays all records when no criteria are supplied, you need to create a criterion that uses the wildcard character. This query either uses the value provided by the user or matches everything. For example, your criterion in the QBE grid might look like this:

```
Like "*" & [Enter a value:] & "*"
```

If the user does not enter a value to match, then the criterion matches all entries in that field because of the * wildcard character. If the user does enter the value, the criterion matches only those values. The wildcard character is ignored, because the value entered is the entire content of the field. When you run the query, you see a prompt like the one shown here. If you type **Johnson**, the query's criterion equals Like "*Johnson*". If you do not type anything, the criterion equals Like "**".

Enter Parameter Value	✕
Enter a value:	
[ ]	
	OK Cancel

Can I create a parameter query that returns all records in which the Text field's entry starts with the single letter the query prompts for?

Yes, you can create a parameter query that returns all records in which the entries in a Text field start with a single letter provided by the user. You do this by combining the letter entered with the * wildcard character for that field's criterion. For example, you can make this entry in the QBE grid:

```
Like [Enter first character:] & "*"
```

This criterion matches any entries starting with the letter the
user enters.

RELATIONAL QUERIES

 How do I create a relational query?

You can use a query to draw relationships between two or
more tables, by following these steps:

1. Click the Queries button in the Database window and
   then click New.

2. In the New Query window that appears, click Design
   View and then click OK. A new Query window appears,
   containing a Show Table dialog box, as shown here:

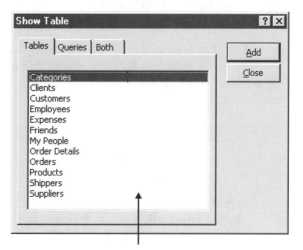

The Show Table dialog box can be used
to add multiple tables to a query design

3. In the Show Table dialog box, add each table needed in
   the query by selecting the table and clicking the Add
   button (or by double-clicking the table).

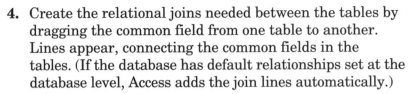

4. Create the relational joins needed between the tables by dragging the common field from one table to another. Lines appear, connecting the common fields in the tables. (If the database has default relationships set at the database level, Access adds the join lines automatically.)

5. Add the needed fields to the query by dragging the field names from the field lists to the columns of the window.

6. Add any needed sorting and selection criteria to the query design.

7. Save and run the query.

 Tip: *If you add more than two tables to a query, the join lines may cross in ways that make the relationships hard to follow. You can rearrange the field lists, as desired, to make the join lines easier to see.*

 ### How do I join tables when one of the tables is in a different database?

You can join tables from different databases in a single query by linking to the table that's in the other database. Do this by using the following steps:

1. Make the Database window the active window.

2. Select File | Get External Data | Link Tables.

3. In the Link dialog box that opens, find the database containing the table that you want to join, and click Link.

4. In the Link Tables dialog box that appears, select the desired table and click OK.

The linked table from the other database appears in the Database window of the current database, and you can use it along with the existing tables and queries while designing your relational query.

I can edit some fields in my relational query, but not others. Why?

Some limitations exist in editing data through relational queries. If you add referential integrity at the database level, you won't be able to edit any key fields used in the query that are on the "one" side of a one-to-many relationship.

How can I create a relationship based on more than one field in a table?

You can create relationships based on multiple fields in a query's design. If no single field will work as a primary key, you can base the primary key on a combination of fields. The combination of fields, taken together, must uniquely identify each record in the table. For example, the following shows a relationship between tables that is based on a combination of Last name and First name fields:

A combination of fields are linked to establish a relationship

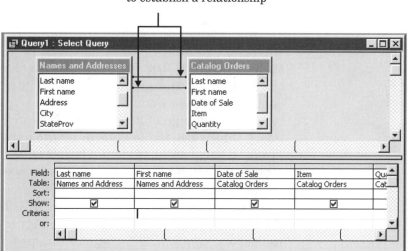

This scheme works as long as no two entries have the same name. To create the relationship, just drag and drop the

fields from one table to the matching fields in the other table, one at a time.

How can I create a relational query based on a comparison other than equality?

When you create a relational query via a join line between two tables, Access bases the join on *equality*—in other words, based on entries in the joined fields of the two tables being equal. However, in rare cases, you may need a join that's not based on equality, but is instead based on finding matching records when the value in one table is between two values in the other table. Access does not let you use join lines to create joins based on an operator other than the equal symbol (=). However, you can accomplish the same end result by intentionally omitting the join line, and instead specifying the join as part of the criteria for the linking field. In the Criteria cell of the linking field for the first table, you use the expression

> Between [*second table name*].[*first field*] and [*second table name*].[*second field*]

where *second table name* is the name of the other table in the relationship, *first field* is the name of the field containing the first value, and *second field* is the name of the field containing the second value.

As an example of how this works, consider a relational query that is needed to determine the appropriate letter grade to be given to students, based on the students' test scores. If a student's test score falls between 93 and 100, the student receives an A; if the score falls between 84 and 92, the student receives a B; if the score falls between 73 and 83, the student receives a C; and so on. Figure 6-1 shows two tables, one containing the student names and their respective test scores, and the other containing the appropriate letter grade that a student should receive based on the test score.

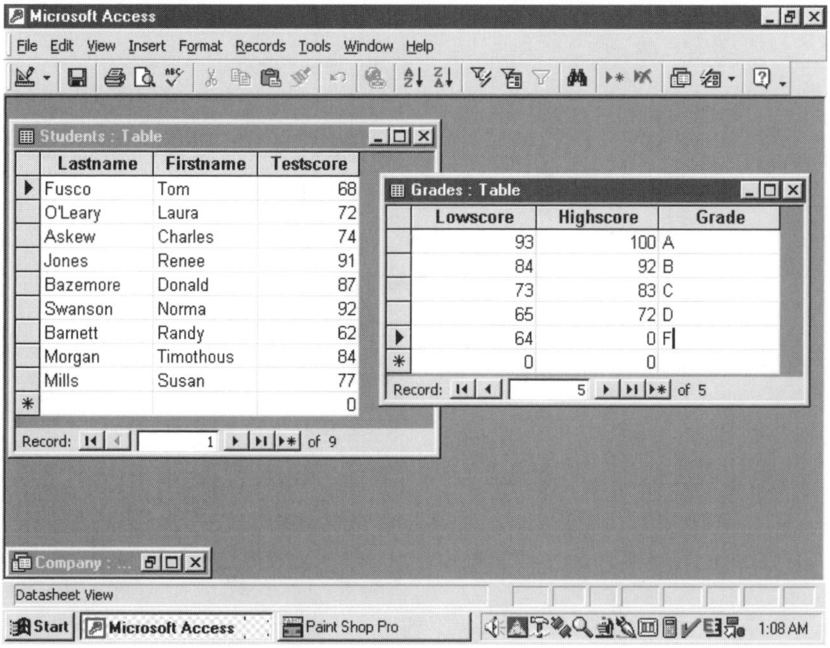

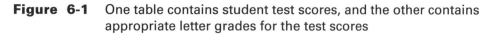

Figure 6-1   One table contains student test scores, and the other contains appropriate letter grades for the test scores

The typical Access relational query can't be used to match a letter grade to a student test score, because this situation requires a relationship based on the Between operator rather than the Equals operator. For example, if a student's test score falls *between* 65 and 72, the student receives a D. Figure 6-2 shows an example of the query design that can be used to provide a listing of appropriate letter grades for each student. Figure 6-3 shows the results when the query runs.

In the example, the expression used in the Criteria row for the Testscore field is

```
Between [Grades].[Lowscore] and [Grades].[Highscore]
```

which establishes the relational link, using the Between operator, between the Testscore field of the Students table and the Lowscore and Highscore fields of the Grades table.

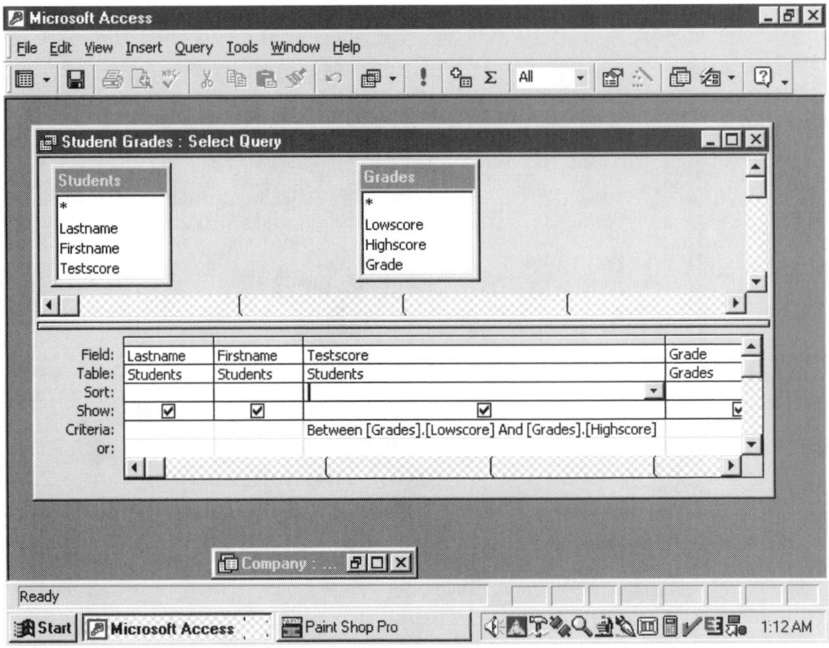

Figure 6-2 An example of a query that uses the Between operator within criteria to join two tables

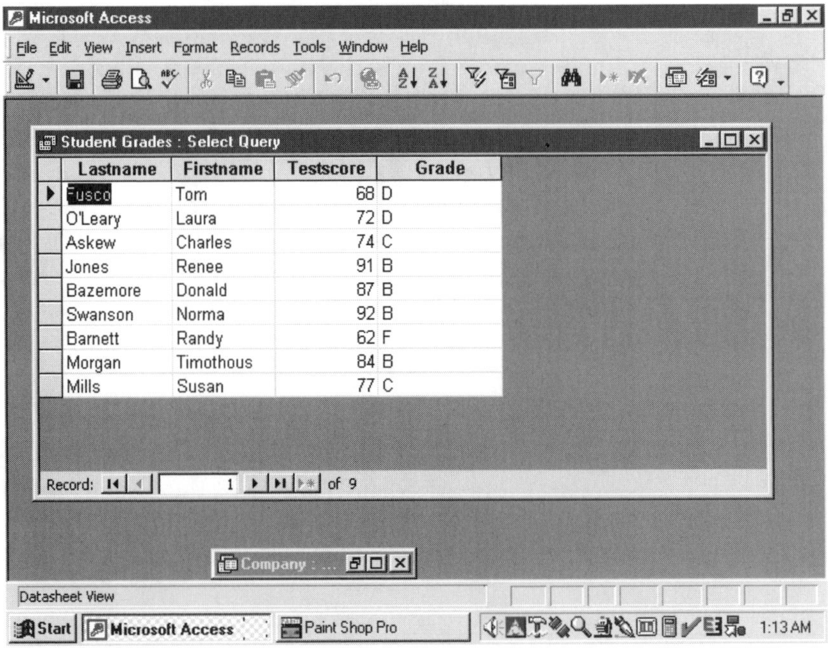

Figure 6-3 The results of the query that uses the Between operator

Why does my relational query fail to run and instead display the message "Query contains ambiguous outer joins"?

Occasionally, Access gets confused when you join multiple tables and define one of the links as an outer join. When this happens, Access displays the preceding error message. The way around this is to break the query into two queries, and use those two queries as the basis for the final query, as in this example:

1. Link the two tables with the outer join in one query and call it **Query One**.
2. Create a second query containing the equi-joins and call it **Query Two**.
3. Create a third query and add Query One and Query Two as data sources to that query, establishing the needed link between the related fields.

I want to use a query to show the relationship between employees and their managers, but all the employees and managers are in a single table. How can I do this?

You need to create a type of join called a *self-join*. In Access, to create a self-join, you add the same table to the Query window twice, and then link one field to another field in the same table.

For example, Figure 6-4 shows a self-join, with the ReportsTo field in an Employees table related to the EmployeeID field in the same table. (Both the ReportsTo field and the EmployeeID field contain an ID number used to identify each employee.) To show the employees and their managers, the FirstName and LastName fields from the first Employees field list have been placed in the QBE grid, and the LastName field from the second Employee field list (representing the manager's name) has also been placed in the QBE grid. (The field for the manager's name has been renamed Manager: LastName.) The resulting dynaset, shown in Figure 6-5, shows all employees and their managers.

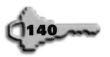

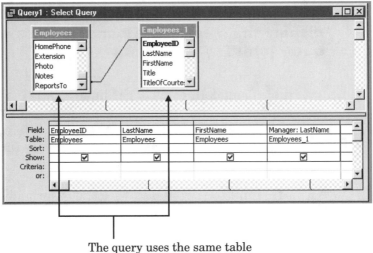

Query1 : Select Query
Employees
HomePhone
Extension
Photo
Notes
ReportsTo
Employees_1
EmployeeID
LastName
FirstName
Title
TitleOfCourte
Field: EmployeeID LastName FirstName Manager: LastName
Table: Employees Employees Employees Employees_1
Sort:
Show:
Criteria:
or:
The query uses the same table added to the query design twice

Figure 6-4 Example of a self-join in a query design

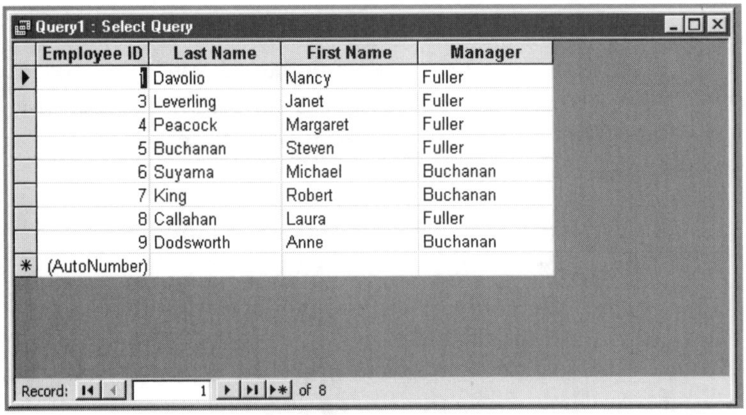

Query1 : Select Query
Employee ID | Last Name | First Name | Manager
1 | Davolio | Nancy | Fuller
3 | Leverling | Janet | Fuller
4 | Peacock | Margaret | Fuller
5 | Buchanan | Steven | Fuller
6 | Suyama | Michael | Buchanan
7 | King | Robert | Buchanan
8 | Callahan | Laura | Fuller
9 | Dodsworth | Anne | Buchanan
(AutoNumber)
Record: 1 of 8

Figure 6-5 The dynaset that results from a self-join

I want to view all records in a relational query, including the records that don't have a match between the two sides of the relationship. How can I do this?

You need to change the *join type* used for the query. By default, Access makes any relationship that you create in a query an *equi-join*, which is one of three possible join types:

- **Equi-joins**   Records appear only when the related field in one table matches an entry for the related field of the other table.

- **Left outer join**   Includes all records in the first table, regardless of whether records in the second table have a match.

- **Right outer join**   Includes all records in the second table, regardless of whether records in the first table have a match.

You can change the join type by performing these steps:

1. Open the relational query in Design view.

2. Double-click the join line between the tables (or right-click the line and choose Join Properties from the shortcut menu). The Join Properties dialog box appears, shown here:

> **Join Properties**   ? ×
>
> Left Table Name   Right Table Name
> [Orders   ▼]   [Order Details   ▼]
>
> Left Column Name   Right Column Name
> [OrderID   ▼]   [OrderID   ▼]
>
> ⦿ 1: Only include rows where the joined fields from both
>   tables are equal.
>
> ○ 2: Include ALL records from 'Orders' and only those records
>   from 'Order Details' where the joined fields are equal.
>
> ○ 3: Include ALL records from 'Order Details' and only those
>   records from 'Orders' where the joined fields are equal.
>
> [OK]   [Cancel]   [New]

3. If you want a left outer join, click the radio button next to option 2 in the dialog box.

4. If you want a right outer join, click the radio button for option 3. (Also, note that the order in which the options are presented—left outer join and then right outer join—can be reversed, depending on which side you started with when you created the join.)

5. Click OK.

CROSSTAB QUERIES

How can I cross-tabulate numeric data?

The easiest way to cross-tabulate numeric data in Access is to create a query by means of the Crosstab Query Wizard. As an example of a crosstab, Figure 6-6 shows one table with a list of prices for television sets, along with the results of a crosstab query that summarizes those sales by sales rep. You can create a crosstab query by performing these steps:

1. Click the Queries tab in the Database window and then click <u>N</u>ew.

2. In the New Query dialog box that appears, select Crosstab Query Wizard and then click OK. The first Crosstab Query Wizard dialog box appears, as shown in Figure 6-7.

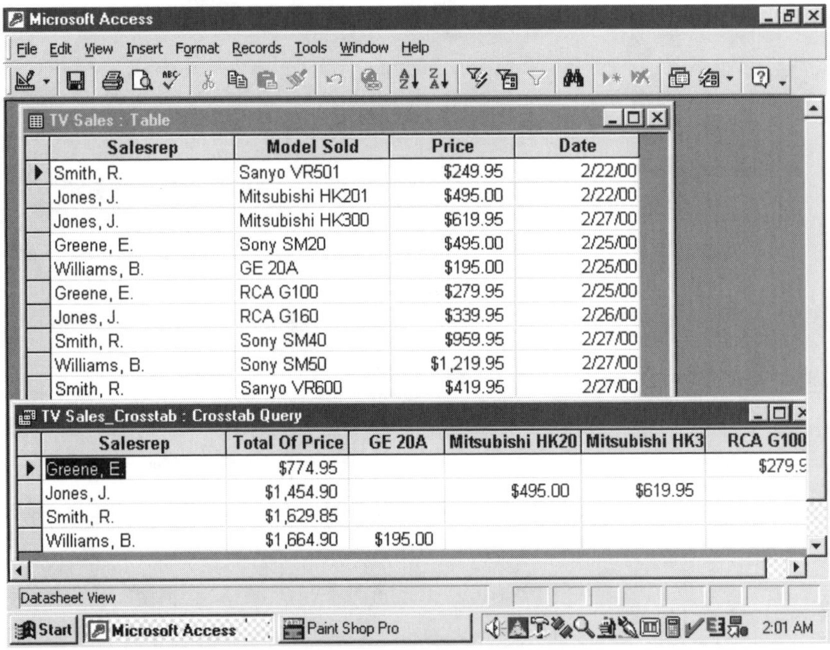

Figure 6-6 A set of numeric data and the results of a crosstab of that data

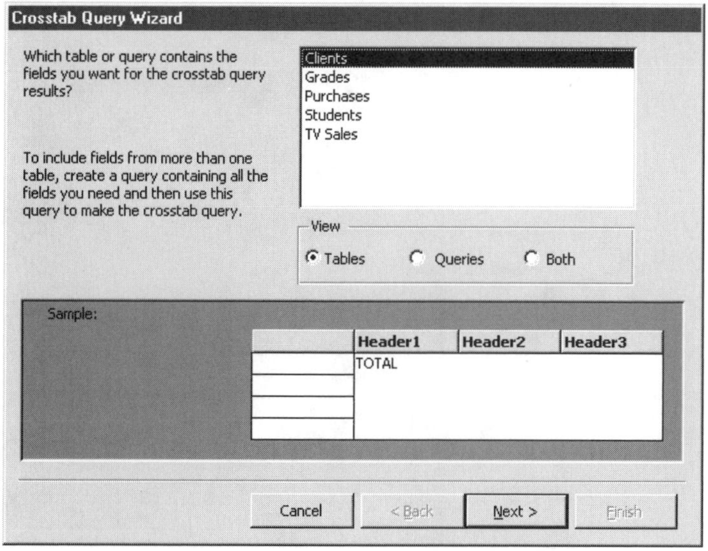

Figure 6-7   The first Crosstab Query Wizard dialog box

3. In the list box, select the table or query that is to serve as the source of data for the crosstab, and then click Next.

4. In the second Crosstab Query Wizard dialog box, choose the fields that should be used as row headings in the crosstab, and then click Next.

5. In the third Wizard dialog box, choose the fields that should be used as column headings. Select each field and then click the right-arrow button, to add the field to the list of column headings. After you are done selecting the column headings, click Next.

6. In the fourth Wizard dialog box (Figure 6-8), choose from the Fields list the field or fields containing the numbers that you want calculated at each column and row intersection. On the right side of the dialog box, choose from the Functions list the type of calculation that you want to use. When done, click Next.

7. In the final Wizard dialog box, enter a name for the query and then click View to view the query's dynaset.

Figure 6-8 lists the Crosstab Query Wizard dialog box:

Crosstab Query Wizard

What number do you want calculated for each column and row intersection?

For example, you could calculate the sum of the field Order Amount for each employee (column) by country and region (row).

Do you want to summarize each row?

☑ Yes, include row sums.

Fields:
- Price
- Date

Functions:
- Avg
- Count
- First
- Last
- Max
- Min
- StDev
- Sum
- Var

Sample:

Salesrep	Model Sold1	Model Sold2	Model Sold3
Salesrep1	Sum(Price)		
Salesrep2			
Salesrep3			
Salesrep4			

Cancel | < Back | Next > | Finish

Figure 6-8 The dialog box for fields and calculation types

 When I press SHIFT-F9 in my crosstab query, it doesn't requery the underlying table to reflect changes. How can I get my crosstab query to display up-to-date information?

A crosstab query displays a static snapshot of data rather than a dynamic dataset. It captures the data to show it in the crosstab query at the moment when you show the crosstab's datasheet. This means that the crosstab query doesn't automatically update when you change the data in the underlying table. To redisplay up-to-date information, close the query and reopen it.

Can I convert my crosstab query into a table?

Yes, you can convert a crosstab query into a table. To do so, create the crosstab query and open it in Design view. Then, convert it into a make-table query by selecting Query | Make Table. Enter the name of the new table in the Table Name text box that appears, and click OK. Note that the table is not

created until you run the query, either by choosing Query |
Run or by clicking the Run toolbar button.

 Note: *The table that you create with a converted crosstab*
query does not use the same layout as the crosstab query's
Datasheet view. Instead, it presents the records as if you had
converted the crosstab query into a select query, using the
usual datasheet orientation and none of the summarizing
available within the crosstab query.

 ## Why can't I update my crosstab query?

A crosstab query cannot be updated. A crosstab query
produces a *snapshot* instead of a dynaset. A snapshot is a
static picture of a set of records. You can edit the data in a
dynaset; you cannot edit the data in a snapshot. This is
simply how Access works, and it cannot be worked around.
When you try to edit a crosstab query, the status line
displays "This recordset is not updateable."

SQL AND PROGRAMMING

How can I use Visual Basic to change the underlying SQL statement that a query uses?

You can use VBA code to change a query's underlying SQL
statement, thereby causing the underlying record source for
the query to change. For example, the following VBA code
changes the underlying SQL statement for a query named
Sales 98, so that the query selects all records in the table
named Sales:

```
SELECT *
FROM Sales;
```

 ## How can I create a pass-through query?

A *pass-through* query sends SQL commands directly to a
database server according to the Open Database Connectivity
(ODBC) standard. A pass-through query enables you to work

with tables on a database server without attaching the tables to an Access database. A pass-through query can also run procedures stored on the database server. You can use a pass-through query to change data in the database being edited, to create a database object, or to perform an action similar to an action query. You do this by entering the correct SQL commands for the desired actions, and these commands are passed directly to the database server. Because Access doesn't process the commands in a pass-through query, when you enter the commands to send to the server, you need to use the syntax that the server expects. Use these steps to create a pass-through query:

1. Click the Query button in the Database window and then click New.

2. In the New Query dialog box that appears, click Design View and then click OK. A new Query window opens, with the Show Table dialog box displayed.

3. Click Close in the Show Table dialog box to avoid adding any field lists to the Query window.

4. Select Query | SQL Specific | Pass-Through. A blank SQL Pass-Through Query window opens.

5. Enter the commands that you want to send to the database server via the ODBC driver.

6. Open the Property window for the query by clicking the Properties toolbar button or by selecting View | Properties.

7. Move to the ODBC Connect Str property and specify the information needed to connect to the database server. You may be able to enter this information by clicking the Build button and making selections.

8. Select Yes for the Return Records property if you want to get information back from this query, or select No if you just want to execute the commands on the database server without returning any information.

9. Choose Query | Run (or click the Run toolbar button) to run the query.

Note: *If you leave the connection string entry in the ODBCConnectStr property blank, Access prompts you for connection information each time that you run the query.*

Do I have to link to the SQL tables that I want to work with in a pass-through query?

No, you do not. This type of query allows you to work with the tables by using their server rather than Access.

Can I convert a pass-through query into a make-table query?

No, you cannot. If you convert a pass-through query to any other type of query, it loses its SQL statement and no longer produces a result.

Tip: *If you want the data from a pass-through query placed in a table, create a separate make-table query that uses the pass-through query as its source of data.*

How can I print the SQL statement for each of my queries?

Access converts all of your queries into SQL statements before they are run. To print the SQL statement for each of your queries, you use the Documentor feature built into Access. Use these steps:

1. Select Tools | Analyze | Documentor and then click the Queries tab in the Documentor window.
2. Click Select All to report on all the queries.
3. Click Options.
4. Clear all the check boxes except SQL and select the Nothing radio buttons for both Fields and Indexes.
5. Click OK twice to create the report. The beginning of the report looks like the window shown in Figure 6-9. In the report, each query's SQL statement appears on a separate page.

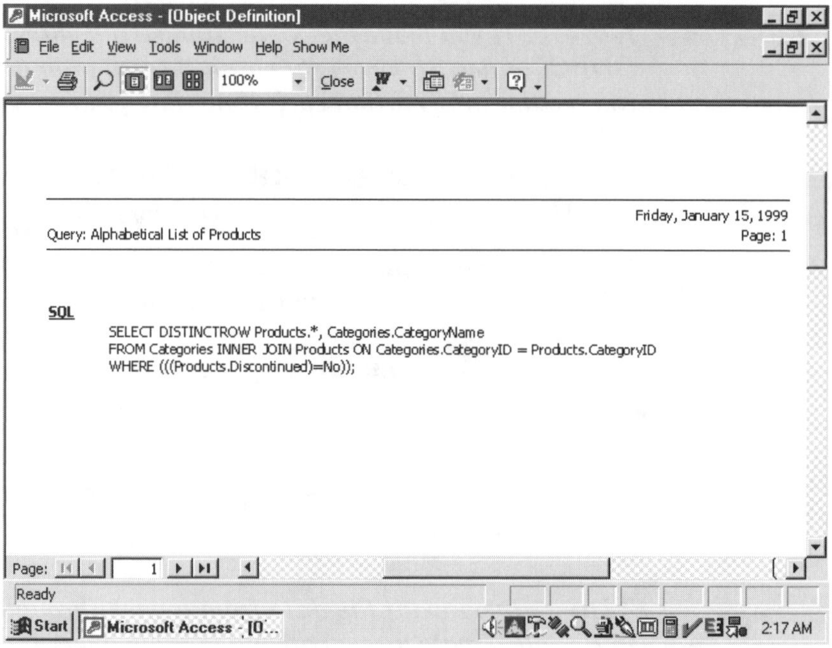

Figure 6-9   A report containing SQL statements created with the Documentor

When I try to run a pass-through query, I get a timeout error. What can I do?

By default, Access waits 60 seconds to get a complete response to your pass-through query. If the response is not complete, it returns a timeout error. This is to prevent you from waiting a very long time for the result of the query. If you suspect that your pass-through query will take longer than one minute to run, open the query's property sheet. Move to the ODBC Timeout property and enter a new number of seconds to wait. If you set the property to zero, Access never prevents a timeout error.

Can I update the records returned by a pass-through query?

No, you cannot edit the records returned by a pass-through query in Access, nor can you enter new ones. The data is a snapshot returned by the database server rather than a dynaset of data in an Access table.

WORKING WITH CALCULATIONS

I need a calculated field in a query that shows a sales tax amount only when the State field contains a specific entry for one state and shows zero for any other states. Is there a way to create a conditional calculation like this in a query?

You can use the IIf() (Immediate If) function in a calculated field of a query when you want to perform a calculation in one way for some records and in another way for other records. The syntax for this function is

IIf(*condition,true,false*)

where *condition* specifies the test that you want to use to determine how to perform the calculation; *true* specifies the results that you want if the condition is true; and *false* specifies the results that you want if the condition is false. *Condition* is an expression, and *true* and *false* can be values, fields, or expressions.

For example, if you want a calculated field in a query to display a sales tax of 6 percent of the Price field if the State field contained NY, and otherwise to display 0 percent for any other state, you could use an expression such as the following in the Field row of a blank column:

```
Sales Tax:IIf([State]="NY",([Price]*0.06),0)
```

After you enter the expression in the field of the query, you can change the formatting property of the field to Currency or Standard.

My query has separate Date and Time fields, but I want to use a parameter query to select records based on a combination of the date and time. How can I do this?

You need to add to your query a calculated field that you use to select records, but that doesn't display. The query's parameters supply entries for this field. For example, create a calculated field by entering **New Time:[Date Field] & " " &**

[Time Field] in the Field row, assuming that your Date and Time fields are named Date Field and Time Field. Next, enter a criterion for this field, including the parameter prompts for where you want the dates and times placed. For example, you can enter **Between [Enter beginning date and time] and [Enter ending date and time]**. If you don't want this field displayed in the resulting dynaset, remember to clear the check box in the Show row of the QBE grid. When the query is run, the query prompts for the beginning and ending dates and times.

Tip: *If you are uncertain that the query's user will correctly enter the dates and times, you can have separate parameter prompts. The criterion can join the dates and times, as in Between [Enter beginning date] + [Enter beginning time] and [Enter ending date] + [Enter ending time].*

My calculated fields are displaying numeric amounts that are actually dollars and cents, but the numbers appear as decimal values, such as 02.5. Can the format for the display of a calculated field be changed?

You can change a calculated field's display in a query by changing the Format value in the Property window for that column in the QBE grid. Use these steps to do this:

1. Open in Design view the query containing the calculated field.

2. Select <u>V</u>iew | <u>P</u>roperties to see the Properties window.

3. Click the column that contains the calculated field.

4. In the Field Properties window, click the General tab (if it isn't already on top).

5. Click the Format property and then click the drop-down arrow to open the list box.

6. Choose the desired type of format from the list. If you want to see the calculations as currency amounts, choose Currency.

I need to calculate both a sum and an average for the same field, but I can choose only one calculation type from the list box in the Total row of the QBE grid. How can I obtain calculations of more than one type for the same field?

When calculating totals, you can add the same field to the QBE grid more than once, to obtain as many totals as you need. After you choose View | Totals to show the Total row in the QBE grid, you can add any field more than once and choose the appropriate type of calculation in the Total row for each calculation type that you need. For example, Figure 6-10 shows a query's design with a Total row, with totals based on Average, Minimum, and Maximum values added for the same field.

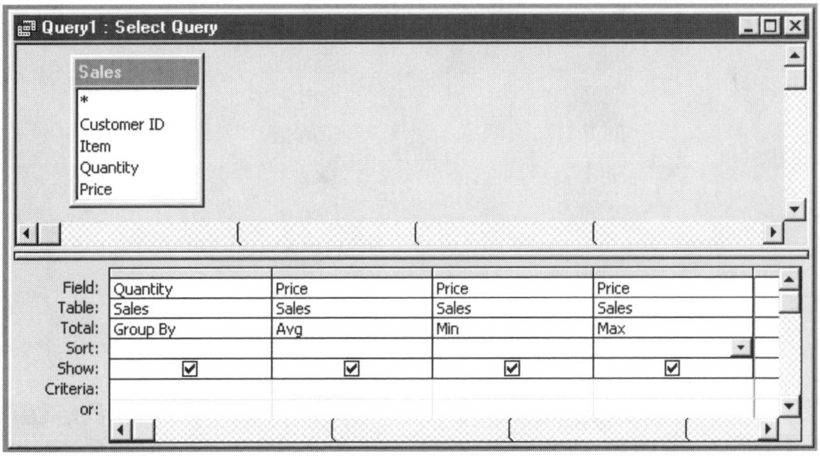

Figure 6-10 A query design with different types of totals for the same field

TROUBLESHOOTING

 ### Can my query extract just the day, month, or year from a Date field?

You could create a calculated field containing the Day(), Month(), or Year() functions to extract just the day, month, or year, respectively, but an easier way exists to do this. Create a custom format for the Date field in the query that displays the date element that you want to extract. The following table shows several custom formats that you can use to do so, and the results of applying each format to the date December 5, 1999. To apply a custom date format, click anywhere within the field while in Design view, select View | Properties, and then click the Format property. Enter the format that you want to use, as shown in the following table. The next time you run the query, you see the new formats.

 Tip: *You can also use these custom formats as the Format property setting for report and form controls.*

Format	Returns
DD	05
DDD	Sun
DDDD	Sunday
MM	12
MMM	Dec
MMMM	December
YY	99
YYYY	1999

My queries print with a header and footer. Can I get rid of them?

Yes, you can print your query from Access without including the default header and footer (which include the query name, the current date, and the page number). Run the query to display the data in a dynaset, and then select File | Page Setup. In the Page Setup dialog box, turn off the Print

Headings check box and then click OK. Finally, choose File |
Print to print the data without the headings.

My relational query is returning an impossibly large number of records. What's wrong?

This happens with relational queries if you add multiple
tables to the design, but leave out one of the join lines
between matching fields. Access then links every record in
one table with every record in the other, resulting in a
Cartesian, or cross, product of the two tables. To fix the
problem, add the missing join line by dragging the field from
the field list of one table to the matching field of the other
table.

My query asks me for a parameter, but I didn't create it as a parameter query. What's wrong?

This problem usually occurs when you misspell a field name
in the QBE grid. The problem can also occur if you have a
field in the QBE grid that refers to a calculated field. If the
field is performing a calculation based on a calculated field,
make sure that the Show check box for the calculated field is
turned on in the QBE grid.

My query runs too slowly. How can I improve the performance of my query?

Besides upgrading hardware (the common but expensive
solution to slow performance), the following are some steps
that you can take to speed up your queries:

- Run Performance Analyzer to obtain suggestions on
  how you might redesign your query to improve its
  performance. Select Tools | Analyze | Performance. In
  the dialog box that appears, click the Queries tab, place
  a check mark in the check box beside the query that you
  want to analyze, and click OK. If Performance Analyzer
  is able to suggest any possible improvements to the
  design of your query, it displays them in a dialog box.

- Try to index the fields on both sides of the join for
  queries using multiple tables.

- Index fields as much as possible, and try to use indexes on any fields that contain selection criteria.

- Compact the database on a regular basis. Compacting a database speeds up queries, because it reorganizes records so that they are placed adjacent to each other by order of the primary key.

- Redesign queries that use the Not In operator, because Access has a hard time optimizing the use of Not In.

 I get an "S_generation" error message when I try to run a query. What does this mean?

Access occasionally displays this message when you run an append query based on more than one table, and the query contains an asterisk in the Field row, to select all fields from one of the tables. Delete the asterisk and add each field individually from the Field list to the QBE grid.

 Why do my queries retrieve too many columns?

Select Tools | Options and click the Tables/Queries tab in the dialog box that appears. Under Query Design, make sure that the Output All Fields option is turned off. (With this option turned on, every field appears in a query dynaset, whether you want it to or not.) This setting in the Tools/Queries tab won't change the corresponding setting for a query that you've already created. To change that setting, open the query in Design view, click any blank area of the query outside the QBE grid, and select View | Properties. In the Query Properties window that opens, set the Output All Fields option to No.

When I try to run a query, I get a "Type mismatch" error message. What's wrong?

This error occurs when you try to use criteria that are of a different data type than the data stored in the underlying fields of the table. For example, if a table's field contains numbers, and you type the criterion **"twenty"**, you see the

"Type mismatch" error, because Access interprets the criterion as a text value and not as a number. If you enter the value as a numeric amount (such as **20**), the query works.

You also get this error if you include the dollar sign ($) in criteria that you specify for a Currency field. Remove the dollar sign to solve the problem.

Chapter 7

Basic Forms

Answer Topics!

- **?** Limiting user actions within Access to a specific form
- **?** Creating reports based on forms
- **?** Sorting records viewed in a form
- **?** Changing the tab order of forms
- **?** Changing a form's title bar caption
- **?** Calculating the total for a single record

TROUBLESHOOTING 186

- **?** Fixing forms that display no data
- **?** Causes for an inability to edit data
- **?** Fixing #Error or #Name values in form controls
- **?** Speeding up slow forms

Basic Forms @ a Glance

An Access form shows and lets you enter your data. You can create a form from a table or query, or combine data from multiple sources. Forms have a wide variety of controls that display data or add visual interest to the forms.

Using forms offers numerous advantages over using datasheets when it comes to viewing and editing your data. With datasheets, you are limited to a display of data in a columnar layout that resembles a spreadsheet; but with forms, you can show your data in a wide variety of possible formats. You can create forms that display data from more than one table, and you can even create multiple forms to provide different views of the same data. And with datasheets, viewing all the fields of a table simultaneously usually is impossible, unless the table has few fields. With forms, you can simultaneously view most or all of the fields in the underlying table.

You'll find that forms are especially important when you create an application for inexperienced users. With careful design, you can create forms that guide users through the steps of entering, editing, and getting data from your database. Well-designed forms also limit the possibility of data error. The questions that you'll see throughout this chapter cover the following areas:

- **Form Design** provides answers to questions about common design techniques used with forms that display data from a single table or query.

- **Using Forms** answers questions that arise when you work with forms in common ways, such as providing the data that you want.

- **Troubleshooting** helps you with problems that arise when use forms.

FORM DESIGN

 ## Should I base my form on a table or on a query?

Because Access lets you base forms on tables or queries, some advanced planning may be a wise idea, to make effective use of forms. If you intend to use the form to examine data from multiple tables, need to examine a selected subset of data, or want to sort the records in a particular order, base the form on a query. If you intend to use the form to examine any or all of the records in a single table, base the form on a table.

 Note: *When you base a form on a query, Access runs the query as the form opens. Hence, forms that are based on complex queries or on queries that process data from large tables can be slow to open.*

 ## How can I create a form quickly?

The fastest way to create a form is to click the New Object toolbar button, shown here, and then use the AutoF<u>o</u>rm menu option.

The AutoF<u>o</u>rm option builds a default, single-column form for whatever table or query is selected at the time that you click the New Object button. You can quickly build a default form with these steps:

1. In the Database window, click the desired table or query.
2. Click the drop-down arrow to the right of the New Object toolbar button and choose AutoF<u>o</u>rm from the menu that appears.

Access builds a default form for the table or query. An example of such a form is shown in Figure 7-1.

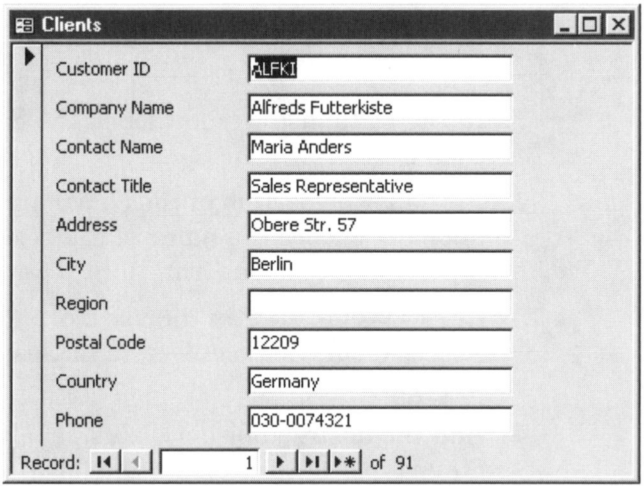

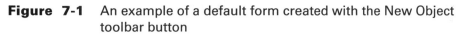

Figure 7-1   An example of a default form created with the New Object toolbar button

 What does creating a form with the Form Wizard involve?

Like other Access wizards, the Form Wizard steps you through the process of form creation by asking a series of questions about the forms that you want to create. The following are the steps that you use to build a form with the Form Wizard:

1. In the Database window, click the Forms button.
2. Click New to display the New Form dialog box.
3. In the lower portion of the dialog box, choose the table or query upon which you want to base the form.
4. Click Form Wizard in the list box and then click OK.
5. Follow the directions in the Form Wizard dialog boxes that appear. In the last dialog box, click Finish to begin entering or viewing data by using the completed form.

 What does manually creating a form involve?

With the manual method of form design, you open a blank form and add desired fields and other design objects (labels, graphics, lines, and boxes) to the form at locations of your

choice. The following are the steps that you need to take to create a form manually:

1. In the Database window, click the Forms button and then click <u>N</u>ew.

2. In the lower portion of the New Form dialog box that appears, choose the name of the table or query that will provide data to the form.

3. Click <u>D</u>esign View in the list box and then click OK. Access displays a blank form in Design view, as shown in Figure 7-2.

4. Add the desired objects (fields, labels, graphics, and any other types of controls) to the form. You can add fields by dragging them from the field list to the form. To add other types of controls to the form, use the Toolbox. Click the desired tool in the Toolbox, and then click the location in the form where you want to place the control.

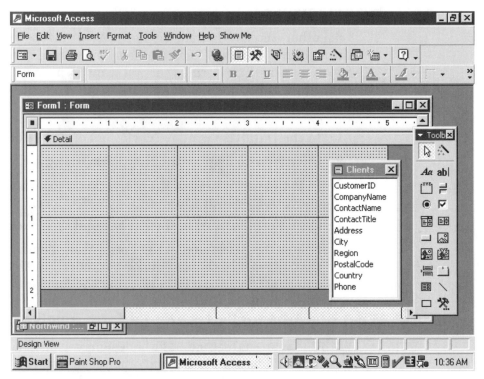

Figure 7-2 A blank form in Design view

> **_Tip:_** _If you open a blank form and the field list doesn't appear, choose **V**iew | Field **L**ist to display it. To add controls other than fields, choose **V**iew | T**o**olbox to display the Toolbox._

5. Save the completed form by choosing **F**ile | **S**ave.

Design Tips for Forms

A perennial danger with any database is that users will enter data incorrectly. By carefully designing the forms that others use to enter, edit, or review data, you can avoid many problems. Some things to consider when designing a form are the following:

- If users will be entering data from a specific source, such as a paper form, match your form's design to the paper counterpart. Users are more likely to enter data correctly if they don't have to search for each piece of it.

- Use rectangles and lines to group sets of controls. That way, users enter related data (such as all of a product's identification information or an entire address) together.

- Don't crowd the controls together, making them hard to read. Users need to be able to easily identify which control they are working with.

- Make sure that the text on the form is meaningful and concise. Two text box controls labeled "Name" won't help a user enter an employee's first and last name correctly.

- Use validation rules to help ensure that entries occur in a logical range. For example, if you know that billing rates in your company vary from $50 to $300 an hour, you can assign validation rules to the Hourly Rate control to prevent a $5,000 entry.

- Use input masks on standardized entries. For example, because you know exactly how many characters are needed to enter a phone number, an input mask—like the one that you use in tables—can make that entry easier.

- Use formatting to make numbers easier to read. You can much more easily see that the salary 1453920.20 is wrong when it appears as $1,453,920.20.

How can I add the current date or time to a form?

You can add the date or time to a form with these steps:

1. Open the form in Design view.

2. Choose Insert | Date and Time. The Date and Time dialog box appears, as shown here:

Date and Time	? X
☑ Include Date	OK
⦿ Friday, January 15, 1999	Cancel
○ 15-Jan-99	
○ 1/15/99	
☑ Include Time	
⦿ 10:37:35 AM	
○ 10:37 AM	
○ 10:37	
Sample:	
Friday, January 15, 1999 10:37:35 AM	

3. To include a date, turn on the Include Date check box and choose a desired date format.

4. To include a time, turn on the Include Time check box and choose a desired time format.

5. Click OK. The Date or Time field appears in the form, and you can drag it to its desired location.

How can I add graphics to a form?

Graphic images as design elements can easily be added to forms by using Windows cut-and-paste techniques. (This answer assumes that you want to add a graphic as a frame. If you want to use the graphic as a background for the form, see the question that begins "Can I use an image of my own as the background . . .," later in this portion of the chapter.)

You can use the Unbound Object Frame tool in the Toolbox to insert an object, but if you need a graphic only, pasting the graphic from the other Windows application

usually is easier. When you paste a graphic selection from another Windows program into a form's design, it automatically appears in an unbound object frame, enabling you to move or size the frame as desired. (Figure 7-3 shows the use of a graphic inside a frame in a form.)

You can use the following steps to paste a graphic into a form as a design element:

1. Open the desired form in Design view.

2. Switch to the graphics program that you are running under Windows, and open the document containing the graphic that you want to use on your form.

3. Using the selection techniques applicable to the graphics program that you are using, select the desired portion of the graphic.

4. From the graphics program's menu, choose Edit | Copy to copy the graphic to the Windows Clipboard.

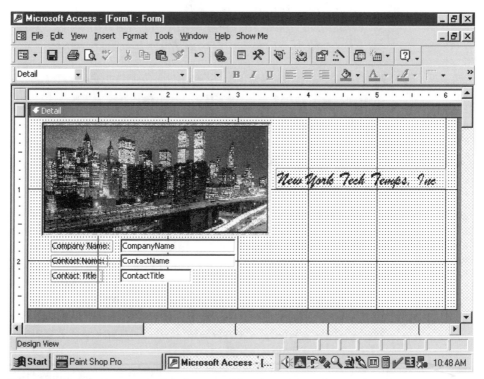

Figure 7-3 An example of a graphic placed in a frame in a form

5. Switch to Access (you can click the button labeled Microsoft Access on the taskbar).

6. Click the section of the form where you want the graphic to appear, and choose Edit | Paste.

7. Use moving and sizing techniques common to form and report design to size the graphic and move it to the desired location in the form.

Caution: *Before you resize an image, be sure that the Size Mode property for the frame containing the image is set to produce the effect that you want. Clip keeps the image at the same size and shape, but some of its content can be lost both horizontally and vertically; Stretch keeps all the content of the image, but its shape can change; and Zoom keeps the shape of the image, but some of its content can be lost either horizontally or vertically.*

Tip: *If you don't need to edit the graphic via OLE, you can convert it into a bitmap. By doing so, you save resources and the form opens faster. Right-click the frame, choose Change To, and then choose Image from the next menu.*

 ### Is there a way to hide the scroll bars or the record selectors that normally appear on a form?

For small forms or forms that are used specifically to add data, you may want to hide the scroll bars, the record selector buttons at the left edge of the form's window, or both. You can easily do this by opening the Properties window for the form while in Design view (choose Edit | Select Form and then choose View | Properties) and setting either the Scroll Bars property or the Record Selectors property, both of which are found on the Format tab. With the Scroll Bars property, you can choose Both, Neither, Horizontal Only, or Vertical Only. With the Record Selectors property, your choices are Yes, to display the record selectors, or No, to hide them.

How can I keep controls horizontally or vertically aligned as I move them?

You can keep controls aligned if you press down the SHIFT key as you move them. When you hold down the SHIFT key as you begin to move a control, the control moves horizontally or vertically, but not in both directions at once. Hence, to keep horizontal alignment of a control while moving it vertically, select the control, hold down the SHIFT key, and drag the control vertically.

Can I use an image of my own as the background for my form instead of the patterns that the Form Wizard supplies?

You can specify a graphic file as a form's background. Figure 7-4 shows an example of a form that uses a bitmap as the background for the form.

You can use files in BMP, ICO, DIB, WMF, or EMF formats. You specify the file to be used as the background in the form's Picture property, by following these steps:

1. Open the form in Design view. If the form is already open, choose Edit | Select Form to select the entire form.

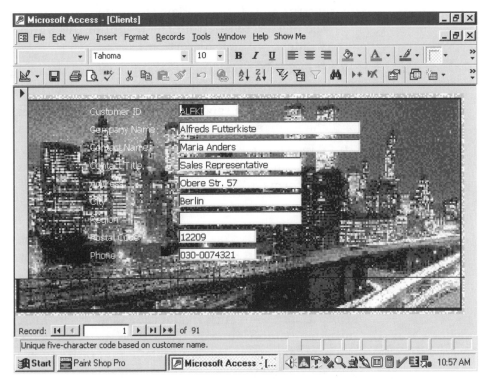

Figure 7-4 A form using a bitmap as the background

2. Choose <u>V</u>iew | <u>P</u>roperties to display the Properties window for the form.

3. Click the Format tab.

4. In the Picture property, enter a path and filename for the image file. (You can click the property and then click the Build button at the far right to open the Insert Picture dialog box, wherein you can locate a file.)

5. In the Picture Type property, specify whether the picture should be embedded or linked. (If you embed it, the image gets stored with the form, and your Access database increases in disk size to store the image—possibly by much more than the size of the image in the original file. If you link the picture, a link to the original file is created, and you must make sure that the original file stays in its present location.)

6. In the Picture Size Mode property, choose Clip, Stretch, or Zoom, as desired. (Clip displays the image at actual size, Stretch changes both the size and shape of the picture to fill the window completely, and Zoom resizes the picture to fit either the height or the width of the window, without distortion.)

7. If you want to change the alignment of the image, choose the setting in the Picture Alignment property.

8. If you want to repeat the image across the background of the form, set the Picture Tiling property to Yes.

9. Save the changes to the form. When you view the form in Form view, the image appears as a background in the form.

 How can I change the label of a control from the default that Access assigns based on the field name?

If you want to change the text within a label, click the label to select it, and then click inside the label. When you do so, an insertion pointer appears within the text, and you can type the new text, using the BACKSPACE and DEL keys as needed to delete existing text.

How can I add a label to a form?

Besides fields, you typically need to include text that's not attached to any object on the forms. Such text may be descriptive or explanatory, such as the text used in titles or captions. Unattached text is added to forms by using a Label tool. Figure 7-5 shows an example of a label in a form, used as a title heading in this case.

You can create a label with the following steps:

1. Open the form in Design view and display the Toolbox (if it is not already visible).

2. Click the Label tool.

3. To create a label that is automatically sized as you type, click where you want to start the label, and then type the label's text. Or, to create a label of any size, click where you want the label to start, drag the pointer until the label is the size you want, and then type its text.

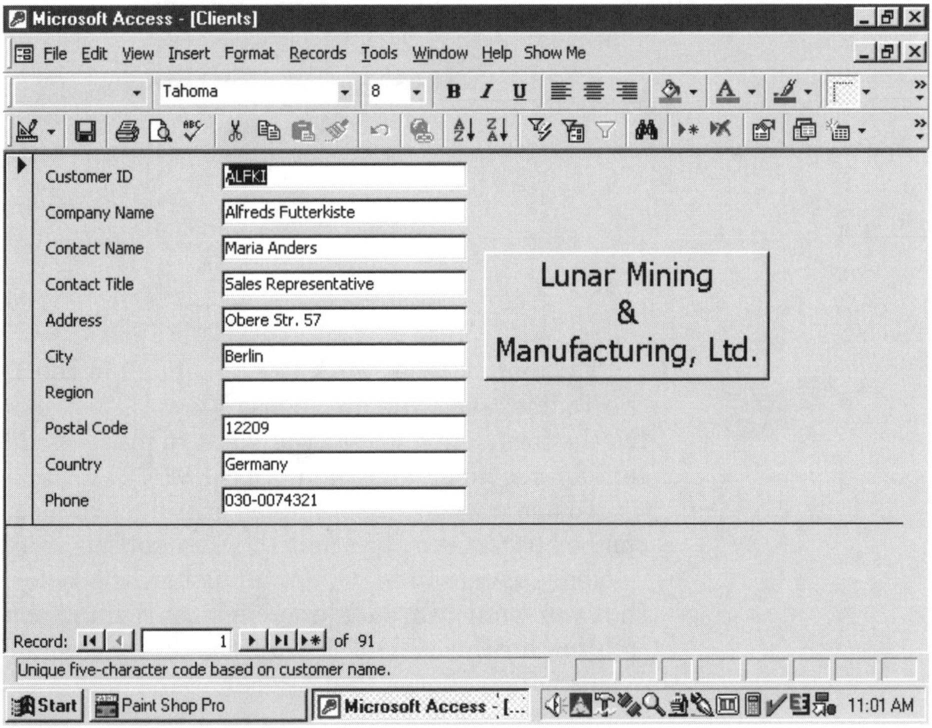

Figure 7-5 An example of a label added to a form as a title

 ## How can I add lines or rectangles to a form?

To add lines or rectangles to a form, click the Line or Rectangle button, respectively, in the Toolbox. Click the form wherever you want to draw the line or rectangle, and hold down the mouse button. Move the pointer to wherever you want the line or rectangle to end. Release the mouse button, and the line or rectangle appears on the form.

How can I manually add controls to a form?

When you manually design forms, the field list offers the easiest way to add controls based on fields. Click the Field List button in the Form Design toolbar or choose View | Field List to display the field list, shown here. Then, to create a control that displays data from the field, drag the field from the field list to the desired location on the form.

To create a label, click the Label tool in the Toolbox. (If the Toolbox isn't visible, choose View | Toolbox to display it.) On the form, click where you want to place the label, type the text for the label, and then press ENTER.

To use a wizard to create a control (such as a list box or a combo box), make sure that the Control Wizards tool in the Toolbox is pressed in. Click the tool for the type of control that you want to create, and click the form at the desired location for the control. Follow the directions in the Control Wizard dialog boxes that appear.

 How can I modify the colors of a form?

Changing a form's colors in Access is very easy, using these three steps:

1. Right-click a blank space in the form.
2. Choose Fi<u>l</u>l/Back Color.
3. Choose the color that you want from the pop-up menu.

 Note: *If a picture has been applied to the form's background, the new color won't be visible. You can't have a background picture and a background color in effect simultaneously.*

 How do I move controls?

To move a control, first select it, and then move the pointer near the edge of the control. When the pointer changes into an outstretched palm, drag the control to the desired location. To move a control apart from any attached label, first select the control (or label) by clicking it, and then place the pointer on the move handle (it is larger than the sizing handles and is in the upper-left corner of the control). When the mouse pointer changes to a hand with a pointing index finger, drag the control to the desired location.

 How can I change an option button to a text box, or vice versa?

You can change an existing control to another type of control. Open the form in Design view and select the control that you want to change. Choose <u>F</u>ormat | C<u>h</u>ange To and then choose from the submenu the type of control that you want to change to.

 Is there a fast way to change the overall appearance of a form?

You can change the overall appearance of an entire form by changing the form's AutoFormat property. Open the form in

Design view, click the AutoFormat button in the Form Design toolbar, and choose a new format from the dialog box that appears.

? How can I add a page break to a form?

In forms that will be printed often, you can add page breaks to indicate where one printed page should end and another page should begin. To add a page break, follow these steps:

1. In the form's Design view, open the Toolbox, if it isn't already open (choose View | Toolbox).

2. Click the Page Break tool in the Toolbox, and then click the form where you want the new page to begin. The page break appears in the form's design as a short dotted line, as shown in Figure 7-6.

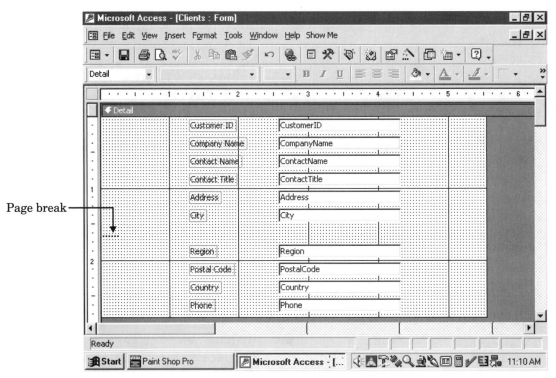

Page break

Figure 7-6 A page break added to a form

 Can I prevent users from adding new records in my form?

You can use the Allow Additions property of the form to prevent users from adding new records. To do so:

1. Open your form in Design view.

2. Display the Properties window for the form either by clicking the Properties toolbar button or by choosing View | Properties.

3. Click the Data tab.

4. Move to the Allow Additions property and set it to No.

5. Save the form and then switch back to Form view. Users will no longer be able to add records using this form.

 Can I prevent users from updating records in my form?

Yes, you can easily prevent users from updating the records displayed in your form, by setting the Allow Edits and Allow Deletions properties to No in the form's Design view. This prevents users from editing the contents of controls that are bound to a table or query. Use these steps:

1. Open your form in Design view.

2. Display the Properties window for the form either by clicking the Properties toolbar button or by choosing View | Properties.

3. Click the Data tab.

4. Set both the Allow Deletions and Allow Edits properties to No.

5. Save the form.

How can I print the data in a form without printing all the records in the underlying table?

To print the data in a form without printing all the records in the underlying table, you need to select the desired record

within the form and then print just the selection, instead of printing all pages. Use these steps:

1. Open the specific form in Form view.

2. To print a single record, find the record that you want to print, and then either click the Record Selector bar at the left edge of the form or choose Edit | Select Record.

3. Choose File | Print, and the Print dialog box appears. Click Selected Record(s) in the Print Range portion of the dialog box.

4. Set any other options that you want in the dialog box and then click OK to begin printing.

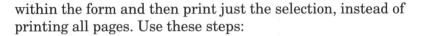 Is there a quick way to select every control on a form, so that I can move them as a group?

You can quickly select every control on a form by displaying the form in Design view and then choosing Edit | Select All or pressing CTRL-A. (You can deselect all selected controls by clicking anywhere outside of a control.)

How do I change the size of a control?

To resize a control, select the control, move the pointer to any of the control's sizing handles (the eight small boxes that surround the control), and then drag the handle until the control is the size that you want.

How can I change the size of my form?

You can increase or decrease the height of form sections individually, but the entire form has just one width. If you change the width of just one section, you change the width of the entire form. (Also remember that you can try changing the size of the window to fit the form while in Form view.) Use these steps to change the size of your form:

1. In the form's Design view, change either the height or the width by placing the pointer on the bottom edge or right edge of the section. The pointer changes to a double-sided arrow.

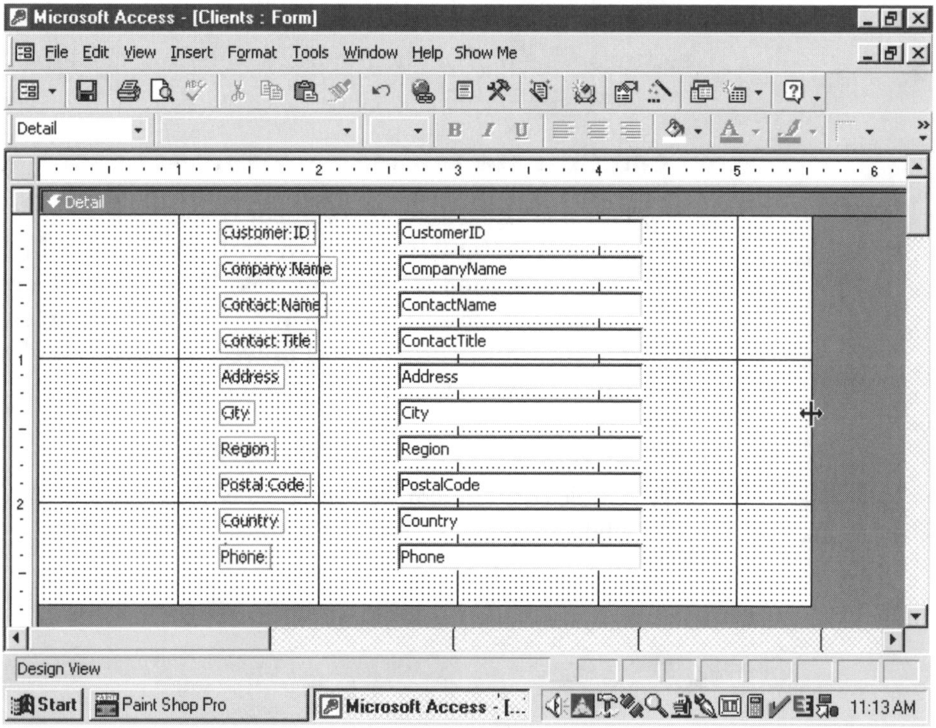

Figure 7-7 Changing the height or width of a form

2. Drag the pointer up or down to change the height of the section.

3. Drag the pointer left or right to change the width of the section, as shown in Figure 7-7.

4. To change both the height and width of a form simultaneously, place the pointer in the lower-right corner of the section, until the pointer takes the shape of an arrow with four heads. Drag the pointer in any direction to adjust the size of the form.

Is there a way to change the grid spacing used in form design?

To change the grid spacing (the number of dots per square inch or per square centimeter), open the form in Design view and choose Edit | Select Form. Next, choose View | Properties.

Click the Format tab and change the Grid X and Grid Y settings. The higher the numbers, the finer the grid (the more dots per square inch).

? How can I create tabbed forms in Access?

You can use the Tab control of the Toolbox to create tabbed forms that resemble the tabbed dialog boxes used in many programs designed for Windows 95, Windows 98, or Windows NT. Figure 7-8 shows the use of a tabbed form; in this type of form, different controls are placed on each tab of the form. Use the following steps to create a tabbed form:

1. Create a new form in Design view.

2. Click the Tab control in the Toolbox. (If the Toolbox isn't visible, choose View | Toolbox to display it.)

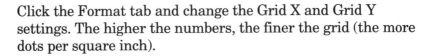

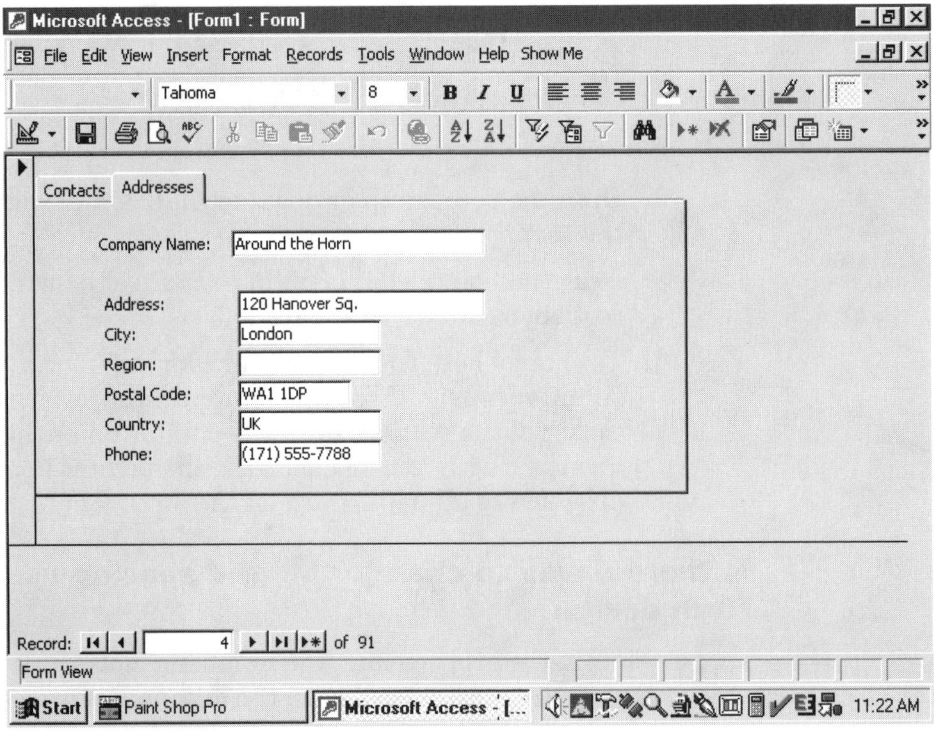

Figure 7-8   The use of a tabbed form in Access

3. In the form, click the point where you want to place the upper-left corner of the Tab control, and then drag to the desired location for the lower-right corner of the control. When you release the mouse button, Access creates a tabbed control containing two tabs, as shown in Figure 7-9.

4. To add the controls that you want to each tab, select the tab and then drag fields from the field list to the tab or add controls from the Toolbox.

5. To change the name of a tab, double-click the tab to open its Properties window, click the Format tab, and enter a name in the Caption text box.

6. To add more tabs, select the tab that the new tab should appear after, and choose Insert | Tab Control Page.

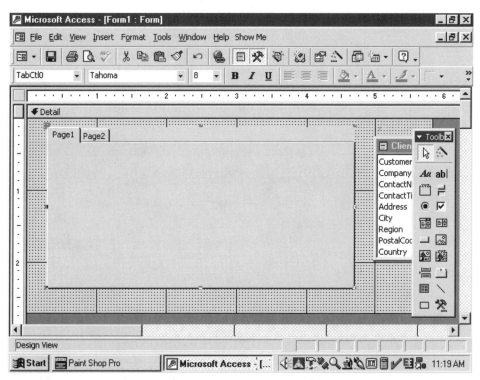

Figure 7-9 A new tabbed control

USING FORMS

How can I add buttons to perform tasks (such as printing or closing the form) to a form?

Command buttons can be added to forms in Access for numerous common tasks, including records management (navigating to records and updating them), opening and closing forms, and printing forms and reports. To add a command button to perform such tasks, follow these steps:

1. In the Design view of the form, turn on the Control Wizards, if they are not already on (click the Control Wizards tool in the Toolbox until it is highlighted).

2. Click the Command Button tool in the Toolbox.

3. Click the location in the form where you want to place the command button. In a moment, Access displays the first Control Wizards dialog box for a command button, shown in Figure 7-10.

4. Follow the steps outlined in the Wizard dialog boxes. (The exact steps vary, depending on what action you want your button to perform.) In the last Wizard dialog box that appears, click the Create button to display the command button while in Design view.

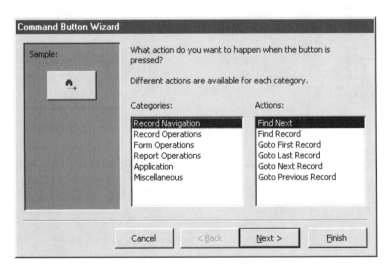

Figure 7-10 The first Command Button Wizard dialog box

Can I add a form button to move to the end of the table so that I can easily add new records?

Yes, you can easily create such a command button in your forms. In fact, Access helps you to do this, with its Command Button Wizard. Use these steps to add this command button to the form's design:

1. Open the form in Design view.

2. If the Control Wizards are turned off, click the Control Wizards button in the Toolbox to turn them on (the button should look pushed in).

3. Click the Command Button tool in the Toolbox (the button with the single raised rectangle).

4. Click the form at the location where you want the button to appear. In a moment, the first Command Button Wizard dialog box appears, as shown earlier, in Figure 7-10.

5. In the Categories list box, choose Record Operations. In the Actions list box, choose Add New Record.

6. Click Finish.

7. Right-click the new button and choose Properties to display the Properties window for the button.

8. Click the Event tab.

9. Move to the On Click property and click the Build (...) button at the right. The form's Module window opens and displays the event procedure created by the Command Button Wizard.

10. Move to the end of the line that reads DoCmd. GoToRecord , , AcNewRec and press ENTER.

11. Type **Forms!**[*form name*]!**[***control name***]**.**SetFocus**, where *form name* is the name of your form, and *control name* is the name of the first control in your tab order.

12. Choose File | Save and then choose File | Close to exit from the Module window.

Now, when you select this button in the form, Access moves you to a new blank record and moves the focus to the first

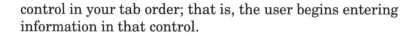

control in your tab order; that is, the user begins entering information in that control.

How can I center a form automatically in the Access window each time it opens?

You can do this by setting the Auto Center property for the form to Yes. Open the form in Design view and choose View | Properties. Click the Format tab in the Properties window that opens, and set the Auto Center property to Yes.

How can I make one of the command buttons on a form the default button?

You can make any command button the default button by changing its Default property. Open the form in Design view, right-click the desired button, and choose Properties. Click the Other tab and set the Default property to Yes.

How can I disable the Datasheet view (or the Form view) for a form?

You can disable the user's ability to switch between Form view and Datasheet view for any form. Use the following steps to do this:

1. Open the form's Design view (if already open in Design view, choose Edit | Select Form).

2. Choose View | Properties to open the Properties window for the form.

3. Click the Format tab.

4. Set the Views Allowed property either to Form, if you want to disable the viewing as a datasheet, or to Datasheet, if you want to disable the viewing as a form.

5. If you set the Views Allowed property to Datasheet, set the Default View property to Datasheet.

6. Save the form.

 I know how to make an entire form read-only, but how can I prevent users from editing in a single control?

Access gives you the ability to restrict editing in a form at the control level by changing the editing properties for the control. In Design view, right-click the control, choose Properties, and then click the Data tab in the Properties window. If you want to make the data readable but prevent editing, set the Locked property to Yes. If you want to disable the control so that it's dimmed and can't receive the focus (that is, so that the user can't get to the control by clicking it or tabbing), set the Enabled property to No.

 How can I filter the display of records while using a form?

You can use a feature called Filter by Form to restrict the records that you view in a form. Use these steps to do so:

1. Open the form in Form view.
2. Click the Filter by Form toolbar button or choose Records | Filter | Filter By Form.
3. Click inside the field for which you want to enter a criterion that records must meet to be included in the filtered records.
4. Enter the criterion that you want to use to select the records, or choose an entry from the drop-down list (you can use more than one field, if needed).
5. If you want to do a search based on an "Or" criterion, click the Or tab that appears at the bottom of the form, and then choose another entry from the drop-down list.
6. Click the Apply Filter toolbar button or choose Records | Apply Filter/Sort.

The form shows only those records meeting your filter criteria. To clear the effects of the filter, click the Remove Filter toolbar button or choose Records | Remove Filter/Sort.

✛ ***Tip:*** *If you want to find records where a check box, toggle button, or option button is selected or deselected, turn on or off the box or button until it appears the way that you want to use it to filter the records. To cancel the filtering effects of the box or button, continue clicking the box or button until it is grayed out.*

 ### Can I find a record by its record number while in Form view?

Although not intuitively obvious, you can easily find a record this way. Click inside the Record Number box (between the navigation buttons) at the bottom of the form or press F5. Delete the existing entry, type a new value, and press ENTER to go to that record. (Keep in mind that this number represents the record number according to the data source used by the form. If your form is based on a query, the record number simply refers to that successive record within the query, which could differ from the actual record number in the underlying table.)

 ### Can I move between the header and detail sections of a form without using the mouse?

Yes, while in Form view, you can press F6 to move between sections of a form. (This assumes that the header contains one or more controls. If no controls are in the header, Access won't let you move into that section of the form.)

Can I open any form in my database by selecting the form by name from a combo box in another form?

Yes, you can open one form by selecting its name from a combo box in another form. You first need to create a combo box that displays the names of all the forms in your database. Then you need to set up the combo box so that selecting a name from the box opens the selected form. To do this, you use Visual Basic for Applications (VBA).

1. On the first form, create the combo box from which you want to select the form to open.

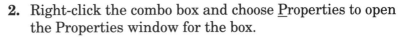

2. Right-click the combo box and choose Properties to open the Properties window for the box.

3. On the Other tab, enter **ListOfForms** in the Name property of the combo box.

4. On the Data tab, select Value List as the Row Source Type property setting.

5. On the Event tab, move to the On Enter property and click the Build button at the end of the field.

6. Select Code Builder in the list box that appears, and then click OK.

7. Enter the following code:

```
Private Sub ListofForms_Enter()
Dim MyDb As Database
Dim MyContainer As Container
Dim I As Integer
Dim List As String
Set MyDb = DBEngine.Workspaces(0).Databases(0)
Set MyContainer = MyDb.Containers("Forms")
List = ""
For I = 0 To MyContainer.Documents.Count - 1
        List = List & MyContainer.Documents(I).Name & ";"
Next I
Me![ListofForms].RowSource = Left(List, Len(List) - 1)
End Sub
```

8. Close the Module window.

9. Move to the After Update property of the combo box and click the Build button again.

10. Select Code Builder in the list box that appears, and then click OK.

11. Enter the following code:

```
Private Sub ListofForms_AfterUpdate()
        DoCmd.OpenForm Me![ListofForms]
End Sub
```

12. Close the Module window.

13. Open the form in Form view and select a form name from the combo box. The form that you select will open.

How can I quickly open a form that I use on a regular basis?

You can do this in either of two ways:

- Create an Autoexec macro that has an Open action for the form as its first event, in which case the form automatically appears whenever you open the database.

- Create a shortcut directly to the form on the Windows desktop.

To create an Autoexec macro that opens the form, create a new macro (click the Macros tab in the Database window, and then click New). In the Action column of the macro, choose OpenForm. Under Form Name in the Action Arguments pane, choose the form that you want to use from the list. Save the macro under the name **Autoexec**. From then on, when you open the database, the form will load automatically.

To create a shortcut from the Windows desktop, size the Access application window so that you can see a portion of the Database window and your Windows desktop simultaneously. Click the Forms tab in the Database window and drag the desired form onto the Windows desktop. A shortcut to the form appears, which you can double-click to launch Access and open the form.

Tip: *Of the two methods, the first is more advantageous if you want to perform other actions in the macro, such as maximizing the form that you want to open or opening other forms or reports. The second method works best if you don't always want to open the same form; you can add desktop shortcuts for each of your commonly used forms. (If you have many forms that you use often, you can create a new folder and store the shortcuts inside the folder.)*

How can I add a button to a form to print just the current record?

You can use the Command Button Wizard to add a button that prints the current record only. You need to be careful

about the selection that you make in the Command Button Wizard dialog boxes to get the desired results, because choosing Form Operations followed by Print Current Form gives you a button that prints every record in the underlying table or query, which is *not* what you want. Use these steps to add a button that prints a single record:

1. Open the form in Design view.

2. If the Control Wizards are turned off, click the Control Wizards button in the Toolbox to turn them on (the button should appear pushed in).

3. Click the Command Button tool in the Toolbox.

4. Click the form at the location where you want the button to appear.

5. In the first Command Button Wizard dialog box that appears, click Record Operations under Categories, and then click Print Record under Actions.

6. Click <u>N</u>ext and follow the directions in the successive Wizard dialog boxes to choose a picture or caption for the button. In the last dialog box, click <u>F</u>inish to add the button.

How can I prevent users from doing anything else within Access while a form is open?

You can force users to stay in the form until they close it, by setting the form's Modal property to Yes. Use these steps:

1. Open the form in Design view.

2. Choose <u>E</u>dit | Select Fo<u>r</u>m.

3. Choose <u>V</u>iew | <u>P</u>roperties to open the Properties window.

4. Click the Other tab and set the Modal property to Yes.

I regularly print data using a form. Is there an easy way to create a report based on the form?

In the Database window, right-click the desired form and choose Save <u>A</u>s. In the next dialog box, change the As drop-down entry to Report. In the upper portion of the dialog box, enter a name for the new report and then click OK.

 Can I use my form to sort the records I view in the form?

You can do this through the form, although you are limited to sorting based on only one field at a time. Click the field that you want the sort to be based on and then click either the Sort Ascending or Sort Descending toolbar button, as desired.

 Tip: *If you want to view the data based on a sort involving more than one field, create a query that sorts your data as you want it sorted, and then use the query as the data source for the form.*

 When I tab through my form, the tab order isn't from top to bottom. How can I fix this?

This often happens when you add a new field to a form, because Access tabs through the fields in the order in which you add them. When you add a new field, it becomes last in the tab order, regardless of the field's location in the form. Use these steps to change the tab order:

1. Open the form in Design view.

2. Choose <u>V</u>iew | Ta<u>b</u> Order to see the Tab Order dialog box, shown here:

3. Click and drag into the Custom Order list box each field that you want to change the order of, placing them in the order in which you want to move between the fields.

4. Click OK to save the changes.

 ## How can I change the title that appears in a form's title bar?

This title is stored in the form's Caption property. If you don't like the default title that the AutoForm button or the wizard assigns, you can easily change it by using these steps:

1. Open the form in Design view.

2. Choose View | Properties to open the Properties window for the form.

3. Click the Format tab.

4. Under the Caption property, enter a new title.

5. Switch to Form view to see the title.

How can I calculate a total for one record in a form?

You do this by adding a *calculated field* to the form. The field is simply a text box that performs the necessary calculation. The expression you place in the text box depends on which fields you want to total. For example, if you want to display the total of two fields called Cost and Shipping, you use the expression **=[Cost] + [Shipping]** in the text box. To add the calculated field to the form, use these steps:

1. Open the form in Design view.

2. Click the Text Box tool in the Toolbox.

3. Click the detail section of the form where you want to place the calculated field.

4. Click the field and then type the expression needed to calculate the total. (Note that the expression must begin with an equal sign.)

TROUBLESHOOTING

 ### My form is blank. Why can't I see any data?

There are two possible causes for this problem:

● *The form is based on a query that is not returning any data.* If the form is based on a query, double-click the query in the Database window to run the query. If it is empty, the form will also be empty. Restructure the query's criteria to provide the needed data.

● *You are in Data Entry mode.* When a form is in Data Entry mode, it displays a blank record that you can use to add data. To see all of your records, choose Records | Remove Filter/Sort.

 ### Why can't I edit data in my form?

If you can't edit data in a form, check for any of the following possibilities:

● The form was created as a read-only form. If the Allow Additions, Allow Editing, and Allow Deletions properties for the form are set to No, you won't be able to make any additions or changes to the data.

● The Locked property for some or all the controls in the form may be set to Yes.

● Another user on the network may be editing the same record.

● The form may be based on a table or query that's not updateable (such as a query based on linked SQL tables).

Why does #Error or #Name appear in a control in my form?

This problem can be due to any one of several causes. Check for any of these possibilities:

● Make sure that field names in the Control Source property for the control are not mispelled.

● If field names used as parts of expressions contain spaces, make sure that brackets surround the field names. For example, [*last name*] is a valid reference to a field name within an expression.

- If you are using a built-in function as part of an expression, make sure that the syntax is correct and that the arguments are in the proper order.

- Make sure that any fields named in the Control Source property for the control haven't been renamed or removed in the underlying table or query.

Why does my form run so slowly?

If your form is slow to open and use, you may be facing the natural challenges of working with large amounts of data. You can run Performance Analyzer, both on the form and on any underlying query, to obtain a report on how you might redesign the form or the query to speed performance. To run Performance Analyzer, close the form and then choose Tools | Analyze | Performance. In the Performance Analyzer dialog box, place a check mark in the check box for the form or underlying query and then click OK. If Performance Analyzer has any suggestions for improving the form or query design, it displays them in a dialog box.

In addition to using Performance Analyzer, you can try the following:

- Close any other forms that you aren't using.
- Avoid using bitmaps, graphic backgrounds, or other unnecessary graphics in the form's design.
- If your form has any unbound object frames containing graphic images, convert them to image controls. (In Design view, right-click the frame, choose Change To, and then choose Image.)
- Avoid sorting records in an underlying query, unless the order of the displayed records in the form is important.
- Index any fields in subforms that are used for criteria in underlying queries.
- If records in a subform won't be edited, set the subform's Allow Additions, Allow Edits, and Allow Deletions properties to No.

Chapter 8

Advanced Forms

Answer Topics!

Advanced Forms @ a Glance

The previous chapter discussed general questions about the design and use of basic forms. This chapter picks up among the more advanced topics of that same subject. When you want to take the design and usage of forms past the ordinary, you often run into the kinds of questions highlighted in this chapter. The questions that you'll see here cover the following areas:

- **Form Design** discusses unusual design techniques and accomplishing useful tasks with list boxes and combo boxes.

- **Form Usage** answers questions that arise about working with forms in more complex ways, such as using validation rules, limiting user manipulation of forms, and exporting data from forms.

- **Relational Forms** helps you to make effective use of forms that display data from multiple tables.

- **Visual Basic for Applications (VBA) and Forms** explores the use of VBA code to manipulate forms.

FORM DESIGN

Can I make a form that changes colors as I tab through the fields?

You can do this by modifying the BackColor property for the form's detail section through the use of VBA code. Your code needs to be attached to the OnEnter event for each field in the form. You also need the numeric values that are equivalent to the colors that you want to use. The easiest way to obtain these values is to look at the value stored in the Back Property entry of the Properties window for any section of a form, after you change that section's color in Design view. Once you know the numeric values for the desired colors, follow these steps:

1. Right-click the first field in the form and choose Properties.
2. In the Properties window that opens, click the Event tab.
3. Click the OnEnter property; then click the Build button (...) at the far right of the property.
4. Click Code Builder in the next dialog box that opens, and then click OK.
5. In the Module window that opens, enter the following code:

    Forms![*form name*].Section(0).BackColor=*nnn*

where *form name* is the name of the form, and *nnn* is the numeric value of the background color.

Repeat steps 1 through 5 for each field in the form, using a different numeric value for the BackColor property, and then save the form. When you run the form, its background color will change as you move through the fields.

Note: *If the form has a background picture, you must first select the form and remove the picture from its Format properties.*

I have a list box with two columns, and I'd prefer that one of the columns remain hidden. How can I hide a column in a list box?

Using the properties for the list box, you can hide any column that you don't want displayed. This can prove useful when

you have a list box that's bound to a field, and you want the field's contents hidden. You do this by changing the Column Widths property for the list box so that the width of the column that you want to hide is zero. The Column Widths property contains a width value for each column in the box, and the values are separated by semicolons. Hence, a three-column list box would have three values in the property, separated by semicolons. In Design view, right-click the list box and choose Properties to open the Properties window for the box. Click the Format tab and change the entry under Column Widths. Assuming that the list box contains three columns, each 3/4-inch wide, and you want to hide the second column, you change the Column Widths property to .75";0;.75".

 How can I add a list box or a combo box to a form?

List boxes and combo boxes are often useful in Access forms. You can use list boxes to present a number of available values from a list, and you can use combo boxes to allow users to enter a value by typing it or by choosing it from a list of items. You can easily add list boxes or combo boxes to forms with the aid of the Control Wizards. Use the following steps:

1. Open the form in Design view.

2. Turn on the Control Wizards in the Toolbox, if they are not already on (if the Control Wizards are on, the Control Wizards button in the Toolbox appears depressed).

3. In the Toolbox, click the List Box tool if you want a list box, and click the Combo Box tool if you want a combo box. (For help identifying the tools, hold the mouse pointer stationary over a tool until the name of the tool appears.)

4. Click the location on the form where you want to place the control. In a moment, Access displays the first Control Wizard dialog box for a list box or a combo box, as shown in Figure 8-1.

5. Follow the steps outlined in the Control Wizard dialog boxes. (These steps will differ, depending on the type of box that you add and the sources that you choose for the choices that appear in the list box or combo box.) In the

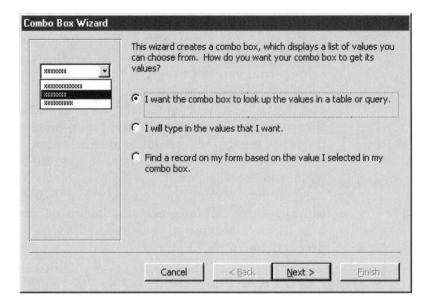

Figure 8-1 Control Wizard dialog box for placing a combo box

final dialog box that appears, click the Finish button to add the list box or combo box to the form.

 I print forms regularly to obtain quick reports of selective data, and most of my forms have command buttons on them. Can I prevent the buttons from printing?

You can prevent command buttons (or any other objects placed on a form) from printing by changing the Display When property for the object. Use these steps to do this:

1. Open the form in Design view.

2. Right-click the command button or other object that you want to prevent from printing, and then choose Properties.

3. In the Properties window that appears, click the Format tab.

4. Set the Display When property to Screen Only.

5. Save the form.

How can I change a text label to display as reverse video?

Text stands out if you create white text against a black background, an effect also known as *reverse video*. (Figure 8-2 shows a form containing a label with its shading formatted as reverse video.) You can apply this effect to a text label with the following steps:

1. Right-click the label, choose Fi̲ll/Back Color from the submenu, and click Black in the color box that appears.

2. Right-click the label, choose Fo̲nt/Fore Color from the submenu, and click White in the color box that appears.

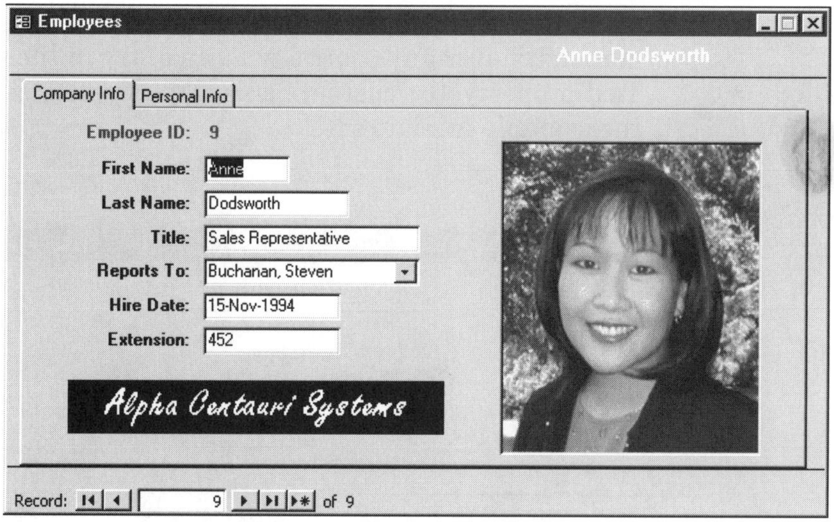

Figure 8-2 A form with a text label displayed as reverse video

? Can I create something on my form similar to the ScreenTips labels that appear when I point the mouse at a toolbar button?

Yes. This took quite a bit of effort in versions of Access prior to Access 97, which may be why Microsoft added a property that lets you easily create customized ScreenTips for any control on a form. Use these steps to do this:

1. Open the form in Design view.
2. Right-click the control for which you want to create a ScreenTip.
3. Choose Properties from the menu that appears, and click the Other tab of the Properties window.
4. Click inside the ControlTip Text property and type the message that you want for your ScreenTip.
5. Repeat this process for any other controls that you want to have ScreenTips for.
6. Save the form.

When you open the form and leave the mouse pointer stationary over any control with an entry in the ControlTip Text property, the custom ScreenTip appears, as shown in the example in Figure 8-3.

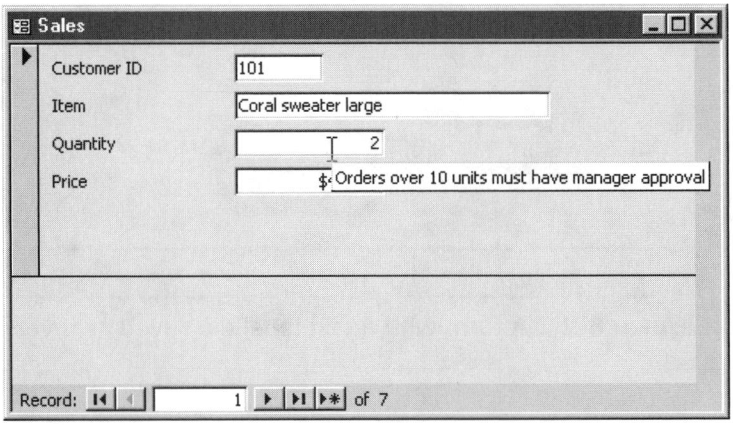

Figure 8-3 An example of a custom ScreenTip

 How can I use a combo box to search for records in a form?

You can use the Control Wizard to add a combo box that displays a drop-down list. When the user types a few characters of a search string and presses ENTER, Access finds and displays a matching record in the form. Use these steps:

1. Open the form in Design view.

2. Turn on the Control Wizards in the Toolbox, if they are not already on (if the Control Wizards are on, the Control Wizards button in the Toolbox appears depressed).

3. In the Toolbox, click the Combo Box tool.

4. Click the location on the form where you want to place the control.

5. In the first Combo Box Wizard dialog box, turn on the last option, titled "Find a record on my form based on the value I selected in my combo box," and then click Next.

6. In the second Combo Box Wizard dialog box, add the field that you want users to search on, and then click Next.

7. In the third Combo Box Wizard dialog box, set the width that you want for the combo box column, and then click Next.

8. In the final Combo Box Wizard dialog box, enter a label for the field, and then click Finish to add the combo box to the form.

9. Save and run the form.

As you type part of a search string into the combo box, Access displays matching entries in the underlying table or query. When you press ENTER, the form moves to that record.

 How can I create a shadow box on a form's controls, similar to the ones created by the Form Wizards?

The shadow boxes that the Form Wizard creates are actually two controls. One control is a text box used to display or edit the data, and the other control is a rectangle that serves as a shadow. You could manually create a rectangle, set its

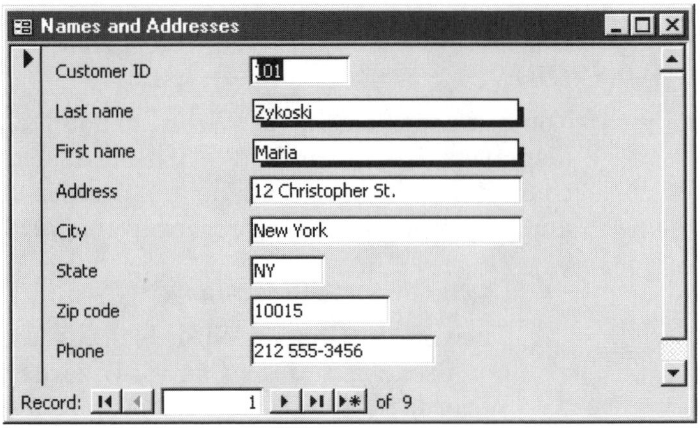

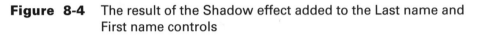

Figure 8-4 The result of the Shadow effect added to the Last name and First name controls

background color to gray, and place it underneath the control, but in recent versions of Access, there's an easier way to give controls a shadow effect. Open the form in Design view and right-click the control. From the menu that appears, choose Special Effect and then choose the Shadow option from the submenu. Figure 8-4 shows two controls, Last name and First name, with the shadow added by using this menu option.

We have a personnel database with employee photos. When we paste the photos into an OLE Object field in a form, large parts of the images are cut off. If we make the field substantially larger to accommodate the photos, it takes up too much room on the form. How can we show the entire photo?

You need to change the default setting for the Size Mode property of the OLE Object field. By default, this setting is Clip, which clips any image that's larger than the control. Use these steps to change the default setting:

1. Open the form in Design view.

2. Right-click the OLE Object frame used to display the photos, and choose Properties.

3. Click the Format tab.

4. In the Size Mode property, choose Zoom to display the entire object with no distortion, or choose Stretch to size the object to fill the control (some distortion may result).

 Tip: *If your photos are all the same size, it's usually best to choose Zoom and then resize the field slightly to eliminate any extra blank space in the field when the photos are displayed.*

FORM USAGE

Can I let users easily cancel editing of a record?

You can add to a form a command button that lets users cancel edits made to the record; the command button uses a VBA procedure to simulate choosing Undo from the Edit menu. Use these steps to add a button that cancels edits to a record:

1. Open the form in Design view.

2. Turn on the Control Wizards in the Toolbox, if they are not already on (if the Control Wizards are on, the Control Wizards button in the Toolbox appears depressed).

3. In the Toolbox, click the Command Button tool.

4. Click the location on the form where you want to place the button.

5. In the first Command Button Wizard dialog box, select Record Operations, select Undo Record, and then click Next.

6. In the second Command Button Wizard dialog box, choose one of the available pictures for the button, or enter text of your choosing to display on the front of the button.

7. Click Finish to add the button to the form.

Can I close a form automatically after a certain period of time?

Yes, you can have a form close itself after a certain amount of time. Use these steps to do this:

1. From the Database window, click the Macros button and then click <u>N</u>ew to open a new Macro window.

2. Click the drop-down list button in the Action column of the first row of the macro, and choose Close.

3. Select <u>F</u>ile | <u>S</u>ave to save the macro (give it any name that you want).

4. Open the form in Design view.

5. Select <u>V</u>iew | <u>P</u>roperties to open the Properties window for the form.

6. Click the Event tab.

7. Move to the Timer Interval property and set it to the number of milliseconds that you want the form to stay open. Remember, 1 second equals 1,000 milliseconds. For example, enter **10000** if you want the form to stay open for ten seconds, or enter **60000** if you want the form open for a minute.

8. Click the On Timer property and choose the macro that you just saved from the list.

9. Save and close the form.

Now, when you open the form, it displays for the amount of time set in the Timer Interval property, and then it closes.

When I double-click an OLE object in Form view, nothing happens. How do I edit an OLE object?

The reason you can't edit the OLE object is that the control's Enabled property is set to No. Access sets the Enabled property differently for OLE objects that are part of the form

design versus those stored in a table. The object that you double-clicked is probably an unbound OLE object. To edit the unbound OLE object while in Form view, you need to return to the form's Design view. Select the control containing the OLE object and select View | Properties. In the Properties window, click the Data tab, set the Enabled property to Yes, and set the Locked property to No. From now on, you can edit your unbound OLE objects in Form view. The bound object frames that display OLE objects stored in a table already have their Enabled property set to Yes.

Tip: *In Form view, to determine whether you can edit a particular OLE object, click it; if it has black marks (handles) around the inside of the frame after you click it, as shown here, then you can edit it:*

Customer ID	101
Item	Coral sweater large
Quantity	2
Price	$49.95

Washington Outerwear, Inc.

Record: 1 of 7

 When I choose File | Export and export a form's data to an RTF file or an XLS file for use with Microsoft Word or Microsoft Excel, the exported file is missing the data from the subform. What's wrong?

The Export command does not output the data from subforms or subreports. This is simply a part of Access's design and cannot be worked around. If you need the related data that is displayed in the subform, create a relational query that

contains the subform fields, and then export the results of that query.

 ## Why doesn't the header that I created appear in Form view?

The header that you created was probably a page header. Two headers are available on forms:

- **Form header** Appears both onscreen and when printed
- **Page header** Displays only if the form is printed

The same is true for footers: page footers and form footers both are available on forms.

 Tip: *To display the Page Header and Page Footer sections, choose* View | Page Header / Footer. *To display the Form Header and Form Footer sections, choose* View | Form Header / Footer.

 ## Can I hide the scroll bars and navigation buttons in my forms?

Yes, on forms, you can hide these elements by changing the Scroll Bars and Navigation Buttons properties. Select View | Properties to display the form's Properties window. Click the Format tab, move to the Scroll Bars property, and choose Neither. Then, select the Navigation Buttons property and enter No. When you save and view the form, your form might look like the example shown in Figure 8-5.

Besides hiding the scroll bars and navigation buttons, you can hide the record selectors by setting the Record Selectors property to No. You can remove the Minimize, Maximize, and Restore buttons in the upper-right corner of the form by changing the MinMax Buttons property to None.

 Tip: *If you want to hide the navigation buttons and scroll bars on a subform, you must modify the subform's design and change the properties there. You cannot hide the navigation buttons and scroll bars for a subform from the Design view for the main form.*

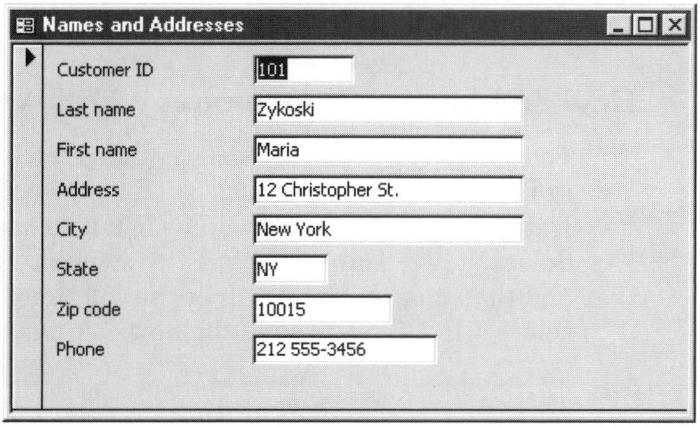

Figure 8-5 A form lacking scroll bars and navigation selectors

Can I prevent users from closing my form with the Control menu box?

Yes; in fact, you can remove the Control menu box from the Form window. That way, you can make sure that users exit the form only the way that you intended. To remove the Control menu box, open the form in Design view. Select View | Properties to display the form's Properties window. Click the Format tab and set the Control Box property to No.

I use different validation rules for certain fields in my form and the underlying table. Which rule actually applies when I enter data in the form?

Actually, both rules apply when you enter data in the form. Access uses the validation rule of both the form and the table when it tests the data that you enter. If the data violates either rule, you can't save the record containing the offending data.

Access evaluates a validation rule when you move the focus to another control or record after entering or editing data. If you leave a field without entering or altering any data, the validation rule is not evaluated. Access also tests entries against the validation rules when you leave the form, switch views, or close the form.

RELATIONAL FORMS

How do I change the column widths of a subform?

To change the column widths, you need to view the subform in Datasheet view. Find the subform by name in the Database window, and double-click it to open the subform. Select View | Datasheet View to switch to Datasheet view, and then change the width of the columns, as needed. Then, select File | Save to save the new column widths.

 Note: *If you widen the columns in a subform, you may want to go into Design view for the form and widen the size of the subform control. This avoids excessive scrolling in the subform when the data is displayed.*

How can I create a relational form, a form that displays data from more than one table?

Two ways exist to create relational forms in Access. One way is to create a relational query and then create a form based on the data in that query. (See Chapter 6 for specifics on creating relational queries.) The other way, which is more common with one-to-many relationships, is to create a form containing a subform. The main part of the form displays the records on the "one" side of the relationship, while the subform displays the records on the "many" side of the relationship. Figure 8-6 shows an example of a relational form that uses a subform.

Although you can create this type of form manually, the easiest way to create a form with a subform is to use the Form Wizard. (Note that to use the Form Wizard to create relational forms, you must first establish default relationships at the table level; see Chapter 4 for specifics on creating a relationship.) Use these steps to create a relational form:

1. Click the Forms button in the Database window and then click New.

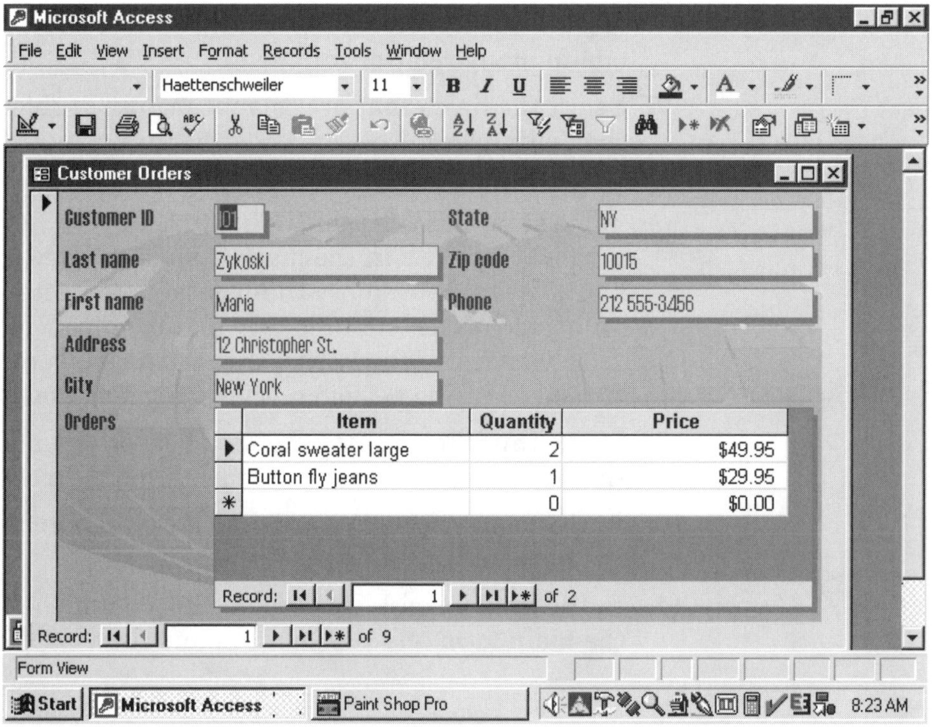

Figure 8-6 A relational form that uses a subform to display the related records

2. In the New Form dialog box that appears, click Form Wizard.

3. In the list box at the bottom of the dialog box, choose the table or query that will supply the data for the main form. (This is the data from the "one" side of the one-to-many relationship.)

4. Click OK.

5. In the first Form Wizard dialog box that appears, choose the fields that will appear in the main part of the form (but don't close this dialog box when done).

6. Click inside the Tables/Queries list box and choose the table or query that will supply the data for the subform.

(This is the data from the "many" side of the one-to-many relationship.)

7. Select the fields that are to appear in the subform, and then click <u>N</u>ext.

8. In the second Form Wizard dialog box (see Figure 8-7), make sure that the table or query that you want to use to view your data in the main form is selected in the list box. (The table or query that contains the data for the "one" side of the one-to-many relationship should be selected.) Leave the Forms with subform(s) option turned on at the bottom of the dialog box, and click <u>N</u>ext.

9. In the third Form Wizard dialog box, choose a layout for the subform (tabular or datasheet) and then click <u>N</u>ext.

10. In the fourth Form Wizard dialog box, choose a style for the form and click Next.

11. In the final Form Wizard dialog box, enter the titles for the main form and the subform and then click <u>F</u>inish.

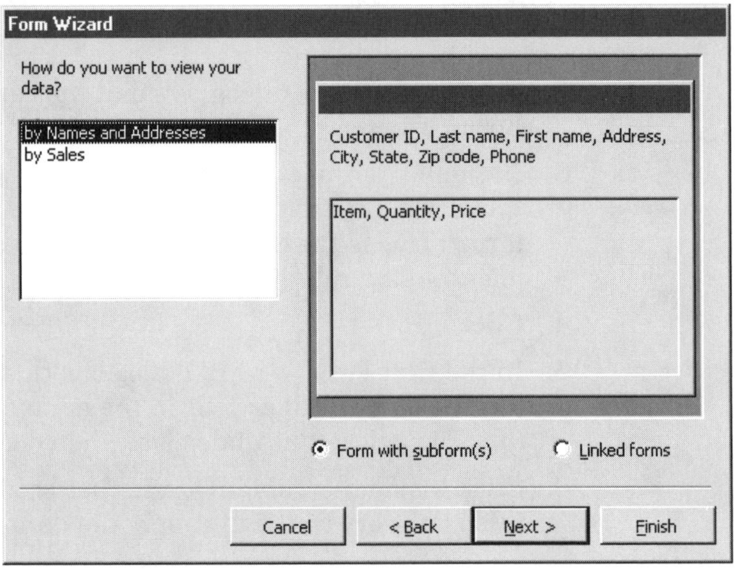

Figure 8-7 The second Form Wizard dialog box asks which table/query should be used to view data

When I open a relational form in Design view, I can change the design of the main form, but I can't change any aspects of the subform, except its size. How do I modify the subform?

The subform is saved as a separate form, so you must specifically open it in Design view to make changes to it. You can find the subform by name in the Database window and open it in Design view, but if you already have the main form open in Design view, you can simply double-click the subform control (the blank rectangle that represents the subform). When you do this, the subform opens in Design view, and you can make any desired changes to its elements.

Can I use multiple subforms on a form?

Yes, you can include more than one subform on a single form. To do so, you need to use the manual methods of form creation instead of trusting the wizards:

1. Create the desired subforms manually, using the same design methods that you would use to create any form.

2. Open the main form in Design view and drag the subforms from the Database window onto the main form, to add subform controls.

3. Open the Properties window for the subforms (click each subform and choose View | Properties) and check the Link Master Fields and Link Child Fields properties, to be sure that Access has selected the proper fields to be used for the relationship between the main form and the subform. The Link Master Fields property must contain the name of the field to link to in the main form, and the Link Child Fields property must contain the name of the field to link to in the subform.

I often print my relational forms, to show all the data related to an entry in the main form. Is there a way to print all the records in the subform, even when they don't fit onscreen?

You can do this by changing the subform's Can Grow property, which allows the size of the subform to expand as needed during printing, to accommodate all the records. Open the form in Design view, right-click the Detail band in the subform, and choose Properties. Click the Format tab and set the Can Grow property to Yes. If you also want to omit the subform from printing if no related records exist, you can set the Can Shrink property to Yes.

How can I make a subform a read-only subform, while allowing changes to the data in the main form?

You can use these steps to make a subform read-only:

1. Open the form containing the subform in Design view.

2. Right-click the subform control and choose Properties from the shortcut menu that appears.

3. In the Properties window that opens, click the Data tab.

4. Set the Locked property to Yes.

5. Select File | Save to save the changes to the form.

How can I synchronize two forms, so that data in the second form shows records that are related to the record shown in the first form?

This question assumes that, for one reason or another, you don't want to use a relational form containing a subform (otherwise, you can easily create a form with a subform by using the Form Wizards). You may want to examine related records on two forms simultaneously. For example, when looking at a customer's record in a Customer form, you might want to see another form containing all sales for that customer. You can create a command button that, when pressed, opens a second form and synchronizes that form so that it displays data related to the record on the first form. Use the following steps to do this:

1. Open the first form in Design view (the form that will contain the button).

2. Turn on the Control Wizards in the Toolbox, if they are not already on (if the Control Wizards are on, the Control Wizards button in the Toolbox appears depressed).

3. In the Toolbox, click the Command Button tool.

4. Click the location on the form where you want to place the button.

5. In the first Command Button Wizard dialog box that appears, click Form Operations in the Categories box, click Open Form in the Actions box, and then click <u>N</u>ext.

6. In the second Command Button Wizard dialog box, choose the form that you want to open and synchronize to the first form, and then click <u>N</u>ext.

7. In the third Command Button Wizard dialog box, select the option titled "Open the form and find specific data to display," and then click <u>N</u>ext.

8. The fourth Command Button Wizard dialog box, shown in Figure 8-8, asks which field contains the matching data used to synchronize the forms. Click the desired field on both sides of the dialog box, click the **<->** button in the center, and then click <u>N</u>ext.

9. In the final Command Button Wizard dialog box, choose text or a picture for the face of the button, and then click <u>F</u>inish to add the button to the form.

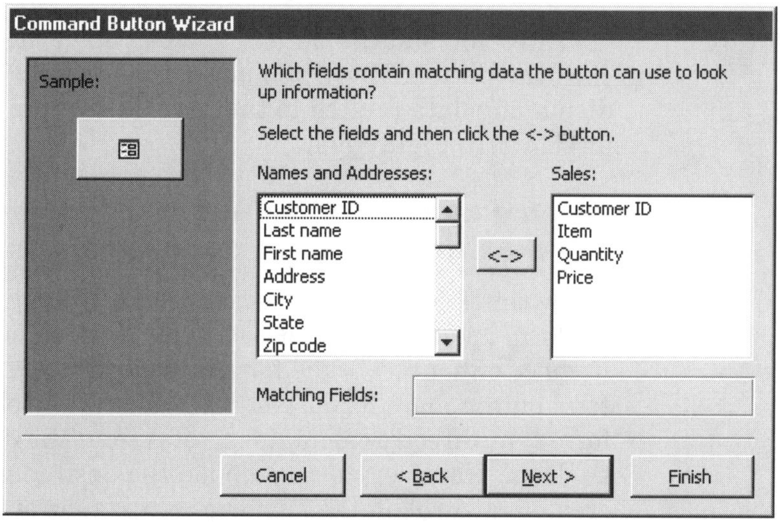

Figure 8-8   Dialog box asking for fields used to synchronize the data in the forms

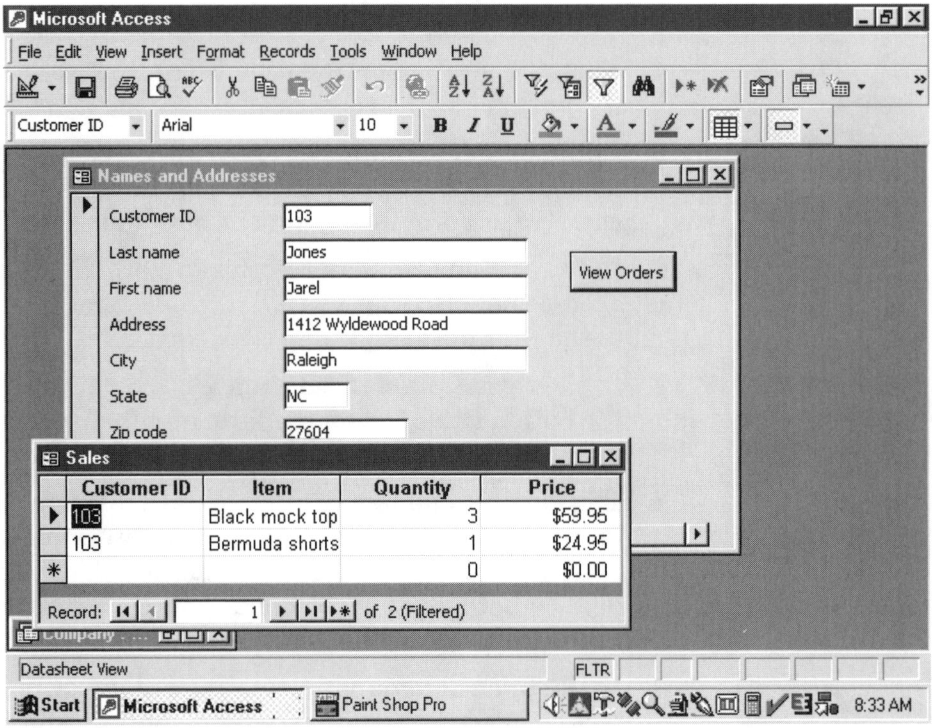

Figure 8-9 Example of data displayed in synchronized forms

After you add the button, you can open the form and click the button. When you do so, the second form opens, displaying data related to the record shown in the first form, as shown in Figure 8-9.

Is there a way to total values in a subform and display that total amount on the main form?

Many times, you may want to total an amount contained in a subform (such as a number of items ordered, or a total number of hours worked for an employee) and display that total on the main form. You can't add a control on the main form that directly calculates a total from the data in the subform. However, to accomplish the desired goal, you can create a control on the subform that is to provide the totals, hide that control, and then reference the hidden control in

the subform from another control on the main form. Use the following steps to do this:

1. Open the subform in Design view.

2. Select <u>V</u>iew | <u>P</u>roperties to display the Properties window for the subform.

3. Drag the border of the subform's footer until no room exists to place a control. (If the subform has no footer, select <u>V</u>iew | Form <u>H</u>eader/Footer to add one.)

4. Add a text box to the footer section of the subform. In the Control Source property for the control, enter an expression that totals the desired field. For example, the Price Subtotal control shown in the footer of the following form contains the expression =Sum([Price]).

5. Enter a name for the control in the Control Name property (and make a note of this name, because you need to refer to it later).

6. Set the Visible property for the control to No.

7. Choose <u>F</u>ile | <u>S</u>ave to save the subform.

8. Open the main form in Design view.

9. Choose <u>V</u>iew | <u>P</u>roperties to display the Properties window.

10. Add to the form a text box that will contain your total. In the Control Source property for the text box, you need to enter an expression that refers to the hidden

control in the subform. The syntax is =[*subform control name*].Form![*subtotal control name*], where *subform control name* is the control name for the subform, and *subtotal control name* is the name that you gave to the hidden control that you added to the footer of the subform. This example uses the expression =[Sales Subform].Form![Price Subtotal], to provide the needed results.

11. Set the Format property for the new control that you added to Fixed or Currency, set the Decimal Places property to whatever is appropriate for the type of value you are totaling (for example, set it to **2** for currency), and set the Visible property to Yes.

12. Save the main form by choosing File | Save.

Data in my subform appears as a datasheet, but I want to view the related records one at a time. How can I view the subform data in Form view?

By default, relational forms that you create by using the Form Wizards display your subform data in a datasheet. If you want to change the way that you view the data during one specific use of the form, you can switch back and forth between Form view and Datasheet view. Just click anywhere in the subform and choose View | Subform Datasheet. This command is a toggle, so each time that you choose it, the data shown in the subform alternates between a form and a datasheet.

If you want to make the subform always display its data in a form, you need to change the Default View and Views Allowed properties for the subform. Use these steps to do so:

1. Open the subform in Design view.
2. Select View | Properties.
3. In the Properties window that opens, click the Format tab.
4. Change the Default View property to Single Form.
5. Change the Views Allowed property to Form.
6. Select File | Save to save the changes to the form.

VISUAL BASIC FOR APPLICATIONS (VBA) AND FORMS

 If I export a form to another Access database, are the procedures that the form uses also exported?

When you export a form, the form's design includes its *module*, which contains all the event procedures. If the form uses only event procedures, then your form design has all the procedures that you need. If the form uses procedures from other modules, these procedures are not included. To get those procedures into the other database, export the module they are contained in.

 Can I look at the VBA code underlying a particular form?

While in the form's Design view, choose <u>V</u>iew | <u>C</u>ode or click the Code toolbar button. A Module window appears. To show the code for a specific object, select it from the Object drop-down list in the top-left portion of the window. To see the VBA code associated with a specific event for that object, select the event from the Procedure drop-down list box in the top-right portion of the window.

 Can I run VBA code within a form?

Yes, you can execute VBA code within a form. To do this for a Function procedure, you need to call the function from a property of the form or a control in it. To do so, move to the property, and enter

=*FunctionName*()

where *FunctionName* is the name of the function. You can also execute VBA code in a form by attaching event procedures to the form, or to controls on the form.

 Can I test to find the view my form is in?

You may need to know a form's current view while running a VBA procedure or a macro. The CurrentView property indicates which view the form is using. This property is available only in macros or in VBA code. The possible settings for this property are listed here:

0   Design view

1   Form view

2   Datasheet view

As an example, a macro could have a condition to test the current view. This entry might look like the following:

[Forms]![*form name*].[CurrentView]=1

Chapter 9

Basic Reports

Answer Topics!

TROUBLESHOOTING 249

? Preventing blank space in reports

? Fixing calculated fields that
appear empty

? Making column headings in a subreport
print

? Preventing blank alternating pages

? Placing a total in a page footer

? Resolving #Error and #Name messages in
report controls

? Resolving prompts for unexpected
parameters

Basic Reports @ a Glance

The questions included in this chapter cover the following areas:

- **Designing Reports** answers questions about common design techniques used with reports that display data from a single table or query.

- **Using Reports** answers questions that arise while working with reports in common ways, such as sorting and grouping data, and printing reports in challenging ways.

- **Working with Mailing Labels** answers questions that are specific to the use of reports formatted as mailing labels.

- **Troubleshooting** provides answers to common problems that arise when using reports.

Types of Reports

Reports in Access are descriptions of how you want to print the data in a table or a query. Unlike forms, reports can't be used to enter data. Reports that you design in Access can be divided into two overall types:

- **Reports that you create with the aid of wizards**   As with forms, you have to answer a few of the Report Wizard's questions about the fields and the report style that you want to use. After you answer these questions, Access creates the report, which you then can save or further modify manually. By default, the field names that you supplied when you designed the underlying table or query are used as headings or labels in the report, but you can change these.

- **Custom reports (reports that you create manually)**   Reports that you create or modify to better fit your specific needs, which may contain any data that you want from your database fields. Custom reports may include numeric information (such as totals or other calculations based on numeric or currency fields) and headings that contain the specified title of the report, the current date, and the page number for each page.

As with forms, you can also save time when designing reports by combining the two methods of report creation. You can use the Report Wizards to create the report initially, and then modify the design as you want, deleting fields, moving the location of fields, changing headings, or adding other text or graphics.

DESIGNING REPORTS

 How can I quickly create a report?

The fastest way to produce a report in Access is to settle for a default tabular report or a default columnar report.

Producing either of these reports is a matter of these simple steps:

1. In the Database window, click the Reports button.

2. Click New.

3. In the New Report dialog box that opens, click either AutoReport: Columnar or AutoReport: Tabular, as desired.

4. In the list box, select the table or query on which you want to base the report.

5. Click OK.

The columnar AutoReport Wizard creates a report with the data arranged in a single column of successive fields, as shown in Figure 9-1. Each field appears on a separate line, with the corresponding label to the left.

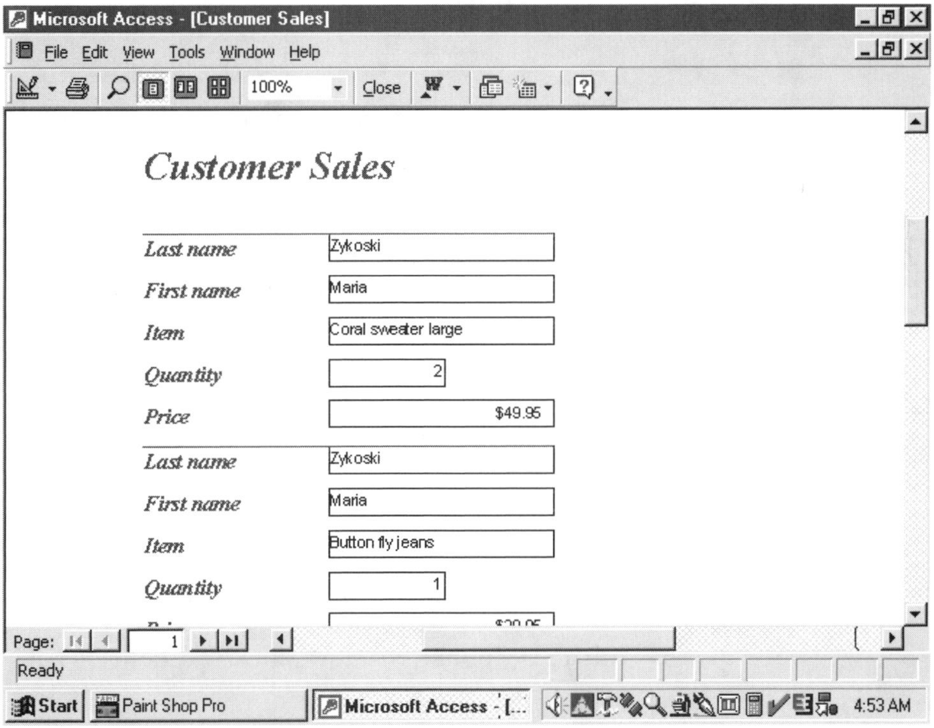

Figure 9-1 An example of a columnar report created with the AutoReport Wizard

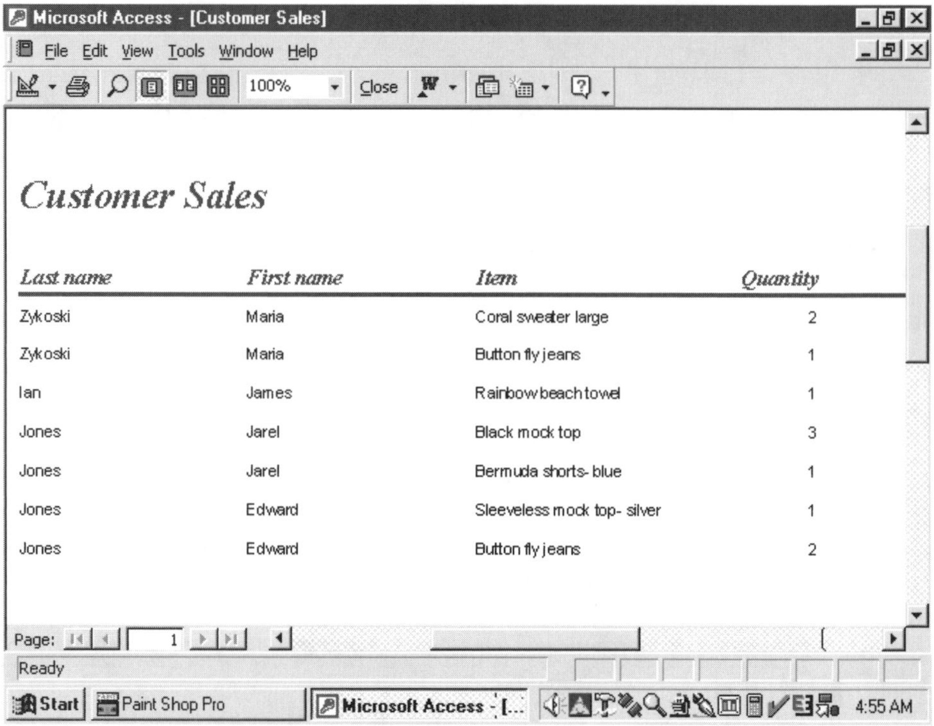

Figure 9-2 An example of a tabular report created with the AutoReport Wizard

The tabular AutoReport Wizard creates a report with the data arranged in the form of a table, as shown in Figure 9-2. Each record appears on a separate line, and the labels print once at the top of each page.

What does creating a report with the Report Wizards involve?

The Report Wizards in Access enable you to create columnar reports, tabular reports, relational reports with subreports, and reports with charts, all by using just a few steps:

1. In the Database window, click the Reports tab.

2. Click <u>N</u>ew to display the New Report dialog box, shown here:

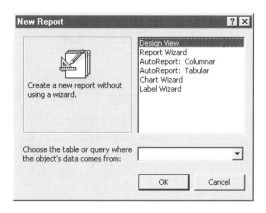

3. Choose the wizard that you want to use from the dialog box.

4. In the list box, choose the table or query on which you want to base the report. (If you want to base the report on more than one table, choose the primary table that will supply data to the main part of the report. You'll be able to choose fields from other tables in dialog boxes that appear later.)

5. Click OK.

If you selected AutoReport Tabular or AutoReport Columnar, Access creates the desired report. If you selected any other report type, follow the directions that appear in successive dialog boxes. (If you are creating a report based on more than one table, the first dialog box that appears requires you to select the desired fields from the first table, choose another table by name, and then select the desired fields from that table.)

 What does manually creating a report involve?

With the manual method of report design, you open a blank report and add fields and other design objects (labels, graphics, lines, and boxes) to the report at the locations that you specify. You also specify sections, such as page header and page footer sections or group header and group footer

sections, that identify groups of data to help divide your report. These are the steps that you need to follow to create a report manually:

1. In the Database window, click the Reports button and then click <u>N</u>ew.

2. In the New Report dialog box, choose the name of the table or query that will provide data to the report.

3. Click Design view in the list box and then click OK. Access displays a blank report in Design view, as shown in Figure 9-3. (If the field list isn't visible, choose <u>V</u>iew | Field <u>L</u>ist to display it.)

4. Add to the report any objects (fields, labels, graphics, and any other types of controls) that you want to include. You can add fields by dragging them from the field list

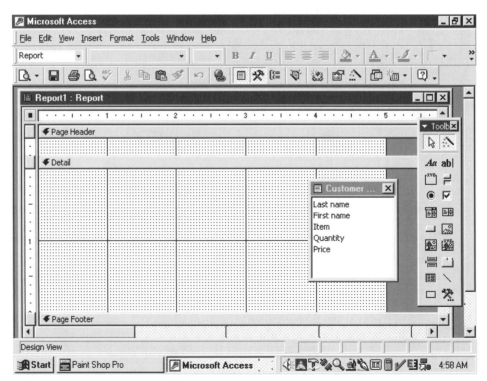

Figure 9-3   A blank report in Design view

to the report. To add other types of controls to the form, click the tool in the Toolbox and click the report at the location where you want to place the control.

5. Add any necessary sections to provide sorting and grouping in the report. Choose View | Sorting and Grouping to open the Sorting and Grouping dialog box, in which you can specify levels of sorting and enable sections in the report for groups of data.

6. Save the report by choosing File | Save.

In Figure 9-4, you can see a report design that prints the report previewed in Figure 9-5. You can see how the sections in the report design are added to the final report.

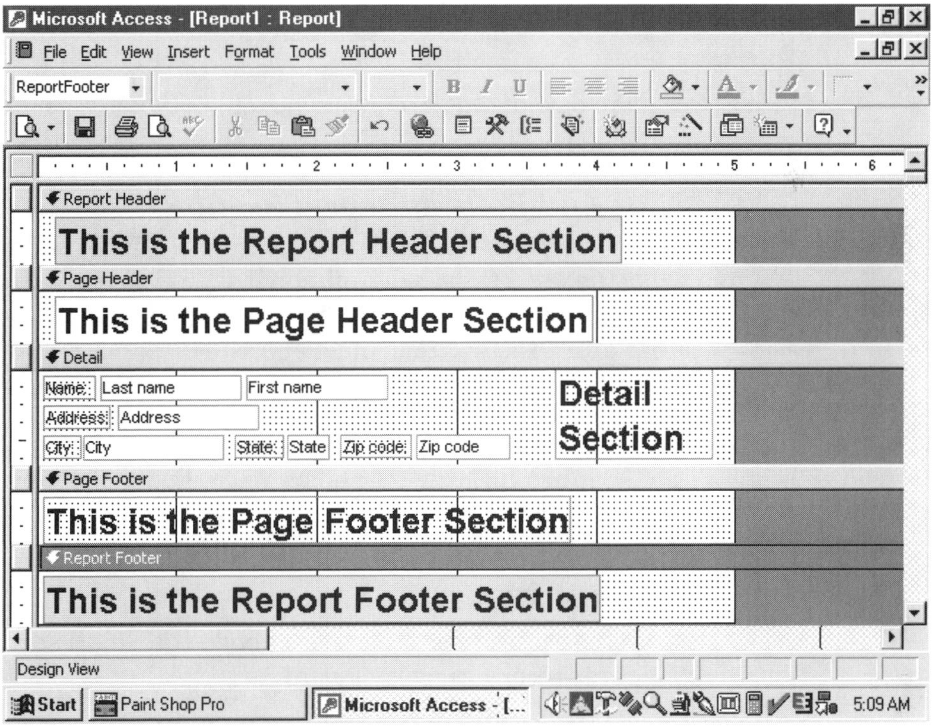

Figure 9-4 Report design showing the different sections of a report

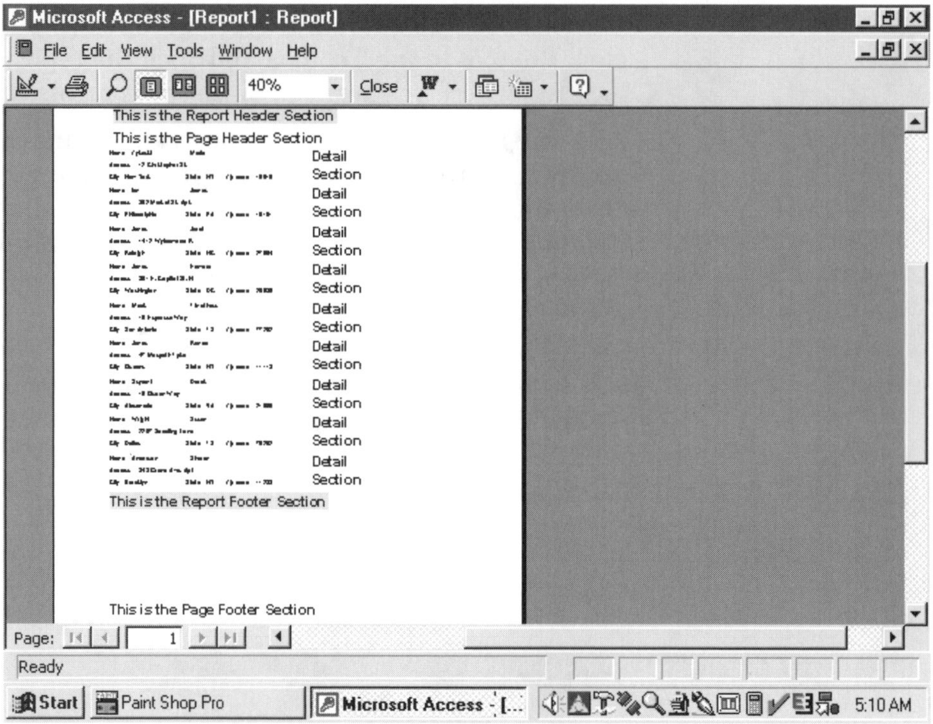

Figure 9-5 Preview of report showing how the different sections
actually print

The Nuts and Bolts of Report Sections

Because reports contain many specific sections, understanding
what these sections are and how they relate to each other is
essential in designing reports. Once you know where and in
what order the sections of a report print, creating an effective
report is much easier. A report can contain the following
sections:

- **Report header**   Appears once, at the beginning of
  the report

- **Page header**   Appears at the top of every page and
  below any report header

- **Group header**   Appears above the detail section of the
  first record in every group

- **Detail sections**   Contain the individual records in
  the report

- **Group footer**   Appears below the detail section containing the last record of every group
- **Page footer**   Appears at the bottom of every page
- **Report footer**   Appears once, at the end of the report

When Access assembles your report for display or printing, it starts by printing the report header and page header sections. Then, it prints detail sections until the page is full. Next, it prints the page footer section, a page break, and the page header section on the next page. Each page contains the page header section, as many detail sections as can fit, and the page footer section. On the last page of the report, the report footer prints before the page footer section.

When a report has group sections, the printing order is basically the same. The only difference is that Access prints the group header section before the first record of each group, and prints the group footer section after the last record of each group.

How can I add the current date or time to a report?

You can add the date or time to a report with these steps:

1. Open the report in Design view.

2. Choose Insert | Date and Time to display the Date and Time dialog box, shown here:

3. To include a date, put a check mark in the Include <u>D</u>ate check box and choose a date format.

4. To include a time, put a check mark in the Include <u>T</u>ime check box and choose a time format.

5. Click OK. The date or time field appears in the report, and you can drag it to wherever you want it located.

How can I add descriptive text to a report?

To add descriptive text to a report, click the Label tool in the Toolbox, and then click the report at the desired location and begin typing the text. As you add text, the text box expands, if necessary, to accommodate the text.

You can also create a label of a fixed size. To do so, click the Label tool in the Toolbox, and then click and drag the label's upper-left corner to the spot where you want the lower-right corner located. When you create a label in this manner, you can make the label's container deep enough for multiple rows of text. The text wraps as you reach the right border; you can also press CTRL-ENTER within the text box to force a new line. When you are done entering text, press ENTER or click outside of the text box to finish the text entry.

Figure 9-6 shows a label added to a report by using this technique; in this case, it is at the top of the page. You can resize the label at any time by clicking and dragging its border sizing handles (the eight small boxes that surround the label's border). An easy way to change the font or font size for the text box is to click the text box to select it, and then choose the font or font size in the Formatting toolbar.

How can I add graphics to a report?

You can add a graphic image to a report as a design object, using the Unbound Object Frame tool of the Toolbox. As an example, Figure 9-7 shows a report that uses a graphic pasted from a Windows Paint file. To add a graphic, follow these steps:

1. Click the Toolbox's Unbound Object Frame tool (choose <u>V</u>iew | T<u>o</u>olbox to display the Toolbox).

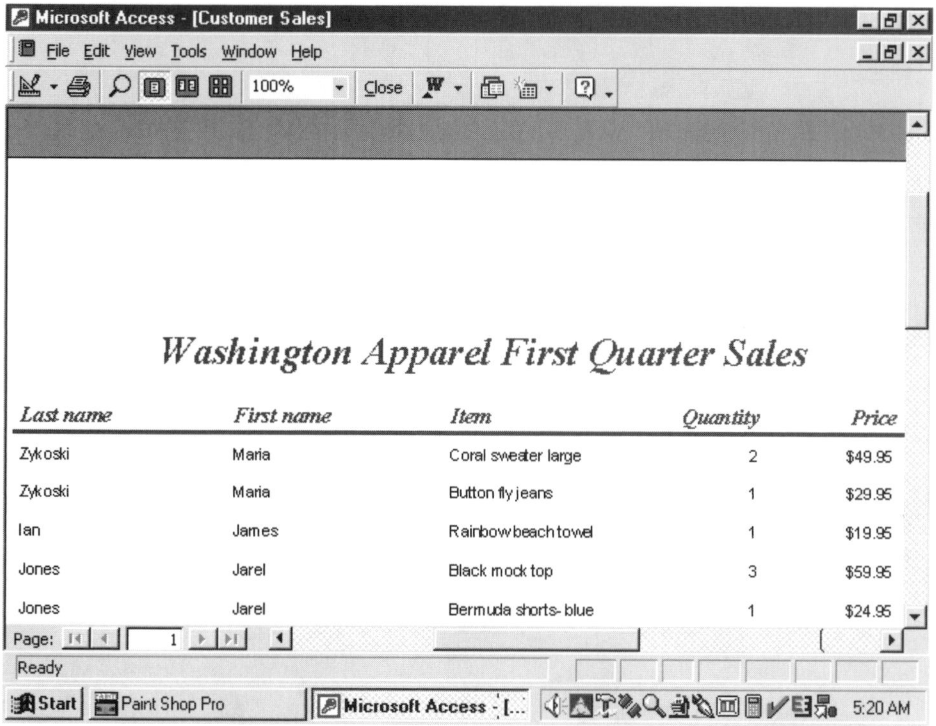

Microsoft Access - [Customer Sales]

File Edit View Tools Window Help

100%   Close

Washington Apparel First Quarter Sales

Last name	First name	Item	Quantity	Price
Zykoski	Maria	Coral sweater large	2	$49.95
Zykoski	Maria	Button fly jeans	1	$29.95
Ian	James	Rainbow beach towel	1	$19.95
Jones	Jarel	Black mock top	3	$59.95
Jones	Jarel	Bermuda shorts- blue	1	$24.95

Page: 1

Ready

Start   Paint Shop Pro   Microsoft Access - [...   5:20 AM

Figure 9-6   An example of descriptive text added to a report as a label

2. Click the location in the report where you want the graphic to start, and then drag the pointer until the frame reaches the desired size. When you release the mouse, an Insert Object dialog box appears, as shown in Figure 9-8.

3. If the image exists in a file, click the Create from File radio button and then use the Browse button to find the image file. To paste the graphic into the report, click Open in the Browse dialog box and then click OK in the Insert Object dialog box.

4. If you are creating a new graphic, click the Create New radio button. In the Object Type list box, click the file type that corresponds to the Windows program that you intend to use to create the graphic. Click OK, and you are taken into the Windows program that you

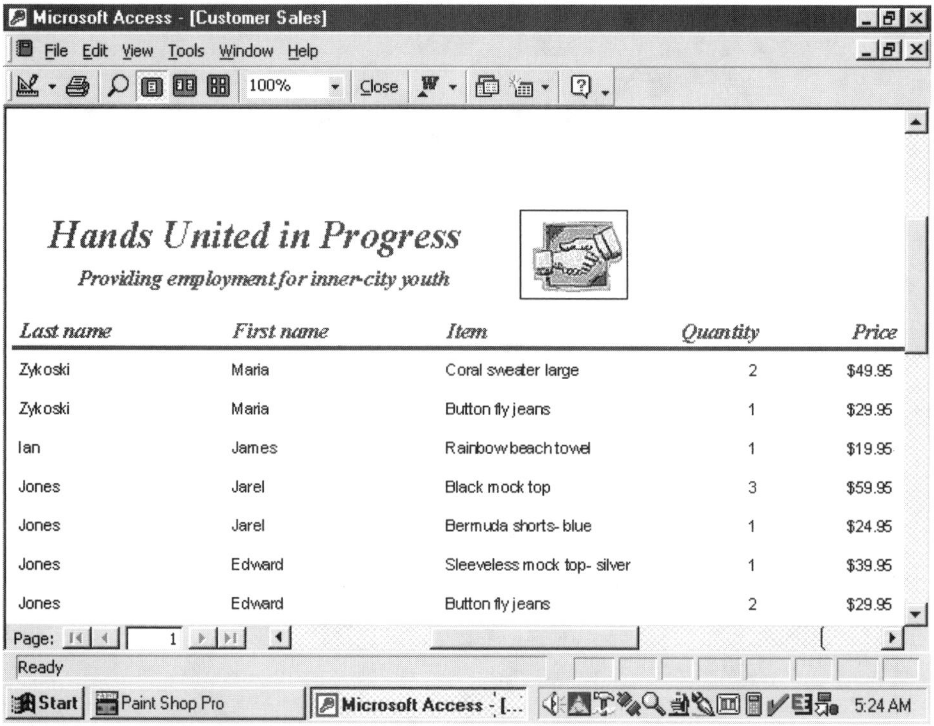

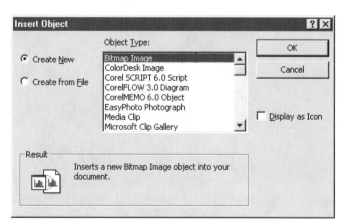

Figure 9-7   An example of graphics within a report

Figure 9-8   The Insert Object dialog box

selected, where you can create the graphic. When you are done creating the graphic, choose File | Exit to return to Access.

 Tip: *If you don't need to edit the graphic by means of OLE, you can convert it into a bitmap. By doing so, you save on resources, and the report opens faster. Right-click the frame, choose Change To, and choose Image from the next menu.*

Can I keep groups of records together on a page rather than let them split between pages?

Yes. To do so, open the Sorting and Grouping dialog box by clicking the Sorting and Grouping toolbar button or by choosing View | Sorting and Grouping. Select the field creating the group that you want to keep together, and then move to the Keep Together property in the bottom half of the window and set it to Yes.

The Keep Together property from the Sorting and Grouping window is the same as the Keep Together property in the Properties window, except that the present property gives you one more option: you can choose With First Detail for the Keep Together property when you want the group's header section on the same page as the first record in the group. This option prevents the unpleasant result of a group header at the bottom of one page and the group's records on the next page.

How can I manually add controls to a report?

The field list provides the easiest way to add controls to a report based on fields. Click the Field List toolbar button or choose View | Field List to display the field list, shown here:

▤ Customer ... ✕
Last name
First name
Item
Quantity
Price

Then, to create a control that displays data from the field, drag the field from the list to the desired location in the report.

To create a type of control other than a text box based on a field, click the control's tool in the Toolbox (if the Toolbox isn't visible, choose View | Toolbox), and then click the location in the report where you want to place the control.

 How can I modify the appearance of text in a control?

Select the control that contains the text, by clicking anywhere on the border of the control. Then, use the Font Size and Font Style list boxes on the toolbar to change the appearance of the text. You can also use the Bold and Italic toolbar buttons to bold or italicize the text, and use the Left, Center, or Right alignment toolbar buttons to align the text.

How do I get my report to print on multiple columns?

Decide how many columns you want and how much room you have on the page. After you are sure that all the columns will fit on the page, perform these steps:

1. Open the report in Design view.

2. Choose File | Page Setup and then click the Columns tab in the Page Setup dialog box, as shown here:

Page Setup	? X
Margins Page **Columns**	

Grid Settings

Number of Columns: `2`

Row Spacing: `0"`

Column Spacing: `0.25"`

Column Size

Width: `9"`   Height: `0.2708"`

☑ Same as Detail

Column Layout

○ Down, then Across

● Across, then Down

[OK] [Cancel]

3. Enter in the Number of Columns box the number of columns that you want to create.

4. Enter in the Column Spacing box the amount of space that you want between the columns.

5. Choose whether you want the items arranged first down and then across, which arranges the items similar to newspaper text columns, or first across and then down, which arranges the items similar to mailing labels.

6. Click OK.

Note: *If you add more than one column to a report, and the new column either doesn't appear or appears only partially, you need to fix the report design, because the report isn't wide enough to accommodate the added columns.*

How do I make my report use multiple columns only for the detail sections, and use a single column for the other sections?

To create a report that uses different numbers of columns for different sections, you need to use subreports. Figure 9-9 shows a report with a text box at the top occupying a single section, and a two-column middle section. Use the following steps to create such a report:

1. Create a report that shows only the detail sections that you want to appear in the final report. Turn off the Page Header/Footer and Report Header/Footer options in the View menu so that the report has no headers or footers.

2. Choose File | Page Setup and click the Columns tab in the dialog box that appears.

3. Enter in the Number of Columns box the number of columns that you want to create.

4. Enter in the Column Spacing box the amount of space that you want between the columns.

5. Choose whether you want the items arranged down and then across, which arranges the items similar to newspaper text columns, or across and then down, which arranges the items similar to mailing labels.

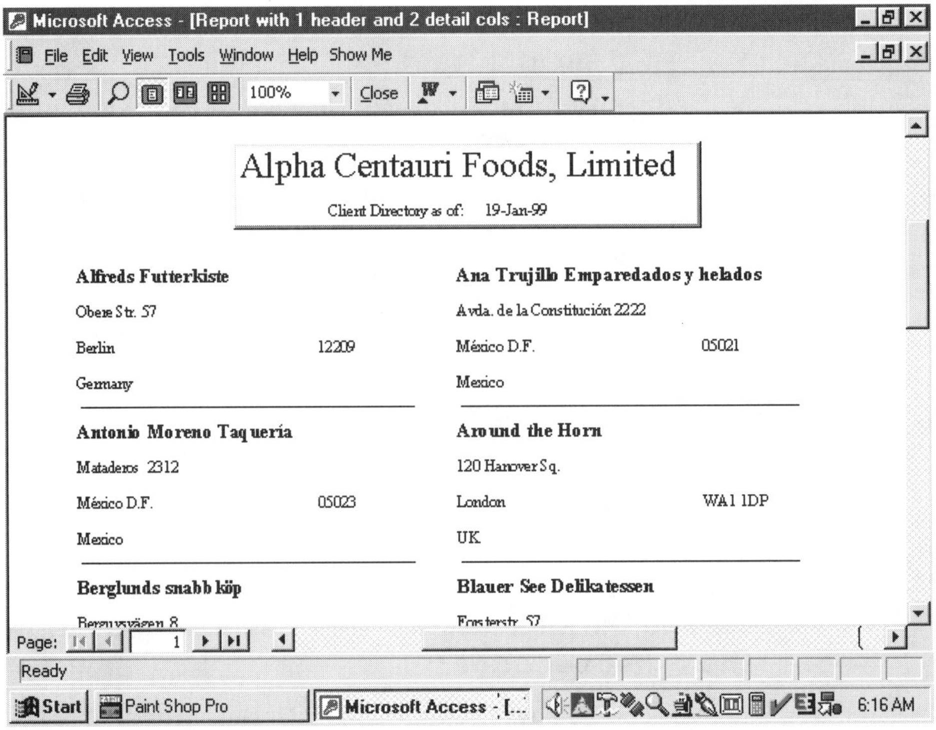

Alpha Centauri Foods, Limited

Client Directory as of: 19-Jan-99

Alfreds Futterkiste

Obere Str. 57

Berlin   12209

Germany

Ana Trujillo Emparedados y helados

Avda. de la Constitución 2222

México D.F.   05021

Mexico

Antonio Moreno Taquería

Mataderos 2312

México D.F.   05023

Mexico

Around the Horn

120 Hanover Sq.

London   WA1 1DP

UK

Berglunds snabbköp

Berguvsvägen 8

Blauer See Delikatessen

Forsterstr. 57

Page: 1

Ready

Start   Paint Shop Pro   Microsoft Access - [...   6:16 AM

Figure 9-9   A report that uses a subreport control to vary the number of columns

6. Click OK and then save the report. If you used a down-and-across orientation, with two columns, your first report might look like Figure 9-10.

7. Create another report.

8. Create the headings and footings that span the columns in the first report.

9. Switch to the Database window, but don't maximize it.

10. Drag the first report from the Database window to the detail section of the second report.

11. Resize the subreport control, if necessary, so that it's as wide as the second report.

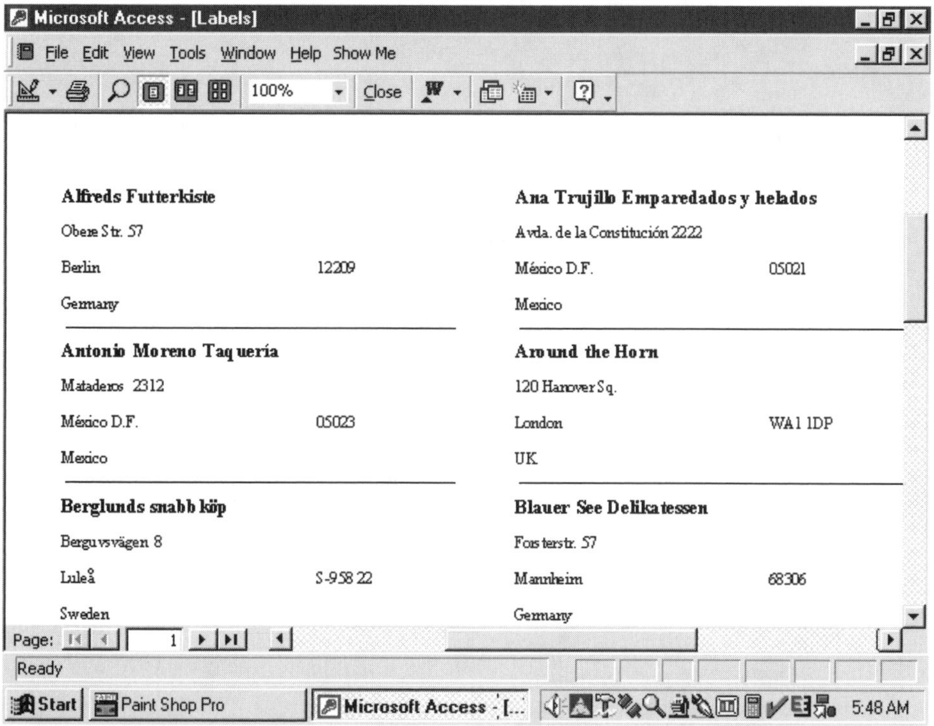

Figure 9-10   A multicolumn subreport in Print Preview

12. Right-click the subreport control and choose Properties, and then click the Format tab in the Properties window that opens. Change the Border Style property to Transparent.

Figure 9-11 shows the completed report design. Note how this report contains the page header section that you want to span across the columns. When you switch from here to Preview, your final report might look similar to the example shown earlier, in Figure 9-9.

Tip: *If you have a problem obtaining the correct data in the main report, make sure that the Record Source property for the main report is empty. You don't want a table or query associated with this report. For the subreport control, make sure that the Link Child Field and Link Master Field properties are empty.*

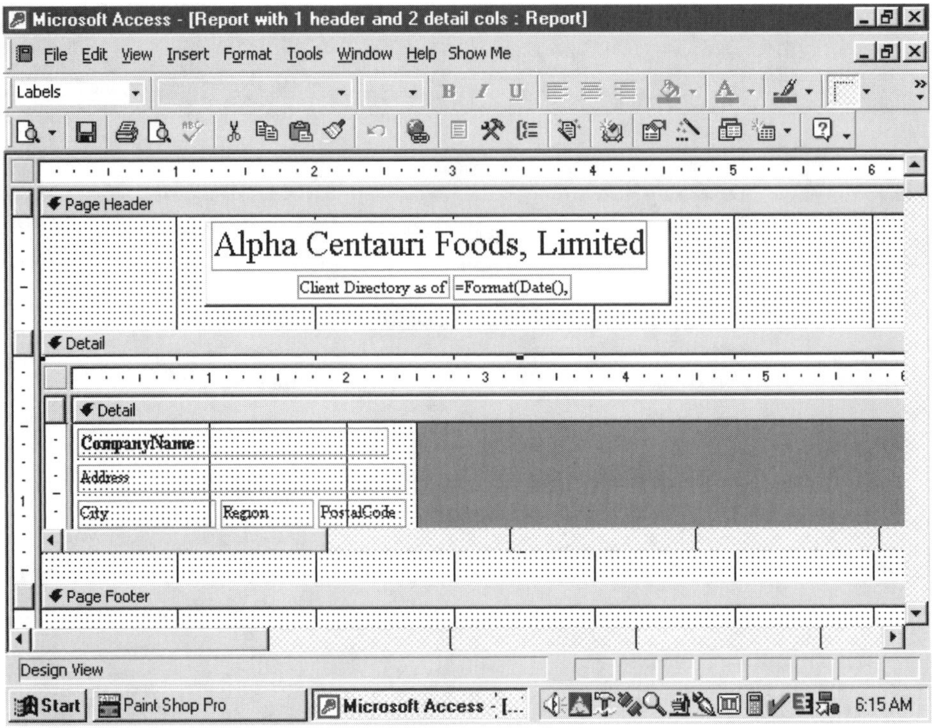

Figure 9-11 The report with varying numbers of columns in Design view

? How can I number the records in the detail section of my report?

You can number records within each group or across the entire report, as follows:

1. Add an unbound text box control to the detail section of the report.

2. Display the properties for this control by clicking the Properties toolbar button or by choosing View | Properties.

3. Click the Data tab, move to the Control Source property, and enter **=1**.

4. Move to the Running Sum property and set it to Over All.

If you have grouped the records in your report and want to start numbering records again at the beginning of each group, set the property in step 4 to Over Group, instead. The records in your report are numbered, as shown in Figure 9-12.

 ## How do I add page numbers to a report?

You can add page numbers to a report by using the Insert | Page Numbers option, as follows:

1. Open the report in Design view.

2. Choose Insert | Page Numbers. The Page Numbers dialog box appears, as shown here:

Page Numbers	? X
Format	**OK**
⦿ Page N	**Cancel**
○ Page N of M	
Position	
⦿ Top of Page [Header]	
○ Bottom of Page [Footer]	
Alignment:	
Center ▼	
☑ Show Number on First Page	

3. From the options shown in the dialog box, choose the desired format, position, and alignment for the page numbers.

4. If you want to include page numbering on the first page, turn on the Show Number on First Page check box.

5. Click OK.

How can I start page numbering with a number other than 1 on a report?

You can start numbering pages at any number that you choose. You do this by manually adding a control that uses an expression to display the page number that you select. If the report doesn't already have a page header or footer, add one

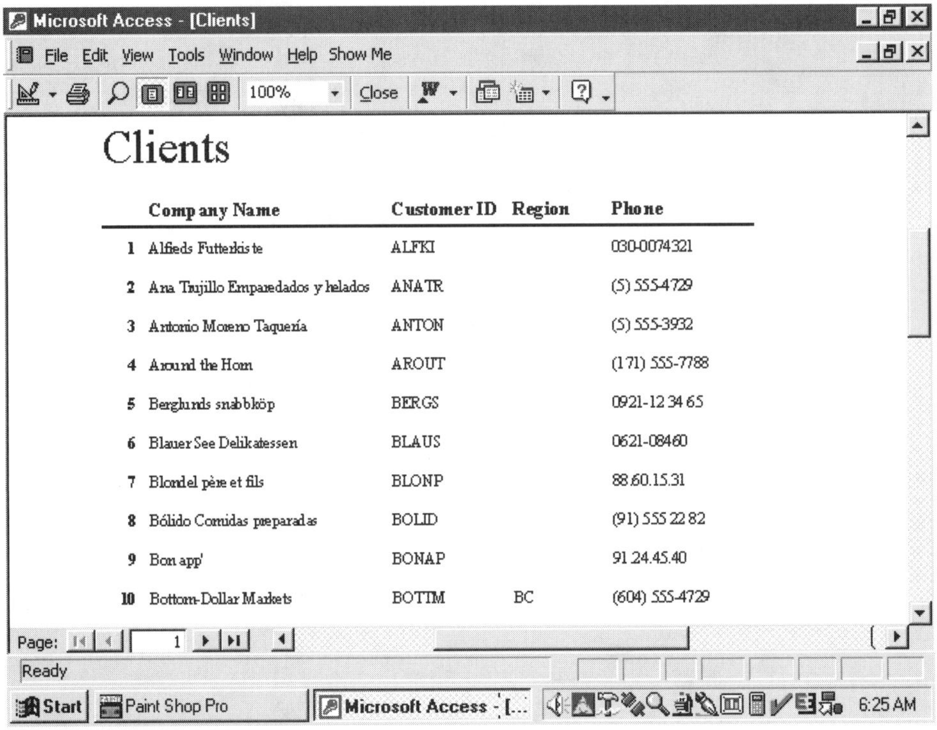

Figure 9-12 An example of a report with record numbers added

by choosing View | Page Header/Footer. Then, add a text box control to the page header or page footer at the point where you want the page numbers to appear. Click inside the control and type the following expression:

=[Page]+*first page number*–1

where *first page number*–1 has a value that is one number less than your desired starting page number. For example, if you want to begin page numbering with 40, you enter the expression **=[Page]+39** in the text box.

Can I have Access prompt me for a value and then use my response as a title in my report?

Yes, in much the same way as Access can ask for values when running a query. Using this trick, you can specify information—such as a report's title—that you want to change each time that you run the report. Use these steps to include such a parameter in a report's design:

1. Create a text box (*not* a label control) that will be used to store the parameter. Place it where you want the information to print. (Usually, you want to place the control in the page header or in the report header.)

2. Click inside the text box and type the expression **=[Enter the title:]**.

3. Format the text box as desired. (You probably want to increase the font size so that the title is displayed or printed prominently.) To produce a centered title, widen the box so that it is as wide as the report's width, and then click the Center toolbar button while the text box is selected.

When you run the report, you see an Enter Parameter Value dialog box, asking you to enter the title for the report. Type an entry and click OK, and that entry appears as the report's title.

How can I include a running sum in a report?

Often, with reports containing numeric values, you want to include a running sum. For example, you may want to see a running total of sales next to the sale amount for each sale. You can include a running sum for each record by using these steps:

1. Open the report in Design view.

2. Add a text box control to the detail section of the report.

3. Right-click the text box and choose <u>P</u>roperties to open the Properties window.

4. Click the Data tab, and in the Control Source property, enter the name of the field that you want to sum.

5. In the Running Sum property, choose either Over All, if you want the running sum to keep a running total throughout the entire report, or Over Group, if you want the running sum to reset to zero for each group.

 ### How do I summarize calculated fields on a report?

To summarize a calculated control, use the Sum() function with the control's formula in a text box control in the report's footer section. For example, suppose that you have a control named Total Billing that has a Control Source property of =[Billing Rate]*[Hours]. The control in the report footer section that totals this field has a Control Source property of =Sum ([Billing Rate]*[Hours]).

USING REPORTS

 ### Can I use a report from another database in my current database?

You can easily copy a report that exists in a different database and use the copy in your current database. The procedure may not be intuitively obvious, but the Windows Clipboard can be used to copy reports (or other Access objects) from one database to another. Open the database that contains the report that you want to copy, select it in the Database window, and then choose Edit | Copy. Close the report's database, open the database in which you want to place the copy, and then choose Edit | Paste. In the dialog box that appears, enter a name for the report.

If the report should use data from a table or query that has a different name than the original report's data source, remember to open the Properties window for the copied report, and change the Record Source property to the current table or query that will be used to supply the data.

✳ *Note:*   *You can't use this trick to copy reports from earlier versions of Access into the current database. To use reports from earlier versions of Access, you first have to convert the database created in the earlier version to the Access 2000 format, and then copy the report from the other database.*

How can use double-spacing when I print reports?

You have to configure this in the report's design, not in the printing process. To double-space a report, include one row of

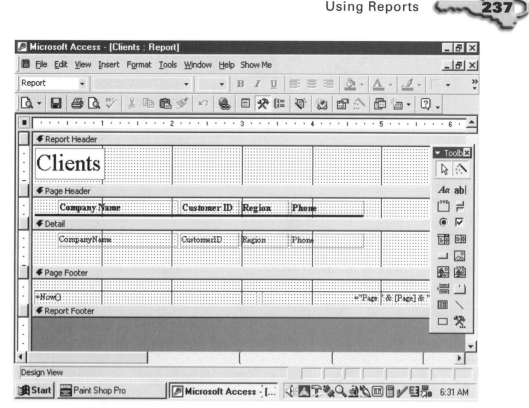

Figure 9-13 A report design with the detail section sized to provide double-spacing

controls for each record in the detail section. Then, below the row containing the controls, leave a space that is the same height as the controls. Figure 9-13 shows a double-spaced report design for a listing of company names and phone numbers.

How can I change the default print margins?

To change the default print margins for all new reports, choose Tools | Options and then click the General tab in the window that appears. Enter the new margins in the text boxes under Print Margins and click OK. Access now uses these default print margins for all new reports, as well as for printing datasheets, open queries, forms, and modules.

If you want to change the print margins for existing reports, you have to do so for each individual report. Open

each report in turn. Choose File | Page Setup, set the print margins, and click OK.

 ### Can I choose not to print a section of my report, depending on a certain condition?

Yes. You can attach a macro to the On Format property of the section that executes the CancelEvent action when a condition is met. Because the CancelEvent action prevents Access from formatting this section, the section doesn't print with the rest of the report.

For example, suppose that you don't want to print the Month of Order footer when a month has less than $1,000 in sales. To configure this, you could create a macro that has a CancelEvent action and the following entry in the Condition column:

```
DSum("[Sale Amount]","[Invoices]","[Month of Order
Date] = Reports![My Report]![Month Text Box]") < 1000
```

This condition sums the Sale Amount field in the Invoices table when the Month of Order Date field entry is the same as the contents of the Month text box control in the report's header. When this sum is less than 1000, Access executes the CancelEvent action, so that this section is neither formatted nor printed.

I have a report that prints invoices, and I need to restrict each record to print on a single page. How can I force a report to print one record per page?

With this type of report, don't use a page header or page footer section. Instead, place any page header information at the top of the detail section. Then, click the detail section to select it, and choose View | Properties to open the Properties window for the detail section. Click the Format tab and set the Force New Page property to After Section.

 I'm using a parameter query as the basis for my report. How can I display the parameters used in the actual report?

When you create a parameter query, include the parameters themselves as fields in the QBE grid. For example, if you are entering a start date and an end date as the parameters for the Date field, you should create Start and End fields in the QBE grid, as shown in Figure 9-14. (When naming the fields, be sure to use the exact same name and case in the grid as you used in the criteria for the parameter.)

Now, when you create your report, the field list for this query displays the two new fields. These fields contain the entries that you made for the parameters. You can add them to your report just as you would add any other field from the query.

For example, a text box control can join text and the parameter entries to tell readers what dates are covered by

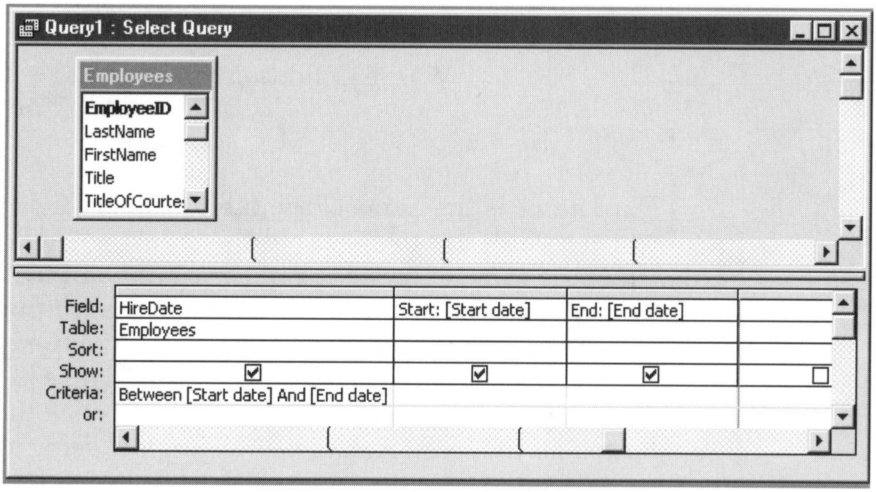

Figure 9-14 A parameter query with the parameters included as fields of the grid

the data in the report. In this case, the expression entered for the control's Control Source property is

= "For the Fiscal Quarter Beginning " & [*start date*] & " and Ending " & [*end date*]

How can I print a report based on the current record shown in a form?

You need to create a macro that opens a report by using the contents of a control on your form to select the current record shown in the form. Attach this macro to a command button on the form, so that you can open the report by clicking the button.

This macro uses the OpenReport action. Set a Where Condition argument to make the report display the same record currently displayed in the form. For example, this macro might contain the following information:

Action: OpenReport
Arguments: Report Name: *name of report*
        View: Print
        Where Condition: [*field name*] = Forms!
                   [*form name*]![*form control name*]

Field name is the name of the table or query field that selects which records are to appear in the report. *Field name* must equal the same entry as one of the controls in the form. You can automatically attach this macro to the On Click property of a command button by dragging the macro from the Database window to the form while the form is in Design view. When you change to Form view and click the command button on the form, Access prints a report using all the records with the same value as the value on the form. If you want the report to show only the record in the form, make sure that the field name contains an entry that is unique to the record. For example, you could use an AutoNumber field, which is unique for each record.

How can I change the record source used for a report?

Each report has a Record Source property that tells Access the name of the underlying table or query providing the records. You can change this property in Design view to base the report on a different table or query. Use these steps:

1. Open the report in Design view (if the report is already open, choose Edit | Select Report).

2. Choose View | Properties and click the Data tab in the dialog box.

3. Click in the Record Source property, open the list box, and choose a table or query as the report's source of data.

4. Save the report.

How can I add sorting and grouping to a report?

You can print the data in your reports in a specified order by sorting it. To highlight or summarize certain information, you also divide the data into individual groups and sort the records within the groups. To add sorting or grouping to a report, perform these steps:

1. Open the report in Design view.

2. Either choose View | Sorting and Grouping or click the Sorting and Grouping toolbar button, to display the Sorting and Grouping dialog box, shown here:

Field/Expression	Sort Order
CompanyName	Ascending

Group Properties

Group Header	No
Group Footer	No
Group On	Each Value
Group Interval	1
Keep Together	No

Select a field or type an expression to sort or group on

3. In the first row of the Field/Expression column, select a field name or type an expression. The field or expression in the first row becomes the first sorting level. The second row becomes the second sorting level, and so on. You can sort or group up to ten fields or expressions.

When you fill in the Field/Expression column, Access sets the Sort Order column to Ascending (A through Z, 0 through 99), by default. To change the sort order, select Descending from the Sort Order list. Descending order sorts from Z through A or from 99 through 0.

To add grouping to the report, use these steps:

1. Set the sort order for the data in the report, as just described.

2. In the upper half of the dialog box, click the field or expression for which you want to add grouping.

3. In the lower half of the dialog box, set the group properties to your preference. Use the Group Header property to add or remove a group header for a field or expression, and use the Group Footer property to add or remove a group footer for a field or expression. Use the Group On property to indicate how you want the values grouped.

 Do I have to sort by a field that I use to group data in a report?

In Access, you can use either a field or an expression to group records within a report. The field or expression that the group is based on also must be sorted—you can't have a grouping in a report and not sort the field or expression used for that grouping. This requirement makes sense, because if Access didn't sort the records by the same expression used for grouping, your report would have several groups for the same field or expression value.

Can I sort data based on a field that's not shown on the report?

Yes, as long as that field is included in the table or query that you based the report on. To sort based on an undisplayed field, simply open the Sorting and Grouping dialog box (choose View | Sorting and Grouping) and enter the field in that dialog box.

If the field by which you want to sort isn't included in the table or query that you are using, you need to add it. If you are using a table, you need to restructure the table to include the field that you want to sort on, and add the needed data. If you are using a query, redesign the query to include all the fields that you want to use in the report, including the field that you want to sort on. Then, open the report in Design view, open the Sorting and Grouping dialog box, and enter the field needed to perform the sort.

When working with reports that are based on queries, remember that you can choose the sort order. You can define the sort order in the query's design and leave blank the Sorting and Grouping dialog box for the report, or you can fill in the Sorting and Grouping dialog box in the report to control the sort order from within the report. If you try to use both approaches simultaneously, the settings in the Sorting and Grouping dialog box for the report take priority over the sort order established in the query.

How can I print my report to a text file?

Printing your report to a text file in Access is very easy. Right-click the report in the Database window, and choose Export. In the dialog box that appears, change the Save As Type option to Text Files, and enter a name in the File Name box. Click Save to produce the file.

WORKING WITH MAILING LABELS

Why do I get a block of blank mailing labels?

You may have blank records in the underlying table on which the report is based. If all the blank records are printing together, then they all contain the same entry in whichever field you are using for sorting. You need to check whether these blank records are the result of a data entry error or just don't have entries in those fields. If the records share a trait that causes them not to have entries in these fields, you can define a query that excludes them.

How can I create mailing labels?

Creating mailing labels is a simple matter, thanks to the Mailing Label Wizard that's built into Access. It supports a variety of mailing label formats, including the popular Avery® label types. You can use these steps to create mailing labels:

1. In the Database window, click the Reports button and then click New.

2. In the New Report dialog box that appears, select Label Wizard.

3. In the list box at the bottom of the dialog box, choose the table or query that contains the data for the labels, and then click OK.

4. In the first Label Wizard dialog box, shown here, choose the size and type of mailing label desired, and then click Next:

Label Wizard		
This wizard creates standard labels or custom labels.		
What label size would you like?		
Product number:	Dimensions:	Number across:
5095	2 1/2" x 3 3/8"	2
5096	2 3/4" x 2 3/4"	3
5097	1 1/2" x 4"	2
5160	1" x 2 5/8"	3
5161	1" x 4"	2

Unit of Measure: ⦿ English ○ Metric
Label Type: ⦿ Sheet feed ○ Continuous
Filter by manufacturer: Avery
Customize... ☐ Show custom label sizes

Cancel < Back Next > Finish

5. In the next Label Wizard dialog box that appears, choose the font and colors that you want for your label, and then click Next.

6. The next Label Wizard dialog box, shown here, asks which fields should appear in the label. Select the first field that should appear on the first line of the label, and click the > button to copy the field to the Prototype Label list box.

Label Wizard

What would you like on your mailing label?

Construct your label on the right by choosing fields from the left. You may also type text that you would like to see on every label right onto the prototype.

Available fields:

Customer ID
Last name
First name
Address
City
State

Prototype label:

Cancel   < Back   Next >   Finish

7. If you want the field that you just added to be followed by a space or other punctuation, type the space or the punctuation character.

8. To have another field appear on the same line, select that field and click the > button.

9. To place the next field on the next line, press ENTER.

10. Repeat steps 6 through 9 for each successive row of the label. As you build the label, the right half of the dialog box shows a representation of how the label will appear.

11. When you have finished adding fields, click Next. Access displays the next Mailing Label Wizard dialog box, shown next, asking how you want the labels sorted.

Label Wizard

You can sort your labels by one or more fields in your database. You might want to sort by more than one field (such as last name, then first name), or by just one field (such as postal code).

Which fields would you like to sort by?

Available fields:

Customer ID
Last name
First name
Address
City
State
Zip code
Phone

Sort by:

> >> < <<

Cancel   < Back   Next >   Finish

12. Select the first field to be used in any sort order, and then click the **>** button.

13. If desired, select the next field to be used in any sort order, and click the **>** button. Repeat this step for each additional field that you want added to the sort order. (You can remove individual fields from the sort order by selecting them in the Sort By list and clicking the **<** button; you can remove all fields from the sort order by clicking the **<<** button.)

14. Click <u>N</u>ext. Access displays the final dialog box of the Label Wizard, which asks whether you want to see the labels as they will be printed or modify the labels (open them in Design view). Make your choice and then click <u>F</u>inish.

Figure 9-15 shows an example of completed mailing labels in a preview window.

How can I print a report that contains a specific number of mailing labels for each record?

You can create a report that lets you choose how many copies of each label you want to print. To do so, create a parameter query that makes as many copies of each record as you need.

Figure 9-15   An example of completed mailing labels

Use these steps:

1. Create a table that contains a single Number field, with a field size of Long Integer. For this example, assume that you named the field **Number** and the table **Copies**.

2. Create a series of records in the Copies table. The first record should contain 1 in the Number field, and each record after it should equal the preceding entry plus 1. For example, enter 1, 2, 3, 4, 5, and so forth. You need to enter only as many records as the largest number of copies of labels you will ever print. So, if you'll never print more than ten labels per record, enter 10 records in the table, with the values from 1 to 10.

3. Create a query that contains all the information that you want to include on your mailing labels. Include the Number field from the Copies table, but don't try to establish any link between the Number field and any fields of the table that contains your label data.

If you switch to Datasheet view, you can see that Access has created a copy of each record for each entry in the Copies table. Because the two tables are unrelated, Access creates a *Cartesian product*, by matching every record in the Copies table to every record in every other table. To print all copies of one label before printing any of the next, sort on a field in the address, such as a Last Name field. Otherwise, you'll print each label once, and then start again.

4. For the Number field, enter a parameter criterion that equals the number of labels you want to print, such as **<=[How many copies?]**. "How many copies?" is the message that Access displays each time this query is run, requesting the entry for this criterion.

5. Create your mailing label report by using the query that you just created, or change the Record Source property for an existing mailing label report to use the new query.

Whenever you attempt to print your report, Access first runs the query. Because it is a parameter query, you get the prompt that lets you choose how many labels to create.

Note: *If you use this method to print multiple labels, you need to enter as many records in the Copies table as the number of copies that you expect you'll ever need. If you add only 10 records but want to print 20 copies of labels, you have a problem, because you get no more copies than the number of labels indicated by the highest value in the Copies table.*

How do I change the field that sorts my mailing labels?

The same sorting and grouping features that change the order of records in a report also set the order of mailing labels when that is what the report prints. With the report in Design view, choose View | Sorting and Grouping or click the Sorting and Grouping toolbar button, to display the Sorting and Grouping dialog box. Enter in the Field/Expression column of the first line the name of the field that you want to sort by. In the Sort Order column of the same line, select the kind of sort that you want (ascending or descending). Include in the following lines any other fields that you want to sort by.

TROUBLESHOOTING

My report has too much blank space. What can I do?

When a report contains too much blank space, you can reduce excess white space by reducing the following:

- The space between sections of the report.
- The space between controls.
- The height of the controls, to the minimum necessary to display the data. Then move the controls up against the detail section's top edge and pull the bottom edge as close as reasonably possible to the controls.
- The height of any header and footer sections in the report, as much as possible.

If every other page of the report is blank, see the question later in this section, "Why is every other page of my report blank?"

Why are some of my report's calculated fields empty?

If some calculated fields on your report are empty and others are not, the calculations with empty results are based on fields in which the field entry equals Null. (In Access, Null means the absence of data.) Calculated fields that use math operators (+, -, *, /, \, ^, or Mod) return Null when part of the expression equals Null. To correct this, convert the Nulls to zero by using the NZ function, which converts any Null values to zeros so that they won't affect the calculation. For example, if a control displays the results of =[Price] + [Tax], change the Control Source property to contain the expression =NZ([Price]) + NZ([Tax]).

Why aren't the column headings in my subreport printing?

Access doesn't print page headers and footers that are in subreports. If you include the labels for your column headings in the page header of the subreport, they won't appear when you print the report. You have two ways around this:

- In cases where the subreport always fits on a single page, put the labels for the columns in the report header of
the subreport.

- In cases where the subreport may span several pages, put the labels for the columns in the group header of the subreport, and set the Repeat Section property of the group header to Yes.

Why is every other page of my report blank?

If every other page of the report is completely blank, the report is too wide for the width of your printed page, minus the page margins. (When you calculate how wide your report sections can be, remember to subtract the combined width of the left and right margins from the width of the paper.) To reduce the report's width, drag the right edge of the report inward. You can also reduce the size of the report's margins: choose File | Page Setup, click the Margins tab, and reduce the amount shown in the Left and Right boxes.

I want to show a total at the bottom of each page in my report, but I keep seeing the message "#Error" instead. What's wrong?

Access doesn't allow the Sum() function in a page footer. To place a total in a page footer, create a control in another section of your report that performs the calculation. Set the Visible property for the control to No to hide it. You may also need to change its Running Sum property from No to either Over All or Over Group, depending on when you want the calculation reset. Then create another unbound text box in the page footer. Enter the name of the control containing the calculation as the text box's Control Source property setting.

For example, suppose that you want to total the sales in the page footer section. Part of your report design might look like the one in Figure 9-16. This detail section includes a calculated control that totals the sales; it has its Visible property set to No and its Running Sum property set to Over All. This control is named Total Calc. The control containing =[Total Calc] in the page footer section returns the value of the Total Calc control for the last record printed on the page, which also is the total up to that point in the report.

Tip: *You can get similar results by adding a macro to the page footer section's On Format property. The Item argument equals the control in the page footer section, and the Expression argument equals the control in the other section.*

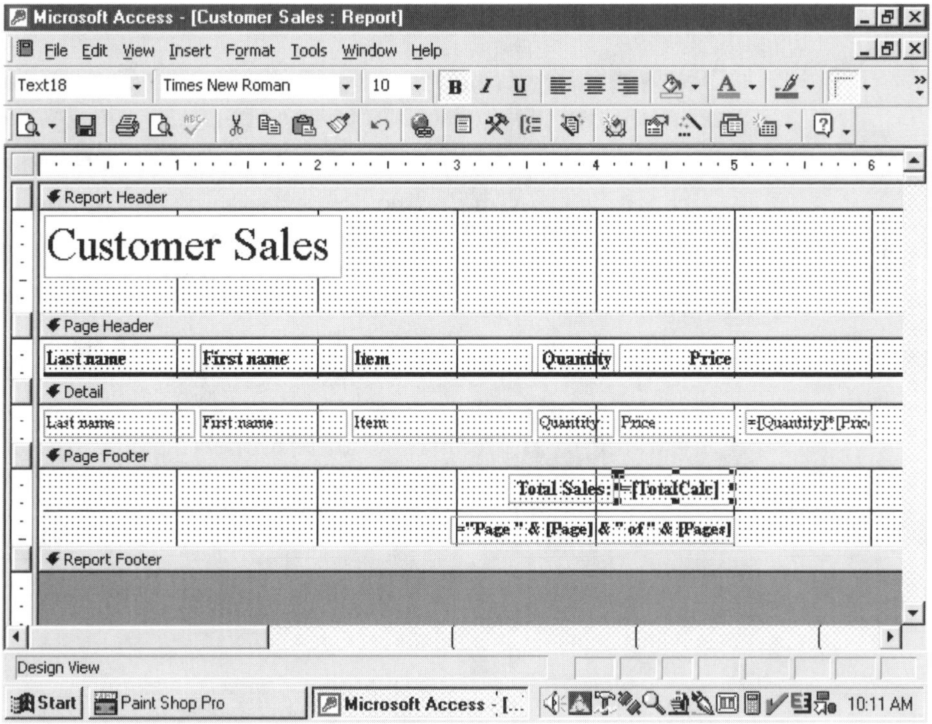

Figure 9-16   An example of a control used to provide a total in a page footer

Why does the #Error or #Name appear in a control within the body of my report?

This problem can be due to a number of causes. Check for any of these possibilities:

- Improper spelling of field names in the Control Source property for the control.

- If field names used as parts of expressions contain spaces, make sure that brackets surround the field names. For example, [*last name*] is a valid reference to a field name within an expression.

- If you are using a built-in function as part of an expression, make sure that the syntax is correct and that the arguments are in the proper order.

- Make sure that any field named in the Control Source property for the control hasn't been renamed or removed in the underlying table or query.

When I run my report, it prompts me for unexpected parameters. Why is this happening?

This problem occurs when you misspell a field name in a control's Control Source property or in the Sorting and Grouping dialog box. Access can't find a field by that name in the underlying table or query, so it thinks that you are referring to a variable that doesn't currently exist in memory. Check to make sure that all field names are spelled correctly in the controls' Control Source properties and in the Sorting and Grouping dialog box. Also, if field names manually entered in any Control Source properties contain spaces, make sure that brackets surround the field names.

Chapter 10

Controls Used with Forms and Reports

Answer Topics!

Controls Used with Forms and Reports @ a Glance

Controls are the basic elements behind the appearance of your forms and reports. They shape the appearance of your data and add other visual elements. With the use of various properties, they can control how your data is displayed or perform certain types of validation. The controls that you use in forms and reports are basically the same. Throughout this chapter, you'll find answers to questions about either type of design. The questions in this chapter fall into the following areas:

Form and Report Design answers questions about the general use of controls in both forms and reports.

Placing Controls answers questions about the sizing, alignment, and placement of controls in forms and reports.

Using Controls in Forms and Reports answers questions about how your controls display and print data when you use your forms and reports.

Calculations and Controls helps you solve problems with calculated controls used in forms and reports.

Troubleshooting helps you handle unexpected error messages and other general problems that arise with controls.

The Nuts and Bolts of Forms and Reports

Controls are the building blocks of your forms and reports, and Access offers many types of controls for your use. Some controls work better in forms than in reports. Others are chosen because they work best at displaying a specific type of data. Here are the types of controls that you can add to forms and reports, along with some ideas about when to use them:

- **Label** Adds text that doesn't change from record to record. You can use labels to add fixed information, such as a company or department name, or to identify data.

- **Text box** Accepts or displays text that changes from record to record. This type of control is commonly used to display and enter data. The control is often used to display the contents of a single field, just as you would see it in a table's datasheet. Text boxes are also commonly used to store or display expressions.

- **Option group** Contains a group of toggle buttons, option buttons, or check boxes.

- **Toggle button** Shows a button that can look pushed in or released. A toggle button, like a check box, often represents a Yes/No field. Toggle buttons may also be used, like option buttons, to show a field that has a limited number of possible values.

- **Option button** Shows an open circle that has a black dot in the center when selected. Option buttons usually show which of a limited set of possible values a field has, like the station selector buttons on a car radio, so they are also known as *radio buttons*. Like a toggle button or a check box, an option button can also be used for a Yes/No-type field.

Check box   Shows a square box that contains a check mark when selected. Check boxes or toggle buttons frequently display the setting of a Yes/No-type field. However, you can also use them in place of option buttons to show the selected value for a field.

Combo box   Shows a drop-down list box, like the ones in Windows dialog boxes. Forms frequently use them to give you a choice of typing an entry or selecting one from a list. They also use less space than a list box. Reports seldom use this type of control.

List box   Shows a list with the current selection highlighted. List boxes work well in forms when a user can only select from a predefined set of choices.

Command button   Adds a button that does something when clicked, such as executing a macro or module. Unlike toggle buttons, command buttons don't stay pressed.

Image   Adds a control used to display a picture. The resulting picture is in display-only format; that is, you can't double-click it to edit the picture in an OLE application. If you want to be able to edit the picture, use an unbound object frame instead.

Unbound object frame   Adds a control that contains an OLE object that isn't linked to any underlying field of an Access table. Use this control when you paste data from another application into your form or report design as a decorative object.

Bound object frame   Adds a placeholder that displays the contents of OLE Object fields. Use this control to store embedded and linked OLE data.

Page break   Divides the form or report into pages. Divide a form into multiple pages when you have lots of data to show or enter, and breaking the form into smaller chunks makes it easier to understand. Divide reports into pages when you have more data than can fit on one page and want to control where the page break occurs. Reports have several page break options, so you can place page breaks by section properties instead of with controls that are in the detail band.

Tab control   Adds a tabbed form control to the form. Clicking one of the tabs causes its own set of controls to be displayed so that the user can enter a particular set of data fields.

● **Subform** or **subreport** Adds a control representing another form or report. This subform or subreport appears in the form or report you are designing. Use subforms and subreports to show records from a related table that are associated to the record currently displayed in the main form or report.

● **Line** Adds a line. Use lines to divide or decorate the form or report.

● **Rectangle** Adds a box. Add boxes to your design to visually group controls or other elements of a form or report.

FORM AND REPORT DESIGN

 Access underlines the next letter when I enter an ampersand (&) in a label. How do I display an ampersand?

The ampersand is a special character in Access. It identifies the letter that you want underlined. Underlining a letter lets you move to the attached portion of a compound control by pressing ALT and the letter; therefore, if you enter an ampersand beside the letter *N* in Name in a label attached to a text box, pressing ALT-N would move you to that text box when in Form view. To tell Access that you want to use the ampersand as an ampersand and not as an underlined letter, type two ampersands next to each other. For example, type **Renee &&Benjie's Cycle Shop** to display "Renee & Benjie's Cycle Shop."

 How can I display information from another table in my form or on a report?

You can do this by using the DLookup function, which returns the value of a field from any table. You can add this function as a calculated field to show a value from another table. DLookup uses three arguments: an expression, a domain, and criteria. The expression argument is the name of the field that contains the data that you want to display.

The domain argument is the name of a table or query that is the source of the data. The criteria argument tells Access which matching record or records should be selected by the function. In most cases, you will want to compare a value in the table or query to a control on your form or report.

As an example, suppose that you have a form for a Payroll table that you use to enter weekly payroll information. When you use the form, you enter the employee's ID number. To make sure that you enter the correct number, this form has a calculated control that displays the employee's name from the Employees table. The entry that you would use for the Control Source property is the following:

```
=DLookup("[Employees]![First name] & ' ' &
[Employees]![Last name]","[Employees]",
"[Employees]![Employee ID] =
Forms![Payroll]![Employee ID]")
```

This formula uses DLookup to return the first name and the last name from the Employees table and separates them with a space. You can see this in both the form and its design, shown in Figure 10-1.

The other domain functions, such as Dcount, Dlast, Dfirst, and Dsum, work the same way. They use the same arguments but perform different tasks with the selected data.

 Note: *A limitation to using the DLookup function is that you can show data from only one field at a time. If you want to show data from several related fields, you need to use a subform or subreport control instead.*

 ## How can I make a text box change colors depending on the value of its data?

You can do this by using Visual Basic for Applications (VBA) code to modify the value of the Fore Color property for the control. In the On Enter property for the control, add an event procedure that contains code that sets the Fore Color property to the desired value. For example, the following code changes the foreground colors of a Salary field depending on

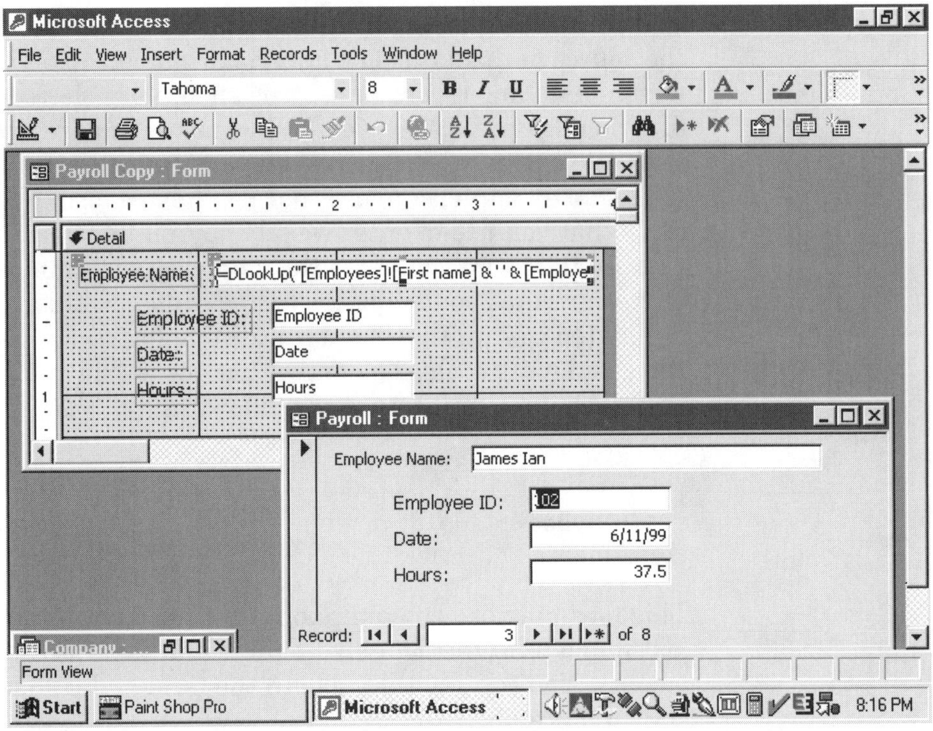

Figure 10-1 A form and the form's design that use the DLookup function

whether or not the amount stored in the field is greater than $6.00. (The Me! operator tells Access that the value assigned refers to the object in whatever form is currently open.)

```
Private Sub Salary_Enter()
    If Salary > 6 Then
        Me!Salary.ForeColor = 255
    Else
        Me!Salary.ForeColor = 8421440
    End If
End Sub
```

If you want to change the color of the background, use the term BackColor in place of the term ForeColor in your VBA code.

How can I attach a bitmap picture to my command button?

To display the contents of a bitmap graphic on a command button, switch to the Design view of the form and use the following steps.

1. Right-click the command button and choose Properties from the shortcut menu.

2. Click the Format tab in the Properties window and click the Picture property.

3. Click the Build button (...) to the right of the property to display the Picture Builder dialog box, shown here:

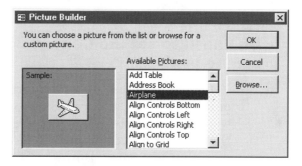

4. Choose one of the available pictures in the list box, or, to use your own bitmap file, click Browse and find the file in the dialog box that opens.

5. Click OK.

Figure 10-2 shows an example of a form that uses bitmaps on various command buttons.

Tip: *If you plan to use your own bitmap file as an image for a button, you should size and position the image in the file, as desired, before you add it to the button. You can't perform any scaling of an image after it is added to a button as a bitmap, so if the image is too large to fit on the button, you must change the size of the image (or resize the button).*

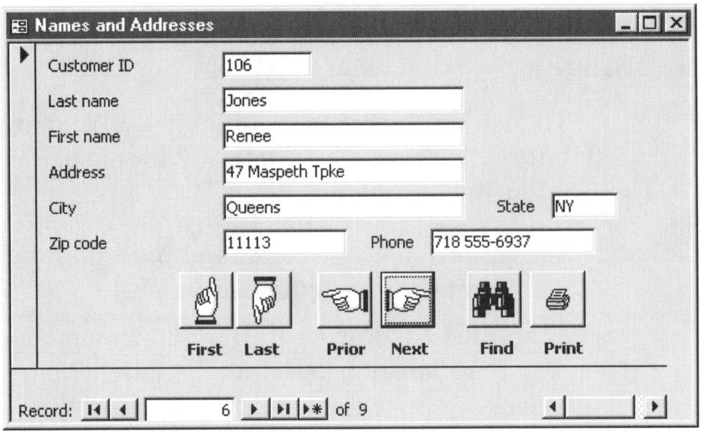

Figure 10-2   A form containing buttons with bitmaps

Do I need to set the Control Source property for a combo box?

You need to set the Control Source property for a combo box only when you use the combo box to enter data rather than to search for records. When you use a combo box for data entry, the Control Source property tells Access where to store the data that you enter. However, if you use the combo box to find records, instead, then you don't need to set the Control Source property—there is no new data to store.

How can I prevent Access from running a Control Wizard every time that I create a button, combo box, or list box?

You can turn off the Control Wizards. Display the Toolbox while in Design view for the form or report, and then click the Control Wizards button in the Toolbox, shown here, so that it no longer appears pushed in:

With the Control Wizards turned off, when you create a command button, option group, combo box, or list box, you simply add an empty control to the form or report design. You must then enter the desired settings in the Property window for the new control.

How do I format numbers as currency in my form or report?

You can change the Format property for the control that displays the data, to display it as a currency value. Use these steps to do so:

1. Open the form or report in Design view, and right-click the control used to display the currency amounts.

2. Choose Properties and click the Format tab.

3. Click the Format property and choose Currency from the list box.

Tip: *When you change the Format property, you may also want to change the Decimal Places property, which sets how many digits appear after the decimal point.*

I created a form with shadowed text. When I edit the text, however, its shadow doesn't change. How do I edit the shadow text?

Many of the Form and Report Wizards create labels that appear as shadowed text. This text is actually a combination of two labels. The second label is darker and is placed slightly to the lower-right of the first label, to create the "shadow" effect. If you change the text of the top label, the text of the shadow does not change. To change the text for both controls easily, click and drag around both controls so that they're both selected, and then right-click either control and choose Properties from the shortcut menu. Click the Format tab in the Properties window and enter your caption under the Caption property. This changes the text for both controls.

 My text displays extra characters that I can't find in Design view. How do I remove the extra characters?

Usually, these extra characters are a result of a control that you can't see because it's behind a text box or other object. Check to see if anything, such as a label, lies behind the text box when in Design view. Click the text box and select Format | Send to Back. If a control was behind the text box, you can now see it. At this point, you can select the control that causes the problem and delete it.

I can hide a control in a subform by setting its Visible property to No, but when the subform appears in Datasheet view, the field is still visible. How can I hide a control's field in Datasheet view?

The Visible property of a control affects only the control itself, which is viewed through the form when in Form view. To hide the column when in Datasheet view, you have to save the datasheet with the column hidden. Open the subform, switch to Datasheet view, right-click the header of the column that you want to hide, and choose Hide Columns from the menu. When you close the subform and later save the form's design, you also save the Column Hidden property of the form's datasheet.

Can I have page breaks in my report that occur only when certain conditions are met?

Yes, you can have conditional page breaks in a report, because a page break is a control with a Visible property, like all controls. But the Visible property works differently with page breaks, because you don't "see" them when a report is printing. If a page break control's Visible property is True (which is the default), the page break occurs. If a page break's Visible property is False, the page break doesn't occur. So, the secret to creating a conditional page break is to change the value of the Visible property for the page break as the

report prints. You can do this with Visual Basic for Applications (VBA) code or with a macro.

As an example, assume that in a report of sales from many countries, you want to force a page break for one particular country. You can add a page break control and use the Property window for the control to give the control a specific name. You can then refer to that control in VBA code that you attach to the On Format property of the report's group band for the Country field. Here's an example of code attached to the On Format property for such a report:

```
Private Sub GroupFooter0_Format(Cancel As Integer, _
                           FormatCount As Integer)
If Country = "USA" Then
    CountryBreak.Visible = True
Else
    CountryBreak.Visible = False
End If
End Sub
```

In this case, the page break control has been named CountryBreak in its Properties window and has been added to the group band for the Country field. The code placed in the On Format property for the Country footer band of the report causes the page break's Visible property to be set to False, unless the Country field for the group currently printing contains the characters "USA," in which case the property is set to Visible and a page break occurs during printing.

 ## How can I make small changes to the position or size of a control on a form?

In Design view, select the control that you want to adjust. To change the size of the field, press SHIFT and use the arrow keys to adjust the size. To move the control, press CTRL and use the arrow keys. Note that you can also type measurements for the Top and Left properties, to move the control to that location. Typing values for the Height and Width properties sets the size of the control.

 Can I change the properties of a group of controls without having to select each one individually?

Yes, you can change properties for controls as a group, by using these steps:

1. Open the form or report in Design view.

2. Select the first control whose properties you want to change.

3. Hold down the SHIFT key and select each additional control that you want to change. (Alternatively, you can click and drag around a group of controls to select them all, if they are adjacent to each other.)

4. Right-click any of the selected controls and choose Properties from the shortcut menu. Notice that the Properties window that opens is titled Multiple Selection.

5. Make the desired changes to the properties. When you close the Properties window, the changes are applied to each of the selected controls.

 Is there an easy way to draw rectangular borders around controls?

When you want to surround a text box or a label, there is an easier way to do this than using the rectangle tool. Right-click the label or control, choose Properties from the shortcut menu, and then click the Format tab. Set the Border Style property to Solid rather than the default of Transparent, and change the Border Color and Border Width properties to your preference.

How do I remove lines, created by a Report Wizard, that I can't find in the report's design?

The Report Wizards routinely add lines as borders at the bottom of report sections, and the placement of these lines often makes them hard to see. The easiest way to remove these lines is to drag the bottom of the section down, so that the lines become clearly visible. Select the line and press DEL to delete it; then drag the bottom of the section back to its previous size.

If you can't locate the line at the bottom of the section, click any text box in the section and press TAB repeatedly to move through all the controls until you get to the line that you couldn't find. Press DEL.

Why won't my report become narrower when I drag the right margin to the left?

The report has a control somewhere on its right side that is preventing you from moving the margin. Access will not let you relocate controls by dragging the margin. You must move the control first and then drag the margin.

Tip: *If a report doesn't appear to have any controls in the way and you still can't drag the right margin to the left, make sure that no lines extend to the right margin. You must also shorten any lines that are adjacent to the right margin, before you can narrow the margin.*

What's the difference between the Row Source and Control Source properties for a combo box?

The Row Source property specifies where the combo box gets the options to display in its drop-down list. For example, in a form for entering customer addresses, the State combo box might get its list from the State Code field of a table of valid states.

The Control Source property specifies where the data selected or entered in the combo box is stored. In the preceding example, the selection in the combo box might be stored in the State field of the Customer table. The field entered for the Control Source property also sets the entry that appears in the combo box when you look at an existing record (that's why it's called a "source").

I have a paper form that is used as a basis for entering records. Can I somehow scan the existing form and use the scanned image as a background for a form in Access?

Yes, you can scan a paper form and use the scanned image as a background for an Access form. (This provides a form with a more familiar environment to your data-entry operators, assuming that they are accustomed to looking at the paper version of the form.) You can use the following steps to do this:

1. Scan a blank form and save the resulting graphic image in Windows Bitmap (BMP) format.
2. Open a new blank form in Design view.
3. Choose Edit | Select Form, and then choose View | Properties.
4. Click the Format tab of the Properties window that opens.
5. Click the Picture property and enter the name (including the path) for the bitmap file.
6. Set the Picture Size Mode property to Stretch.
7. Set the Picture Alignment property to Form Center.
8. Set the Picture Tiling property to No.
9. Close the Properties window to display the form with the bitmap as a background.
10. Add the desired controls and labels to the form, using the usual design techniques for designing forms in Access.

Tip: *To size text boxes so that they match the size of the boxes drawn on the form that you scanned, you may want to disable the Snap to Grid setting that is normally turned on during form design. Choose Format | Snap to Grid.*

How do I refer to my controls in my subforms and subreports?

The syntax for a control on a subform is

Forms![*form name*]![*subform name*].Form![*control name*]

The syntax for a control on a subreport is

Reports![*report name*]![*subreport name*].Report![*control name*]

For example, suppose that you want to identify the Last Name control that appears on the Name Entry subform. The main form is Names and Addresses. The correct syntax is

```
Forms![Names and Addresses]![Name Entry].Form![Last Name]
```

If Names and Addresses were a report and Name Entry were a subreport on the Names and Addresses report, you could enter

```
Reports![Names and Addresses]![Name Entry].Report![Last Name]
```

 Tip: *Expression Builder helps you avoid misspellings in control, form, and report names when entering needed syntax.*

 ## What syntax do I use to refer to controls on my sub-subforms?

You can extend the same syntax that you use to refer to a control to refer to a control in a subform that is in another subform. The syntax is

Forms![*form name*]![*subform name*].Form![*sub-subform name*].Form![*control name*]

For example, suppose that you have a form named Divisions. This form has a subform named Departments. In the Departments subform is a subform named Employees. The Employees subform has a control named Employee Name. To identify the Employee Name control, you can use the following syntax:

```
Forms![Divisions]![Departments].Form![Employees].Form!
[Employee Name]
```

 Tip: *If one of the levels of the reference to the control is for a subreport, change Form! in front of the report name to* **Report!**. *If the main object is a report rather than a form, replace Forms! with* **Reports!**.

When I tab through my form, the order isn't from top to bottom. How can I fix the tab order?

This problem commonly occurs when you add a new field to a form, because Access tabs through the fields in the order that you added them to the form. When you add a new field, by default, it becomes last in the tab order, regardless of where you put it. You can change the form's tab order by using these steps:

1. Open the form in Design view.
2. Choose View | Tab Order. The Tab Order dialog box opens, showing the current order, as shown here:

3. Drag the fields in the Custom Order list box into the order in which you want to tab through them.
4. Click OK to save the changes.

Tip: You can quickly reorganize the tab order for controls from top to bottom by clicking the Auto Order button in the Tab Order dialog box.

How can I choose a check box or a radio button to display the contents of a Yes/No field in a form?

To accomplish this, you click the tool in the Toolbox before you add the field from the Field List, as follows:

1. In Design view, choose <u>V</u>iew | T<u>o</u>olbox to display the Toolbox, if necessary.

2. Click the radio button or the check box in the Toolbox.

3. Drag the Yes/No field from the Field List to the form.

The control that is created is the type that you selected in the Toolbox.

PLACING CONTROLS

Can I add controls to a form without creating associated labels each time?

You can disable the automatic addition of labels to new controls by setting the Auto Label property to No for the desired type of control, as follows:

1. Open a form or report in Design view.

2. Choose <u>V</u>iew | <u>P</u>roperties to open the Properties window.

3. In the Toolbox, click the tool for which you want to disable the addition of labels. When you do this, notice that the title of the Properties window changes to Default *xxx*, where *xxx* is the type of control that you selected.

4. Click the Format tab and set the Auto Label property to No.

Now, whenever you add new controls of the type that you selected in the Toolbox, Access will not automatically add new labels attached to the controls.

Tip: *You can always delete the label portion of a compound control. Select the label portion of the control and press DEL. The rest of the compound control remains on the form or report design.*

In forms created with the wizards, the control and the attached label move together. When I add a text box control and later create a label for it, they move separately. How can I attach the label to the control?

Text box controls added by the wizards are *compound controls*. You can create a compound control by adding a label to the text box control. To do this, select the label control and press CTRL-DEL (or choose Edit | Cut) to cut the control to the Windows Clipboard. Select the text box control to which you want to attach the label, and press SHIFT-INS (or choose Edit | Paste). Both controls in a compound control move together, unless you drag either control separately by dragging the largest handle at the upper-left corner of the control.

How can I move controls as a group?

To move controls as a group in a form or report design, you must first select them all, which you can do in either of two ways:

- Hold down the SHIFT key while clicking each control that you want to move (this method is recommended if the controls are not adjacent to each other).

- If the controls that you want to move are adjacent to each other, click to the upper-left side of the first control and drag to the lower-right side of the last control. When you release the mouse button, the controls appear selected as a group.

After you select the controls, you can move, size, or align them as a group.

You can also define a collection of controls as a group, so that when you move one control, the others always move along with the selected control. To do this, first select the controls that you want to define as a group, using any of the methods previously described. Then, choose Format | Group. (To cancel the definition of a group, select any control within the group and choose Format | Ungroup.)

How can I move just the label for my text box? They keep moving together.

The trick to moving a label separately from the text box lies in how you select the label. When you select the label, it is surrounded by eight small squares, called *handles*. The handle in the upper-left corner is larger than the others. When you point to the larger handle, the pointer turns into a hand pointing with its index finger, like the one shown here. Drag this larger handle to move the label. The text box stays where it is.

Pointer in shape of a hand with a pointing finger

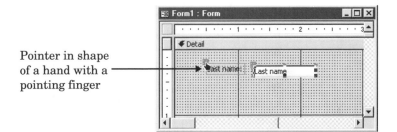

How can I assign a shortcut key to a control?

You can assign an ALT-key combination, also known as a *shortcut key*, to the control's attached label by placing the ampersand (&) immediately in front of the character that you want used as the shortcut key in the Caption property for the control's attached label. In Design view, right-click the label for the control, choose Properties from the shortcut menu, and click the Format tab. Then, in the Caption property, place an ampersand in front of the character that you want to use as the shortcut key. For example, if you want to allow the use of ALT-C to move to a City field in the form, you enter **&City** in the Caption property for the label.

> ***Tip:*** *If you have a control with no label attached to it, and want to add one, create a label, choose* Edit | Cut, *select the control to which you want to attach the label, and then choose* Edit | Paste.

Why doesn't the Format | Size | To Fit command adjust the size of my controls to fit the text in them?

Choosing Format | Size | To Fit does adjust the height and width of labels, command buttons, and toggle buttons. However, it adjusts only the *height* of text boxes, combo boxes, and list boxes to fit the font of the text it contains. This command doesn't change the *width* of these controls, because the width depends on the control's contents. If you want to change the width of these objects, you must do so manually.

How can I draw straight lines on forms and reports?

You can use a little-known keyboard technique to keep your lines straight. Select the Line tool in the Toolbox, and then hold down the SHIFT key as you click and drag in the form or report to draw the line. When you hold down the SHIFT key while drawing a line, Access restricts the line to be perfectly horizontal or perfectly vertical. (After you release the mouse, Access displays the dimensions of the line.)

USING CONTROLS IN FORMS AND REPORTS

How do I open a combo box on a form without a mouse?

Move to the combo box and press ALT-DOWN ARROW.

My Date field has a Long Date format in its table and a Short Date format in a query. When I add the field from the query to my form, what date format does it use?

When you set field properties in a query, they override the field properties that are set for the table. So, if you add the

field with the Short Date format from the query rather than the field with the Long Date format from the table, the control displaying the date field in the form has the Short Date format, by default.

 Tip: *Regardless of what format is used by the table or query, you can change a form or report control to whatever format you want. Open the form or report in Design view, right-click the control, and choose Properties from the shortcut menu. In the Properties window that appears, click the Format tab, click the Format property, and choose the desired format from the list.*

How can I avoid having to click the DOWN ARROW key to display the choices in my combo box?

You can create a macro that simulates pressing the DOWN ARROW key as the user moves into the combo box. Use the following steps:

1. Create a new macro.
2. In the Action column, choose SendKeys.
3. Under Action Arguments, enter %{**Down**} in the Keystrokes entry, and leave the Wait entry set to the default of No.
4. Save the macro (give it any name that you want).
5. Right-click the combo box in Design view and choose Properties from the shortcut menu.
6. Click the Event tab in the Properties window.
7. Click the On Enter property and choose by name from the list box the macro that you just created.
8. Save the form.

When you tab to the combo box field in Form view, the macro sends the keystroke ALT-DOWN ARROW, which opens the combo box.

 Can I set a Memo field's control so that the insertion point goes to the end of the entry when I move to the control?

When you move to a field's entry, the entire entry is selected initially, which means that you can easily accidentally delete a long entry by typing a single character, requiring that you retype the long entry. To avoid this, you can create a macro that simulates pressing F2, by automatically deselecting the entry and placing the insertion point at the end of the text. Use these steps to implement this macro:

1. Create a new macro. In the Action column, choose SendKeys. Under Action Arguments, enter {**F2**} in the Keystrokes entry, and leave the default of No in the Wait entry.

2. Save the macro (you can name it whatever you want).

3. Open the form in Design view.

4. Right-click the Memo field and choose Properties from the shortcut menu.

5. In the Properties window, click the Event tab.

6. Click the On Enter property and choose from the list the macro that you just created.

7. Save the form.

Tip: *This macro works for any type of field, not just Memo fields. If you want the insertion point to be at the beginning of the field instead of at the end, replace {F2} with {F2}^{HOME}. ^{HOME} represents pressing the CTRL-HOME key combination.*

I have a lot of single-character codes to enter. Can I get the form to move to the next field when I complete an entry?

To do this, use the Input Mask and Auto Tab properties. The Input Mask property restricts the entry to just the number of characters set by the property. (Right-click the field, choose

Properties from the shortcut menu, and then click either the Data tab, to get to the Input Mask property, or the Other tab, to get to the Auto Tab property.) For example, you might enter **LL** as the input mask for a field containing state abbreviations, **00000-0000** for ZIP codes, or **A** for a field containing a single letter or number. Next, set the Auto Tab property for each of the fields to Yes. When the Auto Tab property is set to Yes, the focus automatically moves to the next control when the field is filled in.

Tip: *You can also have the Input Mask property set the style of capitalization. Use the < symbol to make letters after this point lowercase, and > to make them uppercase.*

 ### How can I prevent users from moving to a control on a form?

Forms have *tab orders* that set the sequence in which you move through the controls on the form by pressing TAB. You can remove a control from the form's tab sequence so that pressing TAB never moves the user to that control. Right-click the control in Design view and choose Properties from the shortcut menu. Click the Other tab in the Properties window and set the Tab Stop property to No. Note that, regardless of the setting in the Tab Stop property, users can still move to a control by clicking it. If you want to disable the control completely from user access, click the Data tab in the Properties window and set the Enabled property to No.

CALCULATIONS AND CONTROLS

 ### How can I have a text box that combines text with one or more fields?

You can add a calculated control that uses the *concatenation operator* (&) to *concatenate*, or combine, the text and the field contents. You enter an expression that joins the text and the field contents into the Control Source property for the text box. For example, if you want to combine the First Name

and Last Name fields along with some text, you might have this expression stored in the Control Source property for the text box:

```
= "The Employee of the month is " & [First name] & " " & [Last name]
```

If the First Name field contains "Michael" and the Last Name field contains "Jones," the output of this control will show "The employee of the month is Michael Jones."

 ### How can I give a default value to a calculated control?

You can't. If you think about this, you'll realize that you really don't want to. The whole reason for a calculated control is that it equals the value of a calculation.

 ### How do I put an upper limit on the value entered into a field in my form?

You can use the Validation Rule property for a control to specify a maximum value that will be accepted when entering data into that control. Right-click the control and choose Properties from the shortcut menu. In the Properties window that opens, click the Data tab and enter an expression in the Validation Rule property. For example, if a field should have a date prior or equal to today's date, you can enter **<=Date()** as the Validation Rule property. If you want users to enter a number less than 750, you can enter **<750**.

Tip: *When you enter a validation rule, make sure that the person using the form knows what the appropriate limits are. Either add beside the field a label that describes acceptable entries or include an explanation in the Validation Text property. Access displays a message box with the contents of the Validation Text property when you try to leave the field and the validation rule is not met.*

 How can I add expressions to count Yes/No responses in a Yes/No field in a report?

For some reports, having a sum total of responses in a Yes/No field may be helpful. You can use expressions in text boxes to calculate the number of Yes or No responses, and include the Sum() function to produce a sum total. The following expressions can be used in a report group's footers or in the report footer to count the number of occurrences of Yes and No in a field whose data type is Yes/No and whose field name is Insured. Use the same expression, but substitute the name of your field for Insured in the expressions shown.

This expression:	Sums this:
=Sum(IIf([Insured],1,0)	Number of Yes responses
=Sum(IIf([Insured],0,1)	Number of No responses

TROUBLESHOOTING

 Why does #Error appear in my text box when the source of data for the control is a formula that uses a field to supply one of the values?

The most likely reason for this error message is that the control has the same name as one of the fields that you are using in its formula. In such cases, Access gets confused, because it thinks that the formula refers to the control rather than the field, resulting in a circular reference. For example, you might see #Error if a text box is named Unit Price and one of the fields that you are using in the calculation is named Unit Price. To fix the problem, change the name of the control.

? I've added a new record to the underlying table that's supplying data to a combo box on a form, but the choice doesn't appear in the combo box when I open it. What's wrong?

Simply refresh your screen by choosing Records | Refresh. After you do this, the new item that you added to the source table appears in the combo box.

? My report has a calculated field. I want to get a total value, so I tried to sum the control, but I get an #Error message. Why doesn't this work?

To sum the values from a calculated field, you must reference the entire calculation. Access will not correctly interpret your attempt to sum the control name when it refers to a calculated field. Access successfully totals the fields in a table or a query, but in that case, the names of the controls used to display the data are the same as the field names; so Access really is summing the fields. When you want to sum a calculated field, enter the entire calculation within the argument for the Sum function. For example, assume that you have a calculated control named Year_Total, and it has a Control Source property of [Amount Owed] – [Amount Paid]. To get a total, you can't use the expression =Sum(Year_Total) because this would produce the error. Instead, you use the expression =Sum([Amount Owed] – [Amount Paid]) to total the calculation for all records in the report.

Chapter 11

Sharing Data

Answer Topics!

Sharing Data @ a Glance

One of the greatest advantages of Windows is that you can easily exchange data between different applications by using the Windows Clipboard or Object Linking and Embedding (OLE) features. A simple cut-and-paste operation makes it easy to combine graphics, spreadsheet data, and text into a single, attractive document. With OLE features, you can enter and format data in whatever application is the most suitable, and then use the data in any of your other applications that support OLE. Access also shares data with other applications through importing, exporting, and attaching. In fact, the very name of the program, *Access*, comes from the original intent of Microsoft to provide a database product that would work with data stored in a wide variety of formats. These features are all designed so that you can use existing data without the tedious process of retyping it. The questions covered in this chapter are all related to the following two areas:

● **Importing, Exporting, and Linking** answers questions about importing data, exporting data, linking to tables stored outside of Access, and working with data from earlier versions of Access.

● **Working with Object Linking and Embedding** answers questions about OLE and working with OLE objects stored in your Access tables that appear in your forms and reports.

IMPORTING, EXPORTING, AND LINKING

 Why are dates imported from an Excel worksheet four years off?

The date fields that you imported from the Excel worksheet originally came from Excel for Macintosh. Excel for Windows uses the 1900 date system, in which serial numbers from 1 to 65,380 represent dates from Jan 1, 1900, to Dec 31, 2078. Excel for Macintosh uses the 1904 date system, in which numbers from 0 to 63,918 represent dates from Jan 1, 1904, to Dec 31, 2078. You can correct this in Excel for Windows or in Access, as follows:

- **Excel for Windows** Change the date system for the Excel worksheet, and then save the worksheet and import it into Access. (In Excel, choose Tools | Options, click the Calculation tab, and remove the check mark from the 1904 Date System check box.)

- **Access** Create an update query, using the expression [*date field name*] **+ 1462** (the number of days between the two systems) to correct the dates.

 What is a delimited text file?

A *delimited* text file is a text file of data with the fields delimited, or separated, by specific characters. Delimited files can use any character as the delimiter; most commonly, commas are used to separate the fields, text fields are surrounded by quotation marks, and lines are separated by carriage-return characters. A delimited file open in Windows Notepad is shown next.

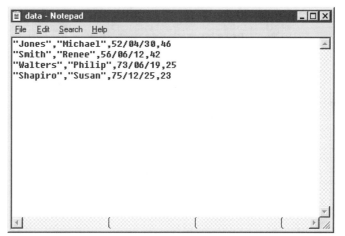

Many programs, when running on larger computers (such as mainframes) can produce files containing data in delimited format, and these files can be imported into Access.

 ### Why are errors reported when I append a spreadsheet or a text file to an existing table?

Appended records must match the structure of the existing table: each field must have the same data type as the matching field in the existing table, and the fields must be in the same order (unless you are using the entries in the first row of the incoming table as field names, in which case the field names must match). For every record that causes an error, Access adds a record to the Import Errors table. You can open this table and examine the data that it contains, to see why the errors are occurring. Here are some common

reasons why errors occur when appending data as part of an import process:

- The data stored in a field of the incoming table doesn't match the data type for the destination field. For example, if the destination field is a Date/Time field, the incoming data may be composed of characters that Access does not recognize as valid dates or times.

- The data in a numeric field of the incoming table is too large for the data type of the destination field in the Access table. For example, if the Field Size of a Number field in Access is set to Integer, the incoming data may contain a number value greater than 32,767.

- One or more rows in the imported table contain more fields than are in the destination table.

- You are attempting to import records that have the same values as primary key values in the existing table.

In some cases, you can get around the errors by editing the data in the tables that you are importing, so that the data does not cause problems. In other cases, you may need to redesign the structure of the destination tables in Access. You may need to change field sizes or field types or rearrange fields to match the layout of the tables that you are importing.

 Is there a fast way to import an Excel worksheet into an Access table?

If you just want to bring a worksheet into a new table, the easiest way, believe it or not, is with the Windows Clipboard. Access is sufficiently intelligent to recognize Excel data pasted into the Clipboard, and Access automatically creates a new table based on that data when you do a cut-and-paste operation. When you do this, it is helpful to include field names in the top row of the selected data of your Excel worksheet. Access automatically assigns those worksheet column headings as field names in the new table. Use these steps:

1. Open the Excel worksheet and select the data that you want to use to create the table in Access. If possible, include column headings in the selection that can be used as field names. (Figure 11-1 shows an example of data in an Excel worksheet, selected for pasting into an Access table.)

2. Choose Edit | Copy.

3. Switch to Access and, with the Tables portion of the Database window active, choose Edit | Paste.

4. When Access asks whether the first row of your data contains column headings, answer Yes, if your selection includes column headings.

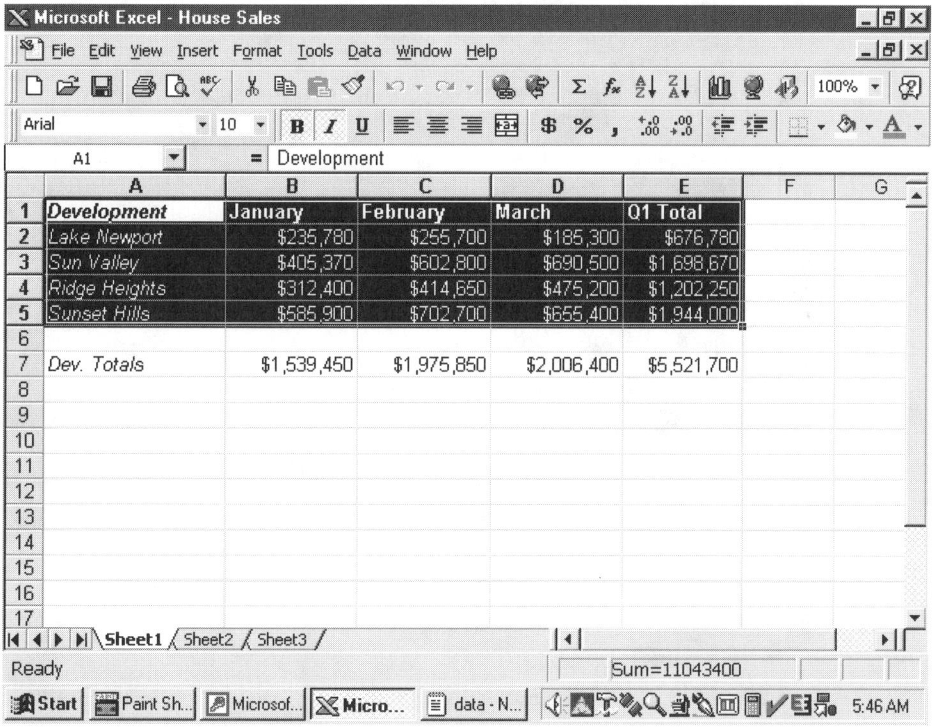

Figure 11-1 Selected data in an Excel worksheet

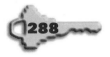

5. When Access prompts that the table was successfully imported, click OK.
6. Access creates a new table with the same name as the worksheet in Excel, as shown in Figure 11-2. If you included column headings in your selection, Access assigns field names that are the same as those column headings; if not, Access assigns field names of F1, F2, F3, and so on. Access assigns field types and formats based on how the data was stored in Excel. For example, if a column consists of date values, Access creates a Date/Time field; if a column contains numbers formatted as currency, Access creates a Currency field.

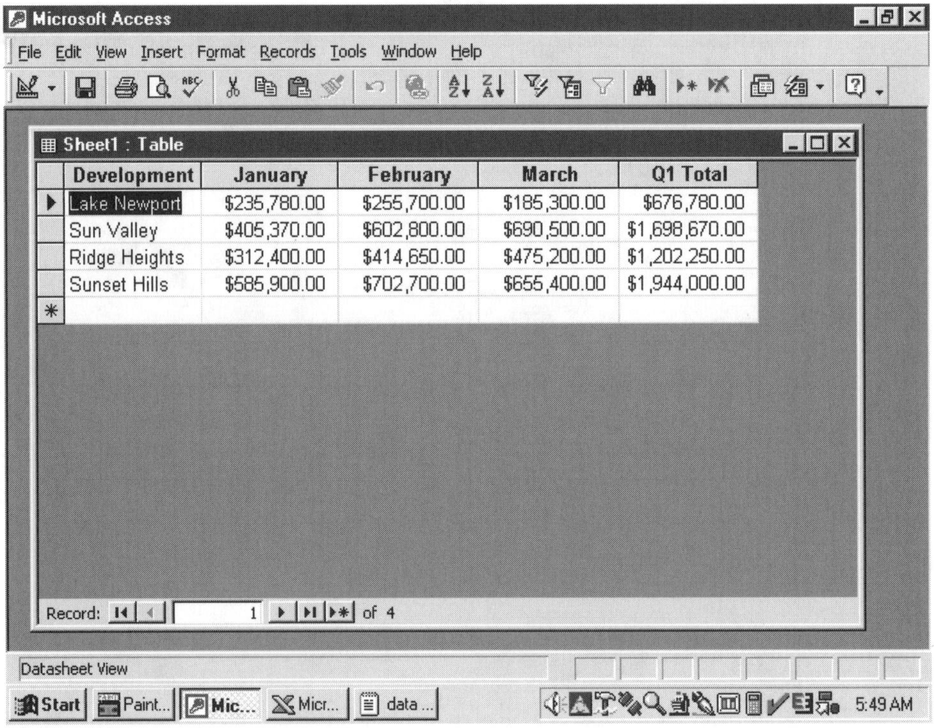

Microsoft Access
File Edit View Insert Format Records Tools Window Help
Sheet1 : Table
Development January February March Q1 Total
Lake Newport $235,780.00 $255,700.00 $185,300.00 $676,780.00
Sun Valley $405,370.00 $602,800.00 $690,500.00 $1,698,670.00
Ridge Heights $312,400.00 $414,650.00 $475,200.00 $1,202,250.00
Sunset Hills $585,900.00 $702,700.00 $655,400.00 $1,944,000.00
Record: 1 of 4
Datasheet View
Start Paint... Mic... Micr... data ...
5:49 AM

Figure 11-2 The results of an Excel worksheet pasted into Access as a new table

Which databases can Access export to?

Access can export to the following databases:

- Paradox 3, 4, 5, 7, and 8
- dBASE III, III+, IV, and 5
- SQL databases via Open Database Connectivity (ODBC)
- Other Microsoft Access databases

Access can also export files in the following formats:

- Microsoft Excel 3, 4, 5–7, 97, 98, and 2000
- Lotus 1-2-3 in WK1, WK3, and WJ2 formats
- Text (delimited)
- Text (fixed-width)
- Rich Text Format (RTF)
- HTML and IDC/HTX (Microsoft Internet Data Connector)
- FoxPro 2, 2.5, 2.6, and 3
- Microsoft IIS (Internet Information Server) and ASP (Active Server Pages) formats

What is a fixed-width text file?

A *fixed-width* text file has fields of a fixed length. The following shows a fixed-width text file open in Windows Notepad:

```
data2 - Notepad
File  Edit  Search  Help
Jones      Michael    52/04/30 46
Smith      Renee      56/06/12 42
Walters    Philip     73/06/19 25
Shapiro    Susan      75/12/25 23
```

Each row, which is a single record, has the same fields. Each field is the same length in all records. In this example, each line contains a last name, first name, date of birth, and age. Many programs running on larger computers (such as mainframes) can produce files containing data in fixed-width format, and these can be imported into Access.

 ## Which databases can Access import from?

Access can import data from the following sources:

- dBASE III, III+, IV, and 5
- Paradox 3, 4, 5, 7, and 8
- Microsoft Excel 3, 4, 5–7, 97, 98, and 2000
- Lotus 1-2-3 spreadsheets in WKS, WK1, WK3, and WK4 format (linked files are read-only)
- Delimited text files
- Fixed-width text files
- HTML 1 (list only), 2, or 3.*x* (table or list)
- SQL databases via ODBC
- Other Microsoft Access databases

Can I import an entire Access database?

You can import all the objects in a closed database into an open database. Use the following steps:

1. Open the database that you want to import the other database into.

2. Choose File | Get External Data | Import.

3. In the Files of Type box, make sure Microsoft Access (MDB) is the selected file type.

4. Click the arrow to the right of the Look In box, choose the drive and folder in which the Access database you want to import from is located, and double-click the icon

for that database. An Import Objects dialog box appears, which lists the objects in the other database.

5. To import all the tables, click Select All. If you want to import only the table definitions (and not the data in the tables), click Options; then, under Import Tables, click Definition Only.

6. Click the Queries tab to display the available queries, and then click Select All to import all queries. If you want to import queries as tables, click Options; then, under Import Queries, click As Tables.

7. For forms, reports, data access pages, macros, and modules, click the respective tab in the Database window, and then click Select All. If you want to include relationships, custom menus and toolbars, or import/export specifications, click Options and then, under Import, choose the items that you want to include.

8. Click OK.

How do I import a text file?

You can import a text file by using the Import Text Wizard, which presents dialog boxes that prompt you for the information needed for an import specification for the text. Use these steps to import the file:

1. Choose File | Get External Data | Import.

2. In the Import dialog box that appears, change the Files of Type entry to Text Files.

3. Enter the filename in the File Name box, or find it in the list box and select it, and then click Import. In a moment, the first dialog box of the Import Text Wizard appears, as shown in Figure 11-3.

4. Click Next and follow the directions that appear in the successive dialog boxes. Depending on whether your data is fixed or delimited, you will be asked to confirm field locations and to indicate a new or existing table in which the resulting data should be stored.

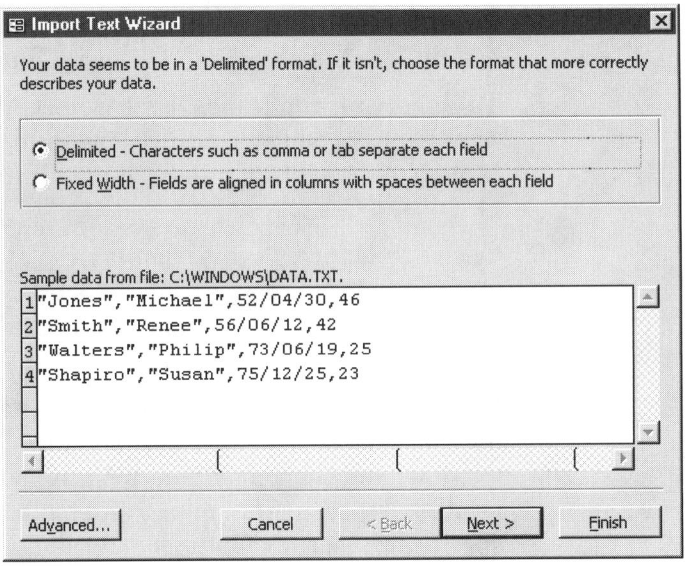

Figure 11-3 The first dialog box of the Import Text Wizard

What are import/export specifications?

Import/export specifications are the entries needed to either import or export delimited and fixed-width text files. For fixed-width text files, these specifications precisely describe each field's name, data type, starting point, and ending point for any given record. For delimited text files, they describe the characters separating field entries and enclosing text entries. To enter the necessary import/export specifications, you click the Advanced button during the process of running the Import Text or Export Text Wizards.

In earlier versions of Access, I used the File | Import/Export Specification command to design a specification for importing ASCII text files. This command doesn't exist in Access 2000. How can I create an import/export specification?

Access 2000 still uses import/export specifications, but they are treated differently. They are created as you run the Import Text Wizard or Export Text Wizard, and they are saved along with

the database that you import to or export from. When you use either the Export or the Get External Data command and specify a file type of text, you can use the Wizard dialog boxes that appear to provide your import or export specification. (You must click the Advanced button when the Wizard dialog boxes appear to make changes to the specifications.)

I can't open a linked Paradox table. Why?

The likely cause of this problem is that Access can't find an associated Paradox index (PX) file or Paradox memo field (MB) file to go with the Paradox table. If you link to a Paradox table that has a primary key, Access must find the Paradox index file in the same directory. If you link to a Paradox table that has memo fields, Access must find the Paradox memo field file in the same directory. If these files have been deleted or moved, Access can't open the table.

If you link to a Paradox table that lacks a primary key, Access can't update the data. You need to go into Paradox and add a primary key, before you can update the data from Access.

Another possibility is that the Paradox table (DB) and index (PX) files are set to read-only. Use My Computer or Windows Explorer to open the folder in which the files are located, right-click the file, choose Properties, and click the General tab. If the Read-Only check box is turned on, clear it and click OK.

Finally, if the Paradox table is stored on a network, you may have insufficient access rights at the network level. Check with your network administrator to be sure that you have rights to any directory in which the Paradox tables and indexes are stored.

Why are my linked SQL tables read-only, when I haven't specified them as such?

Before you can edit linked SQL tables, Access requires that a unique index be defined for each table. SQL views and synonyms are also read-only when no unique index exists. To fix this problem, create a unique index for each of your tables from your SQL server. Then, relink the tables to implement the changes.

Why doesn't Access lock records in my linked SQL table when I have record locking set?

When you work on a linked SQL table, the SQL database controls locking. Therefore, locking doesn't change, regardless of what your setting is in Access. Access always acts as if this is set to No Locks. To change how the records are locked, change them from the SQL database.

How can I export some addresses from Lotus Organizer into Access, when Access doesn't read Lotus Organizer ORG files?

In Lotus Organizer, you need to use the File | Export command to export the data either as a comma-separated values (CSV) file or as a dBASE (DBF) file. You can then import this file into Access. Be aware that Lotus Organizer stores the entire address (including the city, state or province, and ZIP or postal code) as a single field, which makes separating the address data into separate fields a tedious affair. This is just an annoying trait of the way Lotus Organizer is designed.

Tip: *Many experienced Access users report better success using the dBASE format instead of the comma-separated values format when importing Lotus Organizer files into Access tables.*

We need to export data on a weekly basis. Can we automate this process with a macro?

You can automate the exporting (or importing) of data by using a macro. Here are the steps that you need to follow to do this:

1. Open a new macro.

2. In the Action column, choose TransferDatabase to import or export from a database; choose TransferSpreadsheet to import or export to a spreadsheet; or choose TransferText to import or export to a text file.

3. Under Action Arguments, set Transfer Type to either Import or Export, as desired.

4. Fill in the remaining options under Action Arguments, as desired.

5. Save the macro.

After you save the macro, you can perform the import or export at any time by running the macro.

 How can I create a mail merge in Word, based on names and addresses in an Access table?

The easiest way to do this from Access is to use the MS Word Mail Merge Wizard that's built into Access. You can get to this Wizard from the OfficeLinks button on the Database toolbar:

1. Select the table in the Database window, click the drop-down arrow on the right side of the OfficeLinks toolbar button, and choose <u>M</u>erge It with MS Word from the drop-down menu.

2. Follow the directions in the Mail Merge Wizard dialog boxes that appear, to select a new Word document or open an existing one.

3. After the document is open in Word, a Mail Merge toolbar appears in the Word document window. You can then use the Insert Merge Field button, on the left side of the toolbar, to add fields to the document from the Access table or query.

4. After you add your chosen fields, you can use the Merge to New Document button on the Mail Merge toolbar to view the merged data, or you can use the Merge to Printer button on the same toolbar to print the form letters.

Can I merge selected records from my tables into my word processor if I'm not using Word for Windows?

Yes, Access can provide data that most Windows word processors can use as a data source in a merge file. (You need to refer to your particular word processor's documentation, to see how you create the merge document after you export the data.) Most Windows word processors can work with the RTF file format to create merge documents, so you simply need to export a query with your desired records to an RTF file, as follows:

1. Create a query that provides the desired records, in the sort order that you want.

2. Right-click the query in the Database window and choose Export in the shortcut menu.

3. In the Export dialog box that appears, choose Rich Text Format (RTF) under File Type.

4. Enter a name for the file in the File Name box.

5. Click Save to create the RTF file.

Open the RTF file in your Windows word processor, and use the appropriate techniques in your word processor to create the mail merge.

What does ODBC stand for?

It stands for Open Database Connectivity, a powerful means of accessing data stored by a wide range of database management systems. Access uses ODBC drivers to manage information from different sources of data. The ODBC drivers that come with Access include ones for FoxPro, dBASE, Paradox, and Btrieve. You may also have other ODBC drivers on your system that were included with other applications.

How can I link or import to tables stored on an ODBC server?

Before you attempt to link to an ODBC server, you must have the ODBC drivers installed on your system. (They are *not* installed as part of the default Access setup.) If necessary, rerun Setup to add the ODBC drivers. After you install the drivers, you can use the following steps to link to tables stored on an ODBC server:

1. Make the Database window the active window.

2. Choose File | Get External Data | Import to import the ODBC server data into Access tables, or choose File | Get External Data | Link Tables to link to the ODBC server tables.

3. In the next dialog box that appears, select ODBC Databases in the Files of Type box.

4. In the Select Data Source dialog box, click the Machine Data Source tab to see the list of all ODBC sources for the ODBC drivers installed on your computer. Double-click the ODBC data source that contains the data you want to import or link. (If the ODBC data source requires you to log in, you are prompted for a login and password.) Access connects to the ODBC source and displays a list of tables that you can import or link.

5. Click each table that you want to import or link, and then click OK.

6. After you have finished importing or linking the tables, click Close.

 ## What is the Office Links toolbar button used for?

You can use the OfficeLinks button on the Database toolbar to export data quickly from a table, query, or report that is selected in the Database window to a Word document or an Excel worksheet. When you click the drop-down arrow on the right side of this button, you see the three menu options shown here and explained in the following list:

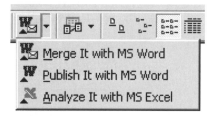

- **Merge It with MS Word**   Launches a Mail Merge Wizard that helps you to create a mail merge document in Word, based on the data in the table or query.

Figure 11-4 shows a Word document titled "Microsoft Word - Customer Sales" containing the following table:

Last name	First name	Item	Quantity	Price
Zykoski	Maria	Coral sweater large	2	$49.95
Zykoski	Maria	Button fly jeans	1	$29.95
Ian	James	Rainbow beach towel	1	$19.95
Jones	Jarel	Black mock top	3	$59.95
Jones	Jarel	Bermuda shorts- blue	1	$24.95
Jones	Edward	Sleeveless mock top- silver	1	$39.95
Jones	Edward	Button fly jeans	2	$29.95

Figure 11-4 An Access table placed in a Word for Windows document

- **Publish It with MS Word** Launches Word (or switches to it if Word is already running) and opens a new document containing the data.

- **Analyze It with MS Excel** Launches Excel (or switches to it if Excel is already running) and opens a new worksheet page containing the data.

Figure 11-4 shows an Access query after it has been exported to Word for Windows by using the Publish It with MS Word option.

How do I export data to an older version of Access?

If you want to use the data in Access 97, you can convert an entire Access 2000 database to Access 97 file format, as follows:

1. Open the database that you want to convert.

2. Choose Tools | Database Utilities | Convert Database | To Prior Access Database Version.

3. In the dialog box that appears, choose a drive and/or directory, and enter a name for the converted database.

4. Click Save.

You cannot directly export data to any Access versions older than Access 97. If you need to do this, use the File | Export command to export the data in Excel 5 format. Then, in the earlier version of Access, you can import the Excel 5 data into new tables.

 In earlier versions of Access, I used the File | Output To command to export Access tables and queries. What happened to this command?

The Output To command found in earlier versions has been replaced with the Save As and Export commands. Just select the desired table or query in the Database window and choose File | Export. In the Save dialog box that appears, you can specify the filename and the type of format for the exported file.

How can I link or import Paradox tables?

You can use these steps to link to Paradox tables:

1. Make the Database window the active window.

2. Choose File | Get External Data | Import to import the Paradox data into Access tables, or choose File | Get External Data | Link Tables to link to the Paradox tables.

3. In the next dialog box that appears, select Paradox in the Files of Type box.

4. Click the drop-down arrow on the right side of the Look In box, choose the drive and folder in which the Paradox tables are stored, and double-click the icon for the Paradox table. (If the Paradox table is password-protected, you are prompted for the password.)

5. Repeat steps 2 through 4 for each Paradox table that you want to link to or import.

6. After you have finished importing or linking to tables, click Close.

 Note: *If you link to a Paradox table that has a primary key, Access must be able to locate the Paradox index file (PX) for the table; otherwise, you won't be able to open the linked table in Access. If you link to a table with Memo fields, Access must be able to locate the associated Memo field file (MB) for the Paradox table; otherwise, you won't be able to open the table. Make sure these files are in the same folder as the Paradox table. Also, if you link to a Paradox table that doesn't have a primary key, you can view the data in Access, but you can't update it. To make the data updateable, go into Paradox and add a primary key.*

When I open my database, I see "Database name was created by a previous version of Microsoft Access. You won't be able to save changes to object definitions in this database." How do I edit my database?

You see this error message whenever you open a database that is saved in an earlier version of Access. The message appears as a warning even after you choose to open the database in the first dialog box that you always see when opening an older Access database. You can edit the data in your tables, but you won't be able to make design changes to objects, such as table definitions, form and report designs, or query designs, unless you convert the database to Access 2000 file format. To convert the database, use these steps:

1. Close any open database.

2. Choose Tools | Database Utilities | Convert Database | To Current Access Database Version.

3. In the dialog box that appears, select the database that you want to convert, and click OK.

4. In the next dialog box, enter the name for the converted database and then click Save.

Caution: *If you enter the same name twice, Access replaces your old database with the updated one. Unless you have a backup of your old database, avoid replacing it, so that if you run into any problems with the converted database, you can go back to the old one.*

 Note: *When you save your converted database with the name of the original database, to replace the original, Access doesn't actually replace the old database until it is finished converting. Thus, you need to have enough space on your hard disk to hold two complete copies of your database for this to work.*

 ### I have data stored in R:BASE for DOS that I need to convert to Access. How can I transfer the data?

R:BASE for DOS uses a rather unique format that is truly a world unto itself. You need to locate a copy of R:BASE Express, a data export utility that is included with the R:BASE system disks. Run the program, and use its menu options to export the R:BASE tables to dBASE format. You can then import the resulting dBASE files into Access.

Can I export only selected records from a table?

Yes; however, you don't do so directly. To export selected records, you first must create a query containing only those records, and then you can export the query. Follow these steps:

1. Design a select query that displays only the records that you want to export.
2. Save the query.
3. Right-click the query in the Database window and choose Export.
4. Choose a desired export file format from the Save as Type list box.
5. Enter a filename for the exported file in the File Name box.
6. Make any other selections that you want in the dialog box, and click OK.

 How can I export a table or query as an Excel worksheet or as a FoxPro or dBASE database file?

You can use the File | Export command to export data from an Access table or query to most common file types. (If you are exporting data for use in FoxPro, you can use the dBASE file format, which is also used by FoxPro.) Use these steps to export the data:

1. Select the table or query in the Database window.

2. Choose File | Export.

3. In the Export dialog box, click the Save as Type list box and choose a desired file format (various versions of dBASE, Excel, and other formats are listed).

4. Under File Name, enter a name for the exported file. (If you are exporting to a product that runs under DOS or Windows 3.*x*, remember to restrict your filenames to eight or less characters, with no spaces.)

5. Click Save to create the file.

WORKING WITH OBJECT LINKING AND EMBEDDING

 When I double-click an OLE object in my form, I see a message that says the file can't be opened. What do I do?

Access displays this message when it can't open the source file for an OLE object. Check these possibilities:

● Make sure the source file hasn't been renamed or moved. Click the object and then choose Edit | OLE/DDE Links. The Links dialog box that appears displays the original filename and path. If the file has been renamed or moved, click the link in the Links box, and click Change Source to reestablish the link.

● Make sure the application needed to open the file is installed on your computer.

- If the application used to create the source file is already running, make sure that it doesn't have any open dialog boxes.

- If the file is a linked object, make sure someone else doesn't have it open for exclusive use on a network.

- Make sure that you have sufficient memory to open the other application (close down unneeded applications, if necessary).

- If you are on a network, check with your network administrator to be sure that you have access rights to the directory in which the source file is located.

 I want to see the content of my OLE object in my form or report, but all I see is an icon. How can I change this?

The default display property for your object is set to an icon rather than the contents of the object. Use these steps to change this:

1. Open the form or report in Design view.
2. Click the icon representing the OLE object.
3. Open the Edit menu, choose the appropriate object from the menu (for example, choose Bitmap Image Object for a bitmap), and then click Convert from the submenu that appears. In the Convert dialog box that opens, turn off the Display as Icon check box.

 Can I use OLE to paste an Access table into another application, such as Word or Excel?

No. When you copy and paste entire tables, Microsoft Access doesn't act as an OLE server; it is only an OLE client. This means that you can put OLE data from other applications into Access, but you can't paste an Access table in OLE form into other applications. If you try to paste an Access table into another application, the data is copied—not embedded or linked via OLE—which means that the pasted data has no continuing link with Access.

For example, when you paste an Access table into Word for Windows, the data appears in a Word table within the document. Pasting an Access table into Excel copies the table data in the same column-and-row format that you see in Datasheet view. (Figure 11-5 shows an Excel worksheet that contains data pasted from Access.) The data appears in these applications just as if you had entered it there. However, if the data is later changed in the Access table, it does not change in the Word or Excel document.

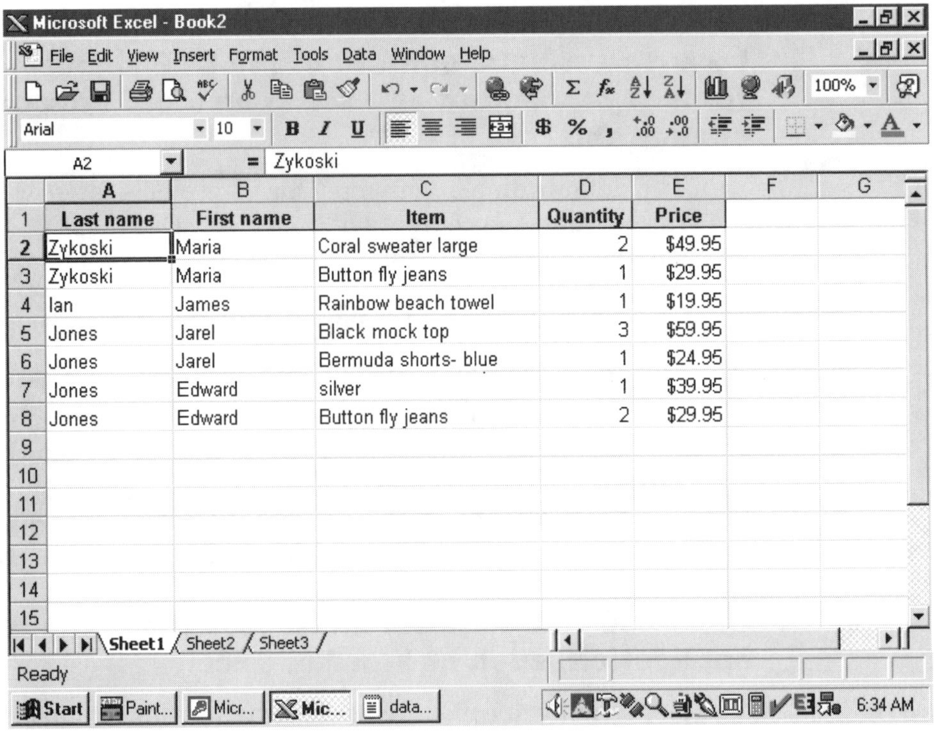

Figure 11-5 Data pasted from an Access table into an Excel worksheet

 I have a Paintbrush image stored as a decorative object in a form. How can I prevent users from double-clicking the picture and editing it in Paintbrush?

In this case, you have a picture placed in an unbound object frame, and you need to convert it to an image. Use these steps to do so:

1. Open the form in Design view.
2. Click the image to select it.
3. Choose Format | Change To | Image.
4. When Access prompts that you can't undo this operation, click OK.

When you use these steps, Access converts the unbound object frame to an image control. The image control is a static representation of the picture, and users won't be able to edit it in its original application.

Caution: *You shouldn't use the preceding procedure with an object frame that contains video. If you convert an unbound object frame containing video to an image, just the first frame of the video remains, and users won't be able to play the video.*

 The original data used to create a linked OLE object in my form or report has changed. How do I update the link?

You can use these steps to update an OLE link manually:

1. If the object is unbound, open the form or report in Design view and click it. If the object is a bound object,

open the form in Form view, find the record containing the object, and then click the object.

2. Choose <u>E</u>dit | OLE/DDE Lin<u>k</u>s.

3. In the Links dialog box that appears, click the link that you want to update. (You can select multiple links by holding down the CTRL key as you click each link.)

4. Click Update Now and then click Close.

Note: *You can use these steps for pictures placed in unbound and bound object frames. Pictures used as backgrounds for forms are updated automatically.*

How can I play video or sound that's displayed in an OLE Object field in a form?

If you store sound or video in an OLE Object field of a table, you can play the sound or video by following these steps:

1. Open the form containing the video or sound data.

2. Locate the record that contains the video or sound clip that you want to play.

3. Open the <u>E</u>dit menu and choose the appropriate command from the bottom of the menu. (For example, to play a video clip, choose <u>E</u>dit | Media Clip <u>O</u>bject.)

4. From the submenu that appears, choose <u>P</u>lay. When you do so, Access plays the sound or video.

Chapter 12

Access Macros

Answer Topics!

Access Macros @ a Glance

This chapter provides answers to questions that arise when you use macros in Access. You can use macros as guides for entering data and to make working with forms and reports easier. Macros may not be as comprehensive as Visual Basic for Applications (VBA) procedures, which provide full programming capabilities, but they are wonderful for less complex tasks.

- **Designing Macros** answers questions about the various design techniques used when creating and modifying macros.
- **Running Macros** answers questions that arise when running, testing, and troubleshooting macros.

If you are familiar with the design of macros in other applications, such as Microsoft Word and Excel, you should be aware that macros in Access are designed differently. Whereas you can create Word and Excel macros by turning on a recorder and performing a series of actions, in Access you design macros by specifying actions that you want the macros to perform in a design grid of a Macro window. If you haven't worked with Access macros in the past, take a look at the following sidebar, "Macro Terms Revealed," to familiarize yourself with some basic terms you need to know.

Macro Terms Revealed

A macro uses some terms you may not recognize. To get the most out of this chapter's tips on macros, you need to understand these terms:

- **Action** A macro command that describes something you want the macro to do, such as open a form or print a report.

- **Condition** A logical statement in the Condition column next to an action that determines whether the action will be performed. When the value in the Condition column is true, the action next to it is performed. Otherwise, the action is ignored. If you want the action to be controlled by the same condition that applied to the preceding action, enter ... (three dots) in the Condition column.

- **Macro** A set of actions to perform. Macros are stored either as individual database objects or as part of a *macro group*, which also is a database object.

- **Macro Group** A collection of named macros stored as a single database object. You name macros within a macro group by displaying the Macro Name column and entering the name in this column. Only the first action in a macro needs a name. All of the other actions after the name and before the next name are part of that macro. To identify a macro in a macro group, enter the macro group name, a period, and the name of the macro.

DESIGNING MACROS

 ### How (and why) would I create a macro?

A *macro* is a list of tasks that Access carries out for you automatically. You should consider creating a macro for any task you perform on a repetitive basis, such as opening and closing forms, printing reports, and setting the values of controls on a form. Figure 12-1 shows a Macro window that contains macros saved in a macro group. The Macro window has the following columns:

- **Macro Name** Contains the macro names next to their first actions. When a Macro window contains only one macro rather than a macro group, this column is empty and can be hidden.
- **Condition** Contains any optional conditions that determine whether to perform the action to its right in the Action column.
- **Action** Contains the instructions to perform. As you move between rows in the top half of the window, the bottom half of the window shows the arguments for the action.
- **Comment** Contains any optional comments that describe the purpose of each action. Comments can be useful in helping you remember the reasons behind the design of a particular macro.

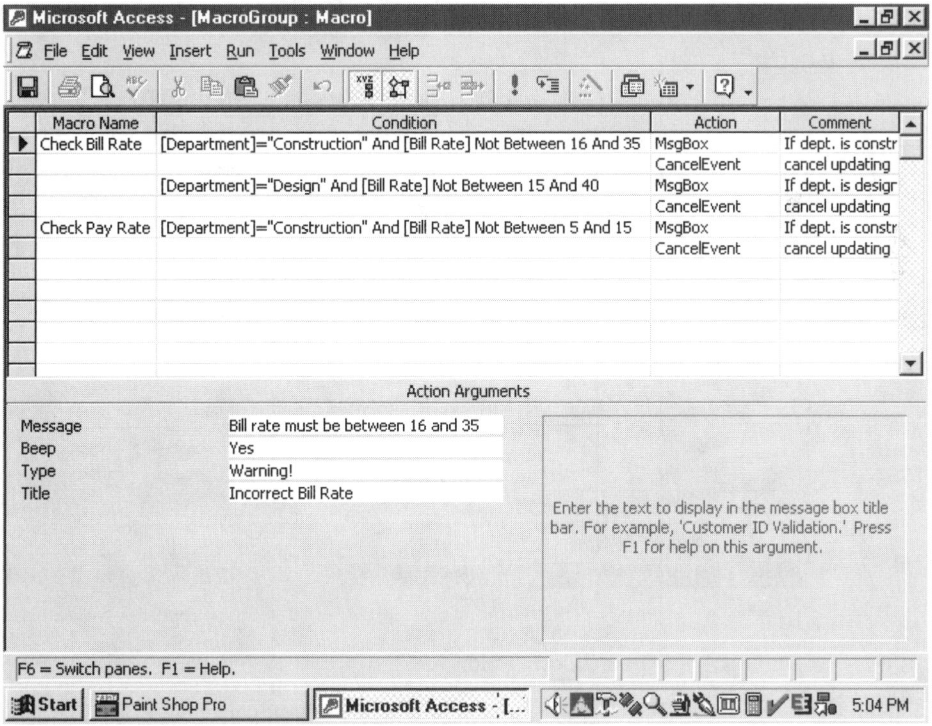
Microsoft Access - [MacroGroup : Macro]
File Edit View Insert Run Tools Window Help
Macro Name
Condition
Action
Comment
Check Bill Rate
[Department]="Construction" And [Bill Rate] Not Between 16 And 35
MsgBox
If dept. is constr
CancelEvent
cancel updating
[Department]="Design" And [Bill Rate] Not Between 15 And 40
MsgBox
If dept. is desigr
CancelEvent
cancel updating
Check Pay Rate
[Department]="Construction" And [Bill Rate] Not Between 5 And 15
MsgBox
If dept. is constr
CancelEvent
cancel updating
Action Arguments
Message
Bill rate must be between 16 and 35
Beep
Yes
Type
Warning!
Title
Incorrect Bill Rate
Enter the text to display in the message box title bar. For example, 'Customer ID Validation.' Press F1 for help on this argument.
F6 = Switch panes. F1 = Help.
Start
Paint Shop Pro
Microsoft Access - [...
5:04 PM

Figure 12-1 A Macro window containing macros saved as a macro group

You create macros from the Macro panel of the Database window. Start a macro with the following steps:

1. In the Database window, click the Macros button.

2. Click the <u>N</u>ew button. When you do so, a new Macro window opens. The parts of a Macro window are shown in Figure 12-2, which already has an action added, so action arguments (the appropriate settings for the chosen action) are visible.

3. In the Macro window, click the first empty row under the Action column.

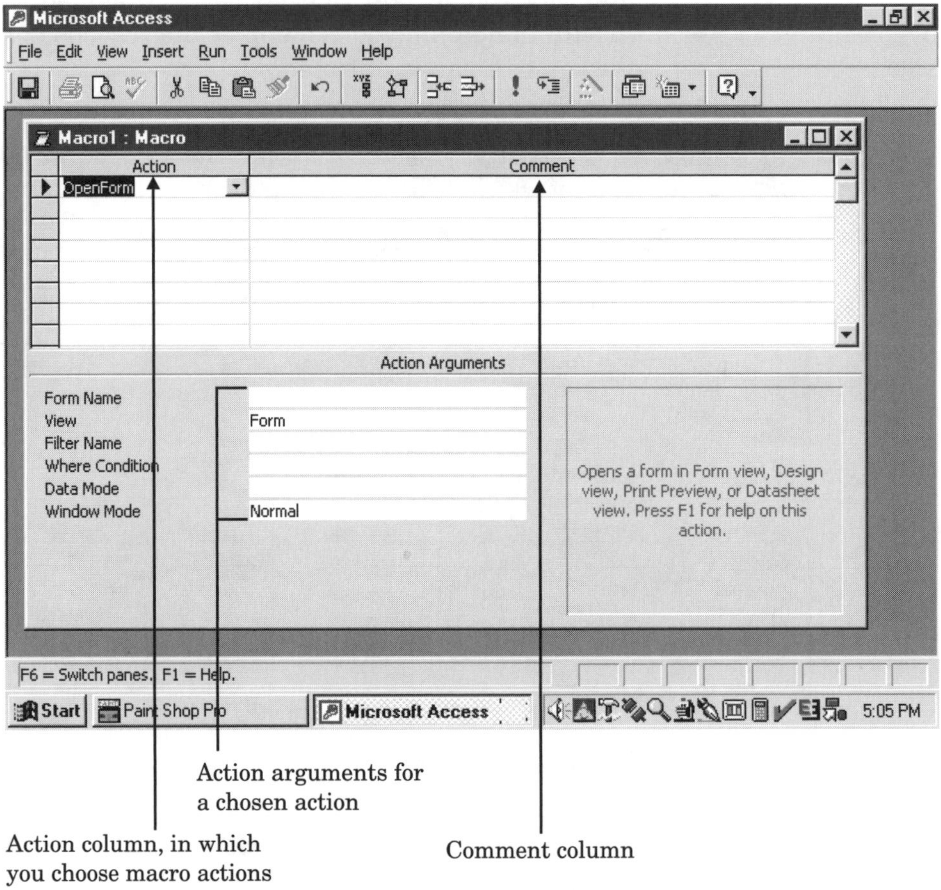

Figure 12-2 The parts of a Macro window

4. Either type the action you want the macro to perform, or click the drop-down arrow to open the list box from which you can choose the action.

5. Enter any optional comments in the Comment column, on the same line as the action.

6. Click the Action Arguments portion of the dialog box (or press F6) and specify any action arguments you want to include with your macro.

7. Save the macro by choosing File | Save.

How can a macro display a message when a user enters an item in a combo box that is not in the combo box's list box?

To execute a macro when a user enters a new item in a combo box, you need to do the following:

● Enter the macro name for the combo box's On Not In List property (on the Event tab of the Properties window for the combo box).

● Set the Limit To List property (on the Data tab of the Properties window) to Yes.

After you do these two things, the macro will execute. The OnNotInList event occurs when a value is entered in the combo box that doesn't appear on its list while the Limit To List property is set to Yes.

How can I use a macro to automate importing or exporting data?

You can use the TransferDatabase, TransferSpreadsheet, or TransferText actions to automate importing or exporting data:

● **TransferDatabase**   Can import or export data to and from other Access databases and from other popular database formats, such as dBASE and Paradox

● **TransferSpreadsheet**   Can import or export data from various Excel and Lotus 1-2-3 spreadsheet formats

● **TransferText** Can import or export data as delimited or fixed-width text or as HTML files (you can also export text as Word merge files)

When you create a new macro, choose TransferDatabase, TransferSpreadsheet, or TransferText, as desired, in the Action column. Then, set the action arguments in the lower half of the Macro window, as appropriate, to the data you are trying to import or export. If you are unsure as to what entry you should make for any argument, you can click within that argument and then press F1, to obtain a Help screen dealing with that specific argument.

 ## Do macro conditions have a length limitation?

A macro's condition can be up to 255 characters. If your condition is longer than this, use a VBA procedure instead.

 ## How many macro actions can I have in one macro?

Your macros may have as many as 999 actions. This limit applies to the contents of a Macro window, so macros within a macro group are limited to 999 actions for the entire group.

 ## What is the maximum number of characters I can have in a comment of a macro?

You can have as many as 255 characters in a macro's comment. Use comments to describe the purpose of each action.

 ## How do I tell my macro to move the focus to a control on a subform?

The GoToControl action moves the focus to a control, such as a subform control. This action accepts only one control name, *not* the full reference syntax of a control on a subform. For example, you can't use the following as a Control Name argument for the GoToControl action:

Forms![*main form*]![*name of subform*].Form![*control on subform*]

However, subforms are considered just another control on an Access form. Therefore, to tell your macro to move the focus to a control on a subform, add the following actions to your macro:

● A GoToControl action that specifies the control name of the subform as the Control Name argument

● Another GoToControl action that specifies the control name of the control within the subform as the Control Name argument

If this scenario includes another layer, such as a subform within a subform, just add one more GoToControl action.

 ## How can I change the order of my macro actions?

You can insert new actions and rearrange existing actions within a macro, as needed, by using any of the following techniques:

● To insert a new row in a macro, select the entire row below where the new row should be added, and then either press the INS key or choose Insert | Rows.

● To delete an existing row, select the row and then either press the DEL key or choose Edit | Delete Rows.

● To move an existing row, first click the row selector button to select it, and then drag the selected row to the desired position.

Can I create a macro that exits Access and shuts down Windows?

If you just wanted to exit Access, you could handle the job with a single Quit action added to a macro. But since you also want to shut down Windows, you need to have a macro call some VBA coding. The VBA code will call a standard Windows API function that shuts down Windows—the equivalent of choosing Start | Shut Down and clicking Yes in the dialog box. Use the following steps.

1. Create a new module (click the Modules button in the Database window and then click <u>N</u>ew). Type the following code into the Declarations section of the module (just below the Option Compare Database line and, if present, the Option Explicit line). The code line appears on two lines here, due to the page width, but you should enter it as one long line in the Module window.

```
Declare Function ExitWindowsEx Lib "user32" (ByVal
uFlags As Long, ByVal dwReserved As Long) As Long
```

2. Type the following procedure into the Module window:

```
Function LeaveWindows()
     Dim z As Long
     z = ExitWindowsEx(1, 0)
     Application.Quit acSaveAll
End Function
```

3. Save the module (giving it any name you wish) and close it.

4. Create a new macro. In the Action column of the macro, choose RunCode. Under Function Name in the Action Arguments, enter **LeaveWindows()**.

5. Save the macro and close it.

You can now run the macro from anywhere in your Access application. When run, it closes Access and shuts down Windows.

Tip: *If you are running Access on Windows NT Workstation and you want to shut down Windows but not log off the user, change the line of code that reads z = ExitWindowsEx(1, 0) to **z = ExitWindowsEx(0, 0)**.*

Caution: *Exiting Windows by making calls to the Windows API can leave undeleted files in the Windows Temp directory. These files then need to be deleted manually at some point, to recover disk space.*

Can a macro make sure that a value entered in a form already exists in a table's field?

Yes, a macro can limit entries to a predefined list of options stored in a field. You do this by placing a condition in front of the macro's actions that tests whether the value is acceptable. When this condition is true, Access performs the actions that handle the new entry. When this condition is false, Access skips over the macro actions. The condition uses the DCount domain aggregate function to test whether the field has a matching entry. (Note that if the values were text values rather than numbers, you could not use DCount to do this.) To add this condition:

1. Create the macro and add the actions that you want performed when the form entry does *not* match any existing entry in a table's field. For example, adding a CancelEvent action stops the updating process. This action, combined with the condition, enables you to halt the updating unless the entry has a match in the field.

2. Click the Conditions toolbar button or choose View | Conditions to add the Conditions column to the Macro window.

3. Move to the Conditions column in the row containing the first macro action.

4. Enter the following condition (all on one line):

    DCount("[*field in table*]","*name of table*",
    "[*match field in table*]=Forms![*form name*]!
    [*control on form*]")=0

    In this condition, *field in table* is the field name from the table to count entries. *Name of table* is the table name containing the entry to match. *Match field in table* is the name of the field to match from the table. *Form name* and *control on form* identify the form and control with the entry you are testing. This function returns the number of matching entries it finds from the table. If

DCount cannot find a matching entry, this function equals 0. This makes the condition true, so Access performs the action next to the condition. You can change the =0 to >0 for conditions used with actions you want performed when Access *does* find a matching entry.

5. Type ... below this condition to repeat it for the other actions that are to be performed if the DCount function does not find a matching entry (or finds one, if > 0 was used).

6. Save the macro.

7. Attach the macro to the event you want to trigger the macro.

8. Use the form. When you make an entry and the event that triggers the macro occurs, Access tests the value you have entered as the condition for the macro's entry.

As an example, suppose you want a form's BeforeUpdate event to run a macro that rejects an entry in the form's FirstName control if it doesn't match any existing entry in the FirstName field in a table called Friends. You would attach a macro to the On Before Update property that has a CancelEvent action and the following condition:

```
DCount("[FirstName]","Friends","[FirstName] =
Forms![Form1]![FirstName]")=0
```

RUNNING MACROS

 How can I assign a macro to a key combination?

Access macros can be assigned to specific key combinations. For example, you might assign to the CTRL-Y key combination a macro that prints the contents of the active window. You can assign a macro to a key combination by performing the following steps:

1. In the Database window, click the Macros button and then click <u>N</u>ew to create a new macro.

2. If the Macro Names column is not visible, choose <u>V</u>iew | <u>M</u>acro Names or click the Macro Names toolbar button.

3. In the Macro Names column, type the code representing the key combination to which you want to assign the macro (see the table below for the acceptable key combinations). Each key or key combination can call one set of macro actions in the macro group.

4. In the Action column, choose the actions you want to run when the key combination is pressed. You can select several actions in sequence by leaving the Macro Name column blank for the rows that follow the key combination.

5. Repeat steps 3 and 4, as needed, to make any additional assignments, assigning an action or combination of actions to each key combination.

6. Choose <u>F</u>ile | <u>S</u>ave to save the macro group. When prompted for a name, call the macro **AutoKeys**. The key assignments are stored for use when you save the macro, and they automatically take effect when the database is opened. The following table shows the key combinations used to assign keys to macros.

Syntax	Meaning
Caret (^) followed by a letter or number (for example, **^P, ^6**)	CTRL key plus that letter or number; hence, ^P would mean CTRL-P
{F1}	Any function key named inside the braces
^{F1}	CTRL plus any function key named inside the braces
+{F1}	SHIFT plus any function key named inside the braces
{INSERT}	INS key
^{INSERT}	CTRL-INS
+{INSERT}	SHIFT-INS
{DELETE} or {DEL}	DEL key
^{DELETE} or ^{DEL}	CTRL-DEL
+{DELETE} or +{DEL}	SHIFT-DEL

 I regularly include detailed message boxes in my macros, using the MsgBox action. Can I force a message to contain multiple lines in a dialog box?

You can force Access to divide a message into multiple lines, with the line breaks inserted where you want them, by entering the Message argument text as an expression that includes the Chr( ) function with the ASCII values of 13 (for a carriage return) and 10 (for a line feed). You need to begin the expression with an equals sign and surround the text with quotes. As an example, you could enter an expression like this one in the Message argument for the MsgBox action in a macro:

```
="Forms cannot remain open for over ten minutes." _
& Chr(13) & Chr(10) & "Form has been closed automatically."
```

When the macro runs, the resulting message box contains multiple lines, with a line break after the first sentence, like the one shown here:

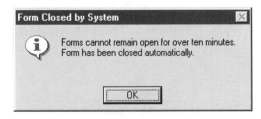

 In a macro that updates a table, can I prevent the message "Updating _x_ records..." from appearing?

Yes. Add the SetWarnings action to the macro. The default for this action is No. This action prevents showing system messages, such as "Updating records" and "Appending records." Access still displays error messages.

My Autoexec macro displays an opening screen for my application. Can I prevent this screen from appearing every time I open my database?

To keep an Autoexec macro from executing when you open the database, press SHIFT while you select the database to open.

? Can I make a macro display a "Please wait" message while a query runs?

You can manage this by running the query from within a macro and having the macro display a small form containing the text of your desired message. The first macro action opens the form with the message, the second action runs the query, and the last action closes the form. Use these steps:

1. Create a new form that is not based on any table or query. Add a label to the form, containing the message you want displayed as the query runs. In the All tab of the form's Properties window, set the form's Scroll Bars property to Neither, the Modal property to Yes, the Popup property to Yes, and the Record Selectors and Navigation Buttons properties to No.

2. Save and close the form. Call it **Waiting**.

3. Create a new macro. For the first action, choose Open Form. Under Action Arguments, set the Form Name to **Waiting**.

4. For the second action of the macro, choose Open Query. Under Action Arguments, set the Query Name to the name of the query you want to run. Set the View and Edit options as you want them for your query.

5. For the last action of the macro, choose Close. Under Action Arguments, set the object type to Form. Set the object name to **Waiting**.

6. Save and close the macro.

When the macro runs, the form containing the desired message is displayed on the screen as the query runs. Once the query finishes running, the form closes. Note that if the computer running the query is very fast or the underlying table is not very large, the message may not remain on the screen long enough for the viewer to see it.

? How can I cause a macro to run automatically when I open a database?

In Access, any macro that is named Autoexec runs when the database containing that macro is opened. To start any macro

automatically, create the new macro and add the desired actions. Save the macro, and when prompted for a name, call it **Autoexec**. Thereafter, each time the database is initially opened, the macro runs automatically (unless the user holds down the SHIFT key while opening the database).

 ## How can I make macros run conditionally, depending on the data in a form?

You can do this by adding a conditional expression to the macro's design. To enter a conditional expression in a macro, perform the following steps:

1. If the Condition column is not visible in the Macro window, choose View | Conditions or click the Conditions toolbar button.

2. In the Condition column, enter an expression in the row where you want to establish the condition.

3. In the Action column, choose the macro action you want Access to perform when the condition is true.

I have a macro that uses a SendKeys action to send keystrokes to a dialog box, but the keystrokes aren't being sent. What's wrong?

Dialog boxes suspend the operation of macros. Since this occurs by design in Access, you must place your SendKeys action prior to the action that opens the dialog box, and set the Wait argument to No to prevent any pauses in processing of the keys.

I have a macro that uses a SendKeys action to send keystrokes to a form. The keystrokes are valid when typed manually, but when the macro runs, I hear beeping and I don't get the desired results. What's wrong?

This usually happens due to a timing conflict; the macro is sending the keystrokes before some other part of Access is ready to receive them. Open the macro in Design view, click the SendKeys action, and set the Wait argument under

Action Arguments to Yes. This causes the macro to wait until the keystrokes are processed before it moves to the next macro action.

? Can I use a macro to store a date and time in a field, to indicate when a record in a table was last edited?

You can use a macro to add a *timestamp* to records, indicating the date and time of the last update, by having the macro store the current date and time in a control of a form used to edit the records. The following steps assume that your table contains a date/time field called Last Modified, and that your form used to edit the field contains a corresponding control named Last Modified.

1. Create a new macro. In the Action column, choose SetValue. Under Item in the Action Arguments area, enter the name of your form's control, surrounded by brackets. For example, assuming the control is named Last Modified, you would enter **[Last Modified]** under Item.

2. Under Expression, enter **Now()** and note that you should *not* precede the expression with an equal sign.

3. Save the macro and name it **Last Modified**.

4. Open the form used to edit the table in Design view.

5. Choose <u>V</u>iew | <u>P</u>roperties to display the Properties window for the form.

6. On the Event tab, set the Before Update property to the name of the macro (in this example, **Last Modified**).

7. Save and close the form.

When you use the form to edit a record, the value of the current date will be stored in the field once you move to another record. If it isn't important for users to see the contents of the Last Modified field, you can go into Design view for the form and set the Visible property for the control to No. The control won't appear, but the macro will still store the current date to the field as edits are made.

 ## How can I have a macro temporarily ignore a line while I test the macro?

You can disable any line by putting a condition in front of it that is always false. Choose <u>V</u>iew | <u>C</u>onditions or click the Conditions toolbar button. Type **0** (zero) into the Conditions column for the lines you want to ignore. An action executes only if the condition evaluates as true. The 0, which equals false, prevents the macro from executing that particular line. Remember that this affects *only* the line to which you add the 0 (and subsequent lines that have ... in the Condition column). When you no longer want this line ignored, remove the 0.

 ## How can I troubleshoot problems I'm having with my macros?

You can use a number of different techniques to find the cause of problems in the design of your macros, including the following:

● **Using the Action Failed dialog box**   Whenever a macro halts due to an error, Access displays the Action Failed dialog box, as shown here:

Action Failed	? X
Macro Name:	Step
RunMyQuery	Halt
Condition:	Continue
True	
Action Name:	
OpenQuery	
Arguments:	
Student Grades 3, Datasheet, Edit	

The dialog box contains the name of the macro that was halted, the value of any expression in the Condition column at the time the macro stopped, the action name of the action where the macro halted, and the arguments

for the action. You can use this information to narrow down the source of the problem, and click Halt to stop the macro.

- **Single stepping** You can run a macro one step at a time to analyze what happens during each step. Open the macro in Design view and choose Run | Single Step (or click the Single Step toolbar button). Close the macro and run it. As the macro executes its first step, you see the Macro Single Step dialog box, shown here:

Macro Single Step	? X
Macro Name:	Step
RunMyQuery	Halt
Condition:	Continue
True	
Action Name:	
MsgBox	
Arguments:	
Query may take some time to execute., Yes, Information, Begin Processing	

You can click the Step button each time you want to proceed to the next step of the macro. When you are done using the single-step process to test the macro, open the macro in Design view and again choose Run | Single Step to turn off the Single Step feature.

- **Using the MsgBox action** If you suspect that a value of a control may be causing a problem at some point within the macro, you can add a MsgBox action that displays the value of that control at any point in the macro. Add a MsgBox action where desired among the steps of the macro, and for the Message argument, enter the name of the control you want to check. For example, if you want to show the value of a control named Amount Due in a form named Billing, you would enter the following expression in the Message argument:

```
=Forms![Billing]![Amount Due]
```

 How can I run a Visual Basic function from a macro?

To run a VBA function from a macro, add a RunCode action to the macro. In the Function Name argument, enter the name of the desired function.

 Can I prevent the warning messages and dialog boxes that may appear as a result of a macro's actions?

You can suppress the warning messages that may appear while your macro runs. At the start of the macro, add a SetWarnings action, and set the Warnings On argument to No. This action is the equivalent of telling Access to press ENTER whenever a warning message box appears. If you use this technique, you may want to add another SetWarnings action at the end of the macro, with the Warnings On argument set to Yes, to turn the warnings back on.

 How can I run another Windows application from a macro?

To run another application, add the RunApp action to your macro. In the Command Line argument, enter the command needed to start the program.

Tip: *If you don't know the precise wording (including the path) for a command line, and an icon exists on the desktop for the program you want to run, right-click the program's icon and choose P̲roperties from the shortcut menu. Click the Shortcut tab in the dialog box that appears. You'll find the text of the command line highlighted in the T̲arget box. While it is highlighted, you can press CTRL-C to copy the command line, and then switch back to Access, go to the macro in Design view, click the Command Line argument, and press CTRL-V to place the command line in the argument.*

Chapter 13

Access Charts

Answer Topics!

Access Charts @ a Glance

Access provides the ability to produce charts in forms and reports, based on numeric data stored in your tables or accessible through your queries. Access uses Microsoft Graph, an application provided with Access and other Microsoft Office 2000 products, to create charts that appear as objects within the forms or reports. The questions in this chapter are divided into two areas:

Working with Charts answers questions about the basic creation and formatting of charts.

Troubleshooting provides answers to problems that arise when using charts in Access forms and reports.

WORKING WITH CHARTS

How do I create a chart?

The easiest way to create a chart is with the aid of the Chart Wizard, which presents a series of questions and, depending on your answers, either summarizes in a single chart the data from all the records or creates a record-based chart that changes as you move from record to record. Figure 13-1 shows an example of a chart in an Access form.

✳ ***Note:*** *To use the Chart Wizard, you must have Microsoft Graph installed on your system. Microsoft Graph is supplied with Access and with Office 2000 Professional, but it isn't installed with Access by default. You may need to rerun Setup to add Microsoft Graph.*

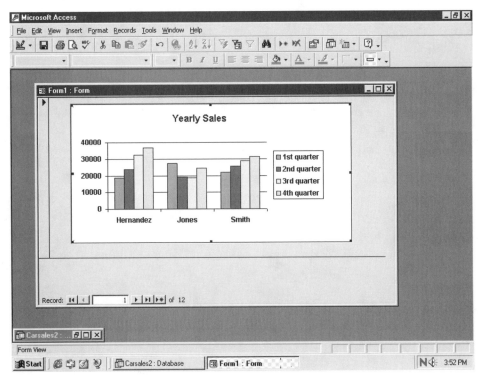

Figure 13-1 A chart placed in an Access form

You can use these steps to add a chart to an existing form or report:

1. Open the form or report in Design view.

2. Choose Insert | Chart.

3. In the form or report, click where you want to place the chart. In a moment, the first Chart Wizard dialog box appears.

4. Follow the directions in the Chart Wizard dialog boxes to create a chart based on the fields that you select within the underlying table or query.

5. Save the form or report. Switch to Form view or Report Print Preview to see the finished chart.

You can use these steps to create a new chart from scratch:

1. In the Database window, click the Forms tab to create a form containing a chart, or click the Reports tab to create a report with a chart.

2. Click New.

3. In the dialog box that appears, select the table or query that will supply the data for the chart.

4. Click Chart Wizard and then click OK.

5. Follow the directions in the Chart Wizard dialog boxes to create a chart based on the fields that you select within the underlying table or query.

6. Save the form or report. Switch to Form view or Report Print Preview to see the finished chart.

I don't like my chart's colors, chart type, and fonts. How can I modify the chart?

You make modifications to charts by editing them within Microsoft Graph (the mini-application that's used to create and edit charts within Access, Word, and PowerPoint). Open in Design view the form or report containing the chart, and then double-click the chart. In a moment, the menus change to reflect the options of Microsoft Graph, as shown in Figure 13-2.

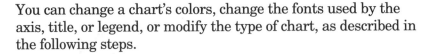

You can change a chart's colors, change the fonts used by the axis, title, or legend, or modify the type of chart, as described in the following steps.

● **Change the color of markers in a chart** First select the marker (make sure that all six selection handles appear on the data marker that you want to format), right-click it, and choose Format Data Point from the shortcut menu. Click the Patterns tab in the next dialog box, click a color to select it, and then click OK.

● **Change the fonts used for labeling an axis, a title, or the chart's legend** Right-click the label, title, or legend that you want to change, and then choose Format from the shortcut menu. (The menu provides an option called either Format Axis, Format Legend, or Format Chart Title, depending on which object you selected.) Click the Font tab in the next dialog box, choose the desired fonts, and then click OK.

● **Change the type of chart (for example, from a bar chart to a line chart)** Choose Chart | Chart Type and click the Standard Types tab in the dialog box that appears (if it isn't already selected). On the left side of the dialog box, click the chart type that you want to use. On the right side, click the subtype and then click OK.

After you make the changes to the chart, click anywhere outside the chart to return to the normal Access menus. When you view or print the form or report, the changes will appear in the chart.

Tip: *More formatting options are available in Microsoft Graph than this chapter can reasonably cover. However, while you are editing a chart, you can get detailed help that is specific to charts. Get into Microsoft Graph by using the steps previously described, and then choose Help | Microsoft Graph Help. The Help screens that appear provide specifics on the use of Microsoft Graph.*

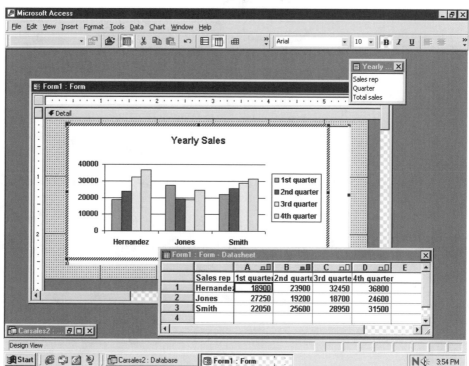

Figure 13-2 The Microsoft Graph window

 How can I change a chart's data series?

In some cases, you may want to swap the data series used by a chart. For example, suppose that you have a column chart that displays sales over 12 months for multiple geographic regions of a sales force. You need the columns to indicate each region, but by default, the columns represent the months. You solve this type of problem by changing the data series used for the chart, as follows:

1. Open in Design view the form or report containing the chart.

2. Double-click the chart to make it active.

3. Select either Series in <u>R</u>ows or Series in <u>C</u>olumns from the <u>D</u>ata menu. After you make a selection, the chart changes in appearance to match your selection.

 ### How can I change the appearance of a 3-D chart?

The Chart Wizard makes certain assumptions about appearance when you create a 3-D chart. You can change the default appearance of a 3-D chart with these steps:

1. Open in Design view the form or report containing the chart.

2. Double-click the 3-D chart to activate it.

3. Choose <u>C</u>hart | 3-D <u>V</u>iew to display the 3-D View dialog box, shown here:

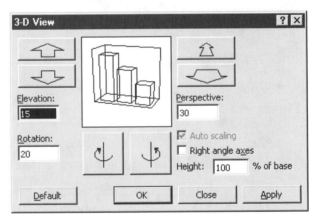

4. To change the elevation of the chart, use the up or down arrow buttons located above the <u>E</u>levation text box, or enter a value in the <u>E</u>levation text box.

5. To change the rotation of the chart, use the left or right rotation buttons located to the right of the <u>R</u>otation text box, or enter a value in the <u>R</u>otation text box.

6. To change the perspective of the chart, use the up or down arrow buttons located above the <u>P</u>erspective text box, or enter a value in the <u>P</u>erspective text box.

7. Click OK.

TROUBLESHOOTING

Why can't I put my chart's columns in the order that I want?

You can't change the actual order of the columns within Microsoft Graph; this is determined by the order of the fields providing the data in your underlying table or query. You could modify the query, by moving the fields around so that they fall in the order that you want, and then rerun the Chart Wizard to build a new chart. But there's another way to do this without discarding the existing chart. You can change the order of the data in the Row Source property for the form or report containing the chart. Use these steps:

1. Open in Design view the form or report containing the chart.

2. Click the chart to select it, and then choose <u>V</u>iew | <u>P</u>roperties to display the Properties window for the chart.

3. Click the Data tab and then click in the Row Source property.

4. Click the Build button to the right of the property. A Query Builder window for the Row Source property opens, like that shown in Figure 13-3.

5. In the window, rearrange the fields in the order that you want them to appear as the markers in the chart, from left to right.

6. Close the query and save the changes.

When you redisplay the form or open the report, the chart columns will appear in the proper order.

Why does my chart appear dimmed or blank?

This problem occurs when the Row Source property for a chart is no longer valid. (Typically, this happens because the underlying query has been renamed or deleted.)

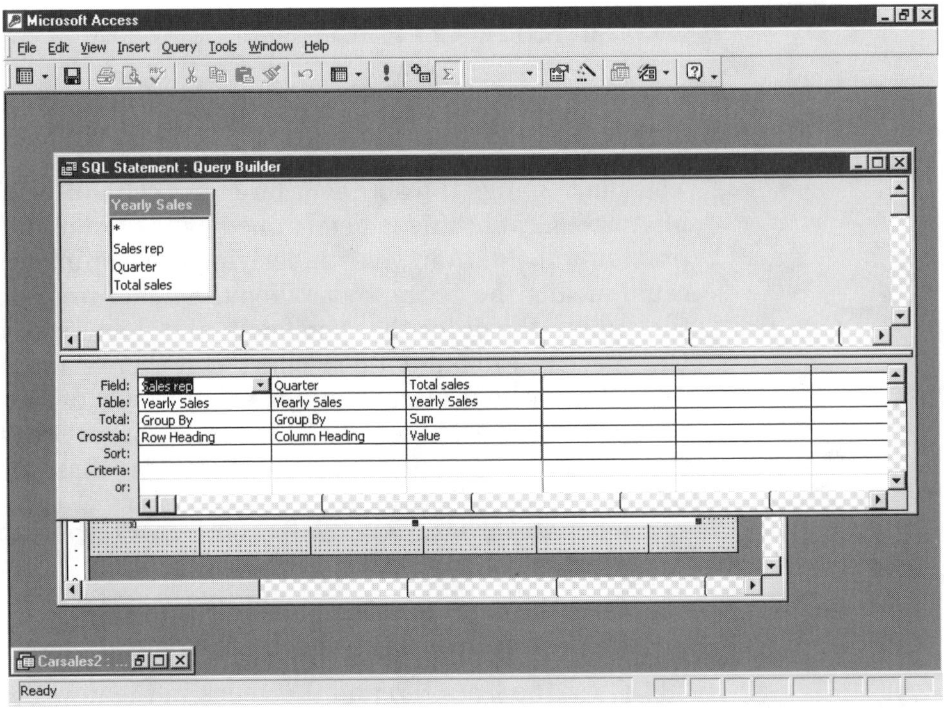

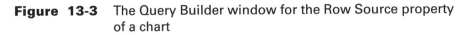

Figure 13-3   The Query Builder window for the Row Source property of a chart

Use these steps to find out if a chart's Row Source property is still valid:

1. Open in Design view the form or report containing the chart.

2. Click the chart to select it, and then choose <u>V</u>iew | <u>P</u>roperties to display the Properties window for the chart.

3. Click the Data tab and then click in the Row Source property.

4. Make sure that the Row Source property box contains a valid entry. Make any needed edits to the entry, and save the form or report.

 Why can't I change the names of the labels on my chart?

When you use Microsoft Graph to change the wording of any labels for chart axes, they are overwritten by the names of

the fields in the table or query that supplies the data. If you want axes labels that are different from your field names, you need to change the query specified by the Row Source property of the chart. Use these steps:

1. Open in Design view the form or report containing the chart.

2. Click the chart to select it, and then choose View | Properties to display the Properties window for the chart.

3. Click the Data tab and then click in the Row Source property.

4. Click the Build button (...) to the right of the property. A Query Builder window for the Row Source property opens, like that shown earlier in Figure 13-3.

5. In the query, enter the name that you want to use, followed by a colon in front of the actual name of the field. For example, if you want a field named Jan to read as January 2000 in the chart, enter **January 2000:Jan** as a name in the Query field.

6. Close the query and save the changes.

When you redisplay the form or open the report, the label will contain the wording that you indicated.

Chapter 14

Access and the Internet

Answer Topics!

Access and the Internet @ a Glance

A major difference between the most recent versions of Access and all versions prior to Access 97 is the addition of capabilities for working with the Internet. The current version of Access provides features for publishing data to static HTML, dynamic HTX/IDC, and ASP formats, ready for uploading to your Web server. Access 2000 also provides hyperlinks as an available data type with Access databases.

This chapter answers questions that arise when you are using the features of Access that are designed to link to the Internet or to a corporate intranet. Questions throughout the chapter fall into these three areas:

- **Working with Hyperlinks** answers questions about hyperlinks, which let you jump to other files, to locations within other Office documents, or to Web sites from within Access.

- **Access and the Web** answers questions about the Web features of Access in general, and how you can produce files that can be published on the Internet or on an intranet.

- **Troubleshooting** helps you quickly overcome problems that arise when working with data on the Web, when using links, and when exporting files for uploading to a Web server.

WORKING WITH HYPERLINKS

What is a hyperlink?

A *hyperlink* is a link from Access to a Web site, to a location in another file on your hard disk or on the local area network (LAN), or to another object in the Access database.

Hyperlink fields in Access tables accept entries that are in the form of either of the following:

- **Uniform Resource Locator (URL)** The standard way of naming locations on the Internet and on private intranets.
  A Web site address, such as http://www.microsoft.com, is a URL.

- **Uniform Naming Convention (UNC)** The standard way of identifying file locations under Windows. UNC addresses include paths to files on an attached hard disk, such as G:\Data\Documents\Smith\sales99.xls, or on other computers on the LAN, such as \\server2\vpath1\ Smith\sales99.xls.

How do I create hyperlinks as part of a table design?

Access 2000 includes the Hyperlink field type as an available field type during the table creation process. Hence, adding a hyperlink to a table is as simple as choosing Hyperlink from the list of available data types. Open the table that you want to add a hyperlink to in Design view, click inside the Field Name column, and enter a name for the field. Then choose Hyperlink from the drop-down list. After you save the table's structure, you can open the table in Datasheet view and enter the desired addresses in the Hyperlink fields of the table.

After the Hyperlink field exists in the table, you can insert hyperlink addresses in the field by clicking the field and then either choosing Insert | Hyperlink or clicking the Insert Hyperlink button on the toolbar. This causes an Insert Hyperlink dialog box to appear (see Figure 14-1), which you can use to specify the hyperlink address. (An alternative method of entering the address is to type the URL or filename and path into the Hyperlink field.)

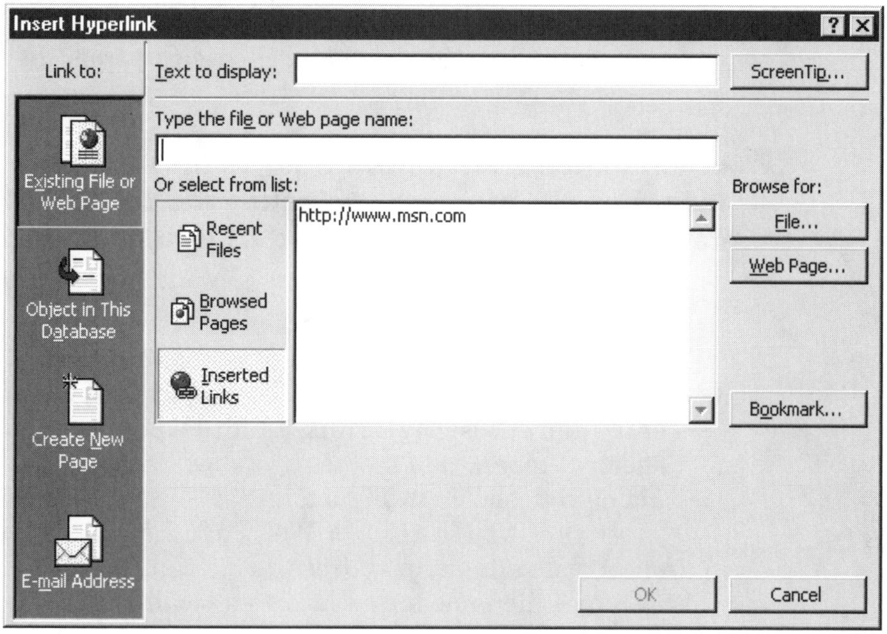

Figure 14-1 The Insert Hyperlink dialog box

Tip: *Hyperlinks can also be used to jump to locations in other Office documents or to files created with other Windows applications. For example, you can use hyperlinks to jump to a slide in a PowerPoint presentation, to a bookmark in a Word document, or to a named range in an Excel worksheet. When you use a hyperlink to identify a file created with another Windows application as the location for the hyperlink, a jump to that file causes it to be opened by the Windows application associated with the file type.*

How can I delete a hyperlink that's stored in a table?

You can delete the entry in a Hyperlink field of a table by performing these steps:

1. Open the table or query containing the Hyperlink field, or open a form that displays the data.

2. Locate the hyperlink entry in the record that you want to delete.

3. In the cell of the datasheet or in the control of the form, right-click the entry and choose Cut from the shortcut menu that appears.

When I click a Hyperlink field to edit the link, Access launches my browser and takes me to the link. How can I edit a hyperlink instead of jumping to it?

If you want to edit the entry that's stored in a Hyperlink field, you can't just click the field. Because Access is designed to use hyperlinks as jump points, clicking the field always results in a jump to the link. To edit the link, right-click the entry and choose Hyperlink | Edit Hyperlink from the shortcut menu. In a moment, you see the Edit Hyperlink dialog box, shown in Figure 14-2.

In the Type the File or Web Page Name text box, you enter the valid jump address. (This can be a URL for a Web site, or a filename for a file stored locally or on an attached

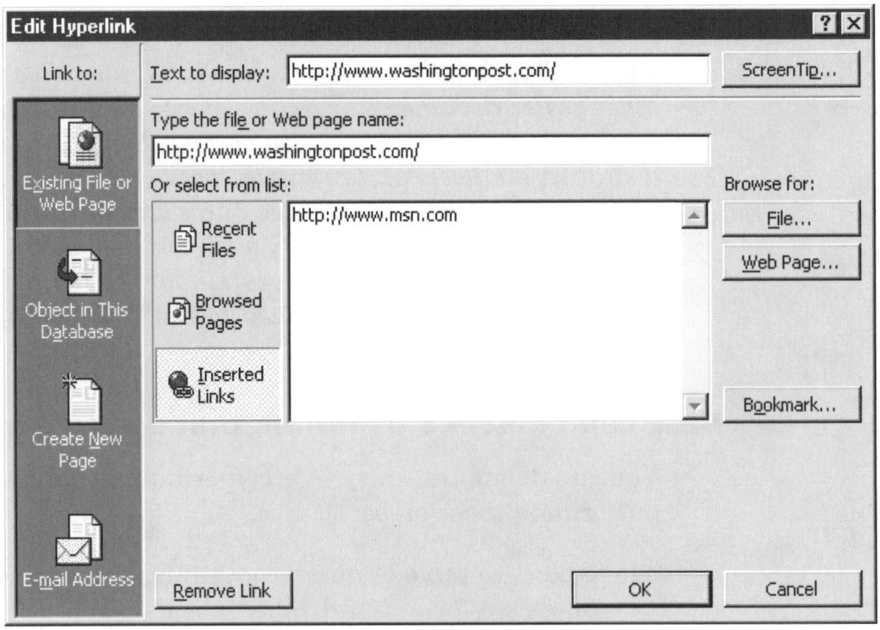

Figure 14-2 The Edit Hyperlink dialog box

network.) Optionally, you can use the File button to browse to another Office 2000 document or use the Bookmark button to browse to a specific location within another Office document that you want to jump to. This can be the name of a Word bookmark, a named range in an Excel worksheet, or a slide number within a PowerPoint presentation. In the Text to Display box, you can enter text that is to be displayed as the title of the link. (If you omit this entry, the text displayed is the same as the entry that you place in the Type the File or Web Page Name text box.)

Can I create a label in a form to serve as a hyperlink?

Yes. If a user of the form clicks the label, Access makes the jump to the link. Use these steps to add a label that serves as a link:

1. Open the form in Design view.

2. Choose Insert | Hyperlink, or click the Insert Hyperlink button on the toolbar. The Insert Hyperlink dialog box appears, as shown earlier in Figure 14-1.

3. In the Type the File or Web Page Name text box, enter the address for the hyperlink. (You can click the File button at the right to open a dialog box in which you can browse for the location of a file.) If you want to create a link to another object in the current Access database, click the Object in this Database icon at the left side of the dialog box, and then select the desired database object within the dialog box.

4. Click OK. Access adds a label to the form, with the text of the label containing the address for the link.

5. Right-click the label, choose Properties, and then click the Format tab in the Properties window that opens.

6. Change the Caption property to your preference and make any changes that you want to the size and fonts used for the label.

7. Save the form by choosing File | Save.

After you save the form, you can test the link by switching to Form view and clicking the label.

How can I add a picture to a form so that users can click the picture to follow a hyperlink?

Using an existing graphic (such as a Windows Paintbrush bitmap or an icon), you can add a picture to a form to serve as a hyperlink. When users click the picture, Access makes the jump to the link. Use these steps:

1. Open the form in Design view.

2. In the Toolbox, click the Image tool. (If the Toolbox isn't visible, choose View | Toolbox to display it.)

3. In the form, click where you want to create the picture.

4. In the Insert Picture dialog box that appears, locate the picture file and click OK to add the picture to the form.

5. With the Image control selected, choose View | Properties to open the Properties window for the control.

6. Click the Format tab and enter the desired address for the hyperlink in the Hyperlink Address property. (You can click the Build button, which appears at the right after you click the property, to open the Insert Hyperlink dialog box, which you can use to enter a URL or browse for the location of a file. If you want to create a link to another object in the current Access database, click the Object in This Database icon at the left side of the dialog box, and then select the database object within the dialog box.)

7. After you enter the URL or choose the file or other database object to serve as the hyperlink, click OK.

8. Save the form by choosing File | Save.

After you save the form, you can test the link by switching to Form view and clicking the image.

ACCESS AND THE WEB

How can I display a Web page on a form?

If you have Internet Explorer 3 or higher installed on your system, you can display Web pages within forms by adding a Web Browser control to the form. (The Web Browser control is an ActiveX control. It is not provided with Access, but is installed automatically as part of the installation of Microsoft Internet Explorer.) Figure 14-3 shows the use of a Web Browser control within an Access form.

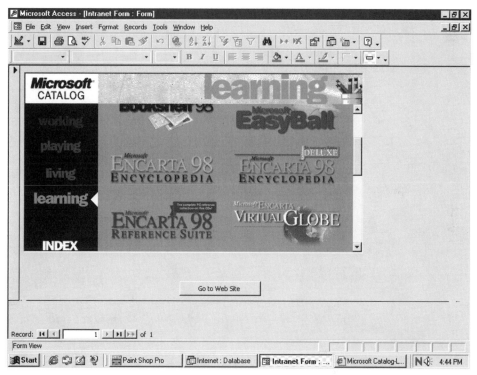

Figure 14-3 A Web Browser control used to display a Web page within a form in Access

Use these steps to add a control that lets you display a Web page:

1. Open the form in Design view.

2. In the Toolbox, click the More Controls tool to open a menu that contains all ActiveX controls installed on your system.

3. In the menu of ActiveX controls, choose the Microsoft Web Browser control.

4. In the form, click where you want to place the control. A rectangle appears, representing the Web Browser control.

5. Size and move the control to the desired location in the form.

After you insert the control, you can use the Navigate method for the control to jump to Web sites. You do this by using Visual Basic for Applications (VBA). The syntax for the method is *ControlName*.Navigate *"Resource-location"*, where *ControlName* is the name of the Web Browser control and *Resource-location* is the URL for the Web site. As an example, you could place a button in the form that, when clicked, would open Microsoft's Web site in the control. Assuming that you named the Web Browser control MyBrowser, the code attached to the On Click property of the command button would look like this:

```
Private Sub Command1_Click
    MyBrowser.Navigate "http://www.microsoft.com"
End Sub
```

 Tip: *If the Web Browser control is too small to show the full width or height of the Web page, the control will include scroll bars; but making the control wide enough to display the full width of the average Web page is usually best, so that your users aren't forced to resort to unnecessary horizontal scrolling.*

What are the differences between the file formats that Access can produce for publishing to the Web?

When you use the File | Export command, Access can produce Web pages in static form or in dynamic form, which differ as follows:

- **Static Web pages** These are saved under the HTML file format. They can be used with all Web servers, but they display static data—when data in the tables or queries changes, the HTML files produced are not updated automatically to reflect any changes.

- **Dynamic Web pages** These can be saved to HTX/IDC (HTML Extension/Internet Database Connector) format or to Microsoft ASP (Active Server Pages) format. These pages automatically reflect any changes made to the underlying Access tables or queries, but they are not compatible with all Web servers. The dynamic files require either the Microsoft Internet Information Server (IIS) with the IDC Add-In, Microsoft Personal Web Server, Windows NT Workstation with Peer Web Services, or another Web server that is fully compatible with the HTX/IDC or ASP file format.

How can I save a table, query, form, or report in HTML format?

Use the File | Export command. You can use these steps:

1. In the Database window, select the desired table, query, form, or report.

2. Choose File | Export to open the Export dialog box.

3. Choose the location and enter a name for the file in the File Name box. In the Save as Type box, change the selection to HTML Documents.

4. Click <u>S</u>ave to create the HTML file in the specified location.

 How can I publish to my company's intranet my HTML files that Access creates?

The precise steps will vary depending on what type of server your company's intranet uses, so contacting the Webmaster at your company for help first is a wise choice. If your company's intranet is running under Microsoft's IIS or Personal Web Server, you can use the following steps to publish your HTML files:

1. Using Windows Explorer, copy the HTML files that you created (choose <u>F</u>ile | <u>E</u>xport in Access) to a folder under the root directory of the Web server. For Microsoft IIS, the default root directory is \Inetpub\Wwwroot. For Microsoft Personal Web Server, the default root directory is \Webshare\Wwwroot.

2. Copy any related files, such as graphics or linked files, to the folder.

3. Using Microsoft FrontPage or your choice of Web publishing software, create the necessary links to the stored files.

TROUBLESHOOTING

 When I try to open a Web page saved in IDC format, I get an error message saying "Error HTTP/1.0 Access Forbidden." What's wrong?

This error occurs if you don't have Read or Execute permission for the virtual directory on the Web server where the files are stored. Contact the Webmaster for the server and request access rights to the appropriate directory on the server.

 After I use the File | Export command to create ASP or Dynamic HTX/IDC files on our Web server, I get the message "Data source name not found" when I try to view the Web page. Why is this happening?

There are two possible reasons for this error. Either you didn't create a system DSN data source on the Web server or the dynamic files that you created in Access for the Web server contain an incorrect data source name (DSN). You can use these steps to check the DSN or add a new DSN:

1. Go to your Web server and double-click the ODBC icon in Control Panel.

2. In the Data Sources dialog box, click System DSN.

3. If you don't see the name of the system DSN that you used in the Output Options dialog box when you created the file, click Add.

4. Click Microsoft Access Driver and then click Finish.

5. Fill in the entries in the ODBC Microsoft Access Setup dialog box that appears. Note that the name you enter in the Data Source Name box is the same name that you must use in the Data Source Name box shown in the Publish to the Web Wizard of Access.

6. Click OK to close the ODBC Microsoft Access Setup dialog box.

7. Click OK to close the ODBC Data Source Administrator box.

8. If the DSN that you entered on the Web server differs from the DSN that you entered when you saved the HTX/IDC or ASP file, use the File | Export command again and rebuild your Web pages, entering the correct DSN when prompted.

 ### When I click a hyperlink, an error message appears. What's wrong?

This problem occurs when, for one reason or another, Access cannot locate the resource that's specified by the hyperlink. If the destination is in another file, the file may have been renamed or moved. Use My Computer or Windows Explorer to check for the existence of the file. If the file has been renamed or is in a different location, you need to change the hyperlink accordingly. To edit the hyperlink, right-click the hyperlink and choose Hyperlink | Edit Hyperlink from the shortcut menu.

If the resource is on the Internet, check to make sure that you have access to the Internet. If you can reach the Internet, the server on which the resource is located is probably busy or unavailable.

If the resource is on your company's intranet, check your network connections to be sure that your company's Web server is accessible. You may want to check with your network administrator to ensure that you have access rights to the resource.

When I try to export an action query as HTML, I get the message, "An action query cannot be used as a row source." What's wrong?

This behavior is an intentional design trait of Access because the purpose of action queries is to create other tables or modify data within tables. You cannot export action queries to any of the Web server file formats (HTML, IDC, or ASP). To work around this, use the action query as a data source for a make-table query. Run the make-table query to create a new table, and then export the table as HTML.

When I export a form with a subform as HTML, only the data from the main form appears in the HTML document. What happened to the data from the subform?

This is a design limitation. When forms containing subforms are exported as HTML, only the records visible in the main form are exported to the file. To get around this, create a relational query that contains all the data that you need, and then export the query to an HTML file.

Why are my subforms blank when I browse Active Server Pages (ASP) files under Windows NT Workstation?

This is a known bug that occurs when using Internet Explorer 3 or 3.01 running on Windows NT 4. Under Windows 95 or Windows 98, when ASP files contain a subform, the subform is displayed in a separate instance of Internet Explorer; but under Windows NT 4, the second instance of Internet Explorer that is needed to display the subform fails to launch. No workaround exists other than to upgrade your version of Internet Explorer or use a platform other than Windows NT 4 to display the subform data at the Web page.

I use a table containing hyperlinks to jump to different links. As I do this repeatedly, my system response slows to a crawl. What's wrong?

This is a trait of the way hyperlinks call needed applications, particularly other Microsoft Office applications such as Word, Excel, and PowerPoint. When you click a series of hyperlinks in succession, all of the programs needed to open those resources are loaded into memory. As you click another hyperlink, the previous program is not automatically released from memory. If you jump to multiple locations on the Internet from the hyperlinks in your Access database, your system may load multiple instances of your Web browser. (We confirmed this behavior with both Microsoft Internet Explorer and Netscape Navigator.) You need to keep track of your system resources visually by glancing at the Windows taskbar. If applications that you no longer need are open, close them by right-clicking the application's icon in the taskbar and choosing Close from the shortcut menu.

Chapter 15

Access and Visual Basic for Applications

Answer Topics!

Access and Visual Basic for Applications @ a Glance

Visual Basic for Applications (VBA) is a programming language that can be used as a part of Access applications. Blocks of VBA code are saved as procedures in modules. You can run these procedures either separately or as part of other database objects. The answers provided in this chapter all deal with VBA and are divided into the following areas:

- **VBA Basics** provides important definitions for various objects you'll work with as you write VBA code.

- **Using VBA with Access** answers questions about performing various operations through the use of VBA code.

VBA BASICS

 What is an event?

An *event* is a specific occurrence that takes place on or inside of an Access object. Events in Access include mouse clicks on buttons, the focus moving into or out of a control, forms opening or closing, and a section of a report being formatted for printing. Events are generally the result of the user doing something to an Access object. Most VBA programming revolves around events and how the Access environment should react to those events.

 What is an event procedure?

An event procedure is a Sub procedure associated with a particular event property of a form or report. When the particular event occurs, Access calls the event procedure. All the event procedures for a form or report are saved with the form or report. Access assigns each event procedure a specific name that indicates the control and the event to which the procedure is assigned. For example, the event procedure in Figure 15-1 runs when you click the button named PrintThis.

 What is a function?

A function (also occasionally referred to as a *function procedure*) is a specialized program that returns a value. When the function is called by an Access object, it performs a calculation of some sort and then returns a value to the object that called it. Access provides numerous built-in functions; for example, the =Now() function returns the current date and time. To construct custom functions that Access doesn't provide, VBA code is commonly used. For example, you could use VBA code to provide a function that would return the date of the first Monday after any given date, or a function that would accept a length and width in feet and return the number of square yards of the measured area.

When you use functions, you provide the function with information in the form of *arguments*. Arguments can be thought of as specific definitions for the function. They provide the additional information VBA needs to handle the

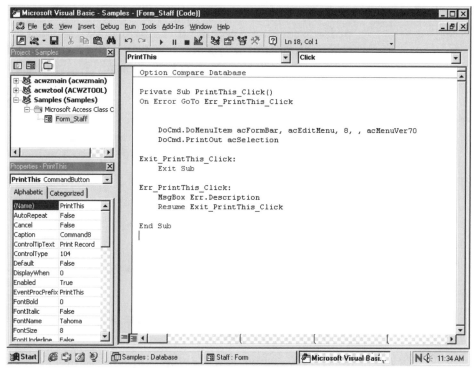

Figure 15-1   An event procedure assigned to an event on a form

task exactly as you prefer. The arguments follow the name of the function, and they are enclosed in parentheses.

 What is a module?

Modules are named collections of VBA code. Access supports two types of modules:

- **Standard modules**   These modules contain code that should be available to other procedures throughout your database. They are visible when you click the Modules button in the Database window.

- **Class modules**   These modules contain definitions for new objects. They are stored as part of forms or reports.

Each module has a declarations section, which stores information such as user-defined data types, global constants, global variables, and references to external procedures in a dynamic link library (DLL). The rest of the module contains Function and Sub procedures. The information in the Declarations section is available to all the procedures in that module.

You can store all of your VBA code in one module or in several different ones. A form or report can have its own module to store the procedures it uses. This module gathers all the procedures for a form or report into one location. However, a form or report can also perform procedures that are in a separate module.

What is a recordset?

Recordsets represent data from a base table or from the result of a query. Access has three types of recordsets: tables, dynasets, and snapshots.

What is the difference between a Sub procedure and a Function procedure?

A *Sub* procedure is a routine that carries out an operation but cannot return a value. A *function* procedure carries out an operation but can also return a value and can be used in an expression. Function procedures can be used in any other place in which you would use one of Access's built-in functions. Function procedures include a statement that assigns a value to the function's name. Figure 15-2 shows both a Function procedure and a Sub procedure.

Tip: *The easy way to differentiate between the two types of procedures is to determine whether the procedure returns a value. If it does, it's a Function procedure. If it doesn't, it's a Sub procedure.*

What is the Variant data type?

The Variant data type is a special kind of data type in VBA. Unlike the other data types, which can hold only a certain data format, Variant variables can hold numbers, strings, dates, and nulls. Variant is the default data type when VBA

Function procedure

```
Microsoft Visual Basic - Samples - [Form_Staff (Code)]
File  Edit  View  Insert  Debug  Run  Tools  Add-Ins  Window  Help
                                                        Ln 11, Col 1
(General)                          HrsMinsSecs

Option Compare Database
Function HrsMinsSecs()
Dim Hrs As Long, Mins As String, Secs As String
If IsNull(TimeVar) Then
    HrsMinsSecs = Null
Else
    Mins = Format(DatePart("n", TimeVar), "00")
    Secs = Format(DatePart("s", TimeVar), "00")
    Hrs = (Fix(TimeVar) * 24) + DatePart("h", TimeVar)
    HrsMinsSecs = Hrs & ":" & Mins & ":" & Secs
End If
End Function

Private Sub PrintThis_Click()
On Error GoTo Err_PrintThis_Click


    DoCmd.DoMenuItem acFormBar, acEditMenu, 8, , acMenuVer70
    DoCmd.PrintOut acSelection

Exit_PrintThis_Click:
    Exit Sub

Err_PrintThis_Click:
    MsgBox Err.Description
    Resume Exit_PrintThis_Click

Start    Samples : Database    Staff : Form    Microsoft Visual Basi...    11:38 AM
```

Sub procedure

Figure 15-2 Module window showing a Sub procedure and a Function procedure

is used within Access, and it is useful in making your module more flexible. Its advantages are that you do not need to declare a data type and that you can switch from one type to another. The disadvantage is that it may use more memory.

You use the Variant data type when you are not sure which data type you will be working with, or when you know that a variable will have more than one type of data.

Macros or VBA?

One question that's common to those who are beginning to extend the limits of Access by programming in VBA is whether to use VBA or to use macros for a specific task. Access is unique among the Office 2000 products in that it provides two ways to handle many complex programming-type tasks: with macros or with VBA. Because many tasks can be performed equally well with either macros or VBA, some guidelines may help in deciding which approach to use with your specific tasks.

Macros work well when you need to automate the opening and closing of forms and the printing of reports. Macros also provide an easy way to quickly prototype simple to moderately complex applications in Access. And some tasks *require* the use of macros, such as an action that is carried out when a database is initially loaded. (Of course, that macro action could be to run a VBA procedure.)

Visual Basic is a better choice when you want tight control over your application or when you want a minimum of clutter. Any complex application built entirely with macros has a Database window with several complex macros, and keeping track of which macro is used for what purpose can be difficult. Conversely, VBA code can be integrated directly into the design of your queries, forms, and reports, resulting in a database that is less cluttered with objects and thus easier to maintain.

VBA is also required when you want to create functions that perform specialized tasks beyond the range of what's possible with the functions built into Access. And you can use VBA to respond to error messages that might otherwise confuse the users of your application.

Finally, VBA is the choice when you want to perform complex operations outside of Access, while under the control of an Access application. You can use a macro to run a Windows or DOS program, but you can't do much else. With VBA, you can do the following:

- Read and write files at the operating system level
- Use Automation or Dynamic Data Exchange (DDE) to communicate with other Windows applications, such as Microsoft Word and Excel
- Call functions stored in Windows DLLs

USING VBA WITH ACCESS

 Where can I add the functions that I have written?

You can place the functions that you create in the same places where you use any of the built-in Access functions, which include several locations throughout your databases:

- The Control Source property of an unbound text box on a form or report, where it provides the contents of the text box.

- An event property of a form or report. For example, to have a procedure be performed when the user clicks a command button, assign the procedure to the button's On Click property.

- The Field/Expression column of the Sorting and Grouping dialog box, used to sort and group data in a report.

- The Field line in a query's QBE grid, where it provides the entry for that field in the query's datasheet.

- The Criteria line in a query's QBE grid, where it tells Access which data to choose with the query.

- The Update To line in an update query, where it supplies the new table entry made by the query.

- The Condition column of a macro, where it chooses when to perform a macro action.

- The Expression argument of a SetValue macro action, where it sets what the item argument equals.

- The Function Name argument in a RunCode macro action.

- Another Function or Sub procedure.

How can I convert macros in my forms to VBA code?

Access 2000 can convert macros on forms and reports to VBA code. To convert your macros to code, open the form in Design view and choose Tools | Macro | Convert Form's Macros to Visual Basic.

 Can a VBA procedure create a form or report?

Yes. Use the CreateForm or CreateReport function to create a form or report by using VBA. These functions create a form or report that is empty, except for what the template places on the design document. (The *template* is simply an existing form or report that is used as the model for the new form or report.) The following is the syntax for these functions:

CreateForm([*database*[, *form template*]])

CreateReport([*database*[, *report template*]])

Database is the name identifying the database that contains the template. *Form template* or *report template* is the name of the existing form or report that is used as the template. Note that if you omit *database*, Access uses the current database. If you omit *form template* or *report template* (or if the named template is missing), Access uses the form or report template specified on the Forms/Reports tab of the Options dialog box, which you can access by choosing Tools | Options. After the procedure creates the form or report, other VBA statements can add controls and make property changes. The statements create forms and reports that are minimized, so you may want to add a DoCmd.Restore statement after creating the form or report, to open it.

As an example, the following code, attached to the On Click property of a command button, creates a new report when the button is clicked. The new report's sections are based on an existing report named Sales.

```
Private Sub Command0_Click()
    Dim MyReport As Report
    Set MyReport = CreateReport(, "Sales") 'Create the
report
    DoCmd.Restore            ' Restore report.
End Sub
```

 Can I use VBA to create a table?

You can manipulate TableDef objects by using VBA to create tables on the fly, under the control of your VBA code. You use the Dim statement to declare your TableDef and Field variables; then, you assign a name to the TableDef variable, and assign field names to the Field variables. Finally, you use the Append and Refresh methods of the TableDef object to add the fields to the table object and store the table in the current database. The following code provides an example of how this can be done:

```
Private Sub Command15_Click()
    ' Declare variables.
    Dim MyDb As Database, MyTable As TableDef, MyField As Field
    ' Assign the current database to the MyDb variable.
    Set MyDb = CurrentDb
    ' Create the new table and assign it to the MyTable variable.
    Set MyTable = MyDb.CreateTableDef("Orders")
    ' Create three text fields and assign them to variables.
    Set MyField = MyTable.CreateField("OrderID", dbText)
    MyTable.Fields.Append MyField
    Set MyField = MyTable.CreateField("ItemName", dbText)
    MyTable.Fields.Append MyField
    Set MyField = MyTable.CreateField("SalesRep", dbText)
    MyTable.Fields.Append MyField
    ' Append the fields to the table object and store it
    ' in the database.
    MyDb.TableDefs.Append MyTable
    MyDb.TableDefs.Refresh
End Sub
```

The code is attached to the On Click event for a command button on a form. When the button is clicked, the code creates a new table called Orders, containing three text fields called OrderID, ItemName, and SalesRep. (If you create and run this code, to be able to see the new table, you need to switch to any other tab in the Database window and then switch back to the Tables tab.)

 Why doesn't my Database window show the TableDef object in the list of tables?

Access does not automatically refresh the Database window when you create TableDef objects. To see the newly created TableDef object in the Database window, choose another list of objects, such as queries, and then switch back to the list of tables. The Database window then refreshes its list, and the TableDef object appears.

 How can I declare the type of data returned by a function?

You can declare the data type that a function returns by specifying the desired data type, preceded by the word *As*, at the end of the statement containing the function. For example, if you wanted Access to use a function called Sales() to return a value, and you wanted that value returned as a currency amount, you would use this syntax:

Function Sales(*amount*) As Currency

 My code is stuck in an infinite loop. How do I stop it?

Press CTRL-BREAK to stop executing a procedure.

 Why is Access ignoring my control's input mask after I added a VBA function to assign a value to the control?

If you use VBA or a macro to assign a value to a control or field that has an input mask, Access ignores the input mask. Therefore, include the effect of the input mask in the VBA code or macro.

 I have a line of code that is very long. Can I continue it on the next line?

Yes. Whenever you want to continue a line of code on a second line, end the first line with a space followed by an underscore. Access uses the space-and-underscore combination as its line-continuation character in VBA.

Can I carry out a macro action from within a VBA procedure?

Yes. Access provides a special object type, DoCmd, that can be used to carry out macro actions from within a VBA procedure. You use one of the available methods for the DoCmd object to

perform the desired macro action. The syntax for the use of the DoCmd object is

DoCmd.*method*[*arguments*]

where *method* is the name of the method that describes the macro action, and *arguments* are the arguments for the macro action, if any are used. For example, you could add the OpenReport method of the DoCmd object to create code that would carry out the OpenReport macro action, opening a report. The following line of code in a procedure would open a report named Quarterly Sales:

```
DoCmd.OpenReport "Quarterly Sales"
```

 I want to print a procedure. When I print the module, all the code in the module prints. How can I print a single procedure in a module?

Open the module and select the entire block of code that you want to print, by clicking and dragging. Then, choose File | Print. In the Print dialog box that appears, click Selection and then click OK.

 How can I protect my VBA code from being read or changed by others?

You can save your database as an MDE file and then distribute that file for use by others. When a database is saved as an MDE file, all editable source code is removed from the database, and only a binary type of code referred to as "p-code" remains. Your VBA code will still run, but it can't be viewed or edited. In addition, users will be unable to open or modify forms or reports in Design view. You can use the following steps to save a database as an MDE file:

1. Close the database that you want to save as an MDE file, if it is open. (If you are on a network, all other users must be out of the database.)
2. Choose Tools | Database Utilities | Make MDE File.

3. In the Database to Save as MDE dialog box that appears, choose the database that you want to save as an MDE file, and then click Make MDE.

4. In the Save MDE As dialog box, specify a name and a location for the MDE file, and click Save.

 Caution: *When saving a database file as an MDE file, be sure that you keep an original copy of the database. You can't change the design of any objects in an MDE file, so if you need to make changes to the code or to forms or reports in the database, you need the original database to do so.*

How can I set the Record Source property of a form at run time?

Use the Me property to specify the current table or query for the Record Source property. An example is shown here:

Me.RecordSource = "*New Record Source*"

New Record Source represents the table or query that the form or report opened with this setting will use.

 Note: *You can also do this in a macro by adding the SetValue action. For the Item argument, enter **Forms!**[form name**].RecordSource**. For the Expression argument, enter the table name, query name, or SQL statement.*

How can I step through my Function procedure so that I can find errors?

You can execute a Function or Sub procedure one line at a time. To do this, add *breakpoints* to your procedure. Breakpoints tell Access to stop executing the code at the line of code where the breakpoint has been added. After Access stops executing the code, you can choose to execute the lines one line at a time. To place a breakpoint on a line of your code, use these steps:

1. Move to a line in the procedure where you want to place the breakpoint.

2. Choose <u>D</u>ebug | <u>T</u>oggle Breakpoint (or press F9).

3. Open the Immediate window by choosing <u>V</u>iew | <u>I</u>mmediate Window.

4. Type **?** *FunctionName*() and press ENTER, where *FunctionName* is the name of your function. Any arguments to the function are placed between the parentheses. For a Sub procedure, don't enter the parentheses. The line of code containing the breakpoint is highlighted in the Module window, and the Step Into and Step Over buttons, shown here, become active in the Debug toolbar. (If the Debug toolbar isn't visible, choose <u>V</u>iew | <u>T</u>oolbars and then choose Debug to display it.)

5. Click the Step Into or Step Over button to step through the procedure. Step Into executes one line at a time. Step Over does too, except that a call to a subroutine or function is treated as a single step.

As an example, Figure 15-3 shows the entry in the Debug window that runs the HrsMinsSecs Function procedure. After encountering the line containing the breakpoint, Access performs the remainder of the procedure one line at a time. The line of code with the circle to its left indicates the setting of the breakpoint. The highlighted line of code with the arrow to its left is the one that Access performs when you click the Step Into button.

 Note: *When you are done testing, you can choose <u>D</u>ebug | <u>C</u>lear All Breakpoints to get rid of your breakpoints.*

I have trouble with syntax in VBA. Is there an easy way to write code?

The online help provided by Access is a great source for finding correct syntax. You can open a window into your VBA code, select any keyword that you need help with, and press F1. A Visual Basic Help window appears, like the one shown at the right side of the screen in Figure 15-4. Once the Help window is

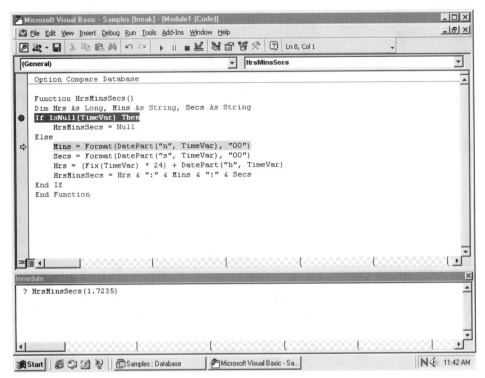

Figure 15-3 Showing a procedure as Access performs it one step at a time

open, you can also click the <u>A</u>nswer Wizard tab in the window, type a question into the text box, and click Search to see a list of help topics that correspond to your question.

Can I test the functions that I've created before I use them in my forms and reports?

You can use the Immediate window (Figure 15-5) to execute any VBA statement. To view the Immediate window, open your module and choose <u>V</u>iew | <u>I</u>mmediate Window. To test a function, in the window, use the Print method (the question mark) followed by the function. For example, you might test a

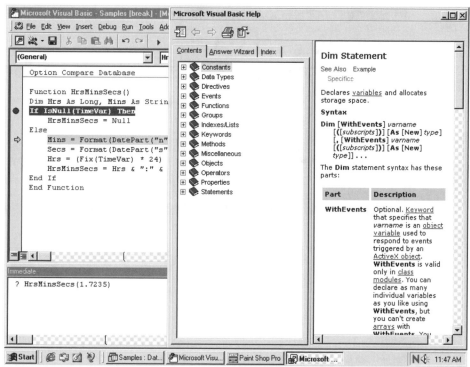

Figure 15-4 The Visual Basic Help window

function called HrsMinsSecs, designed to take a serial time value and return the equivalent hours, minutes, and seconds, by entering **? HrsMinsSecs(1.7235)** into the Immediate window. Figure 15-5 shows the results of such a test.

Can I view two procedures simultaneously?

Yes. Choose <u>W</u>indow | <u>S</u>plit. Access divides the Module window in half. At this point, both halves of the window show the same procedure. You can switch to either half to show another procedure. You can drag the split bar that divides the two halves up or down to change how much of the window

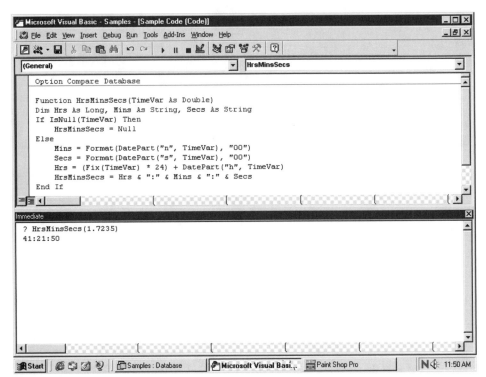

Figure 15-5 Using the Debug window to test a function

each part uses. The Split command is a toggle, so you can again choose Window | Split to remove the split when you are done. Figure 15-6 shows a Module window split between two procedures.

 Tip: *The split bar appears at the top of the right scroll bar for the Module window when the window isn't split. Dragging this split bar down is another way to split a window.*

 ### How do I replace a constant form name in my code with the contents of a variable?

You can replace Forms![*form name*] in your code with a variable name. The following example shows how to do this,

Split bar

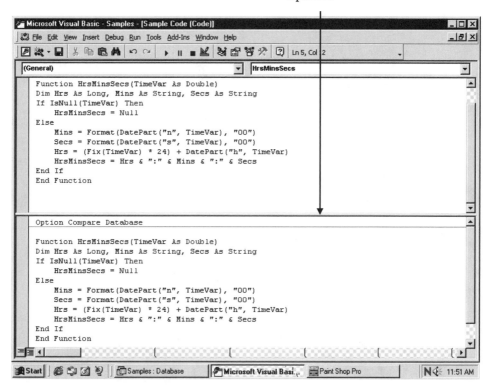

Figure 15-6 A module showing two procedures split across a window

using MyVar as the name of the variable that will equal an acceptable form name:

```
Dim MyVar as String
Let MyVar = "form name"
```

Now, you can replace Forms![*form name*] with Forms(MyVar) everywhere that it occurs in the code. To refer to a different form, just use another Let statement to assign its name to MyVar.

Chapter 16

Miscellaneous Questions

Answer Topics!

Miscellaneous Questions @ a Glance

This chapter addresses some of the miscellaneous problems you may encounter with Access that don't fit neatly into the other chapters of this book. Because these answers represent a potpourri of solutions that don't pertain to a single subject, they are grouped into two broad areas of general usage and troubleshooting. Keep in mind that if you can't find an answer here, you can also check Access's online Help system. Once you familiarize yourself with this Help system, it can provide you with all sorts of useful tips, tricks, and solutions.

- **General Usage** provides answers to challenges that arise in various areas of Access. Many of these questions involve more than one area of Access, which is why they are not tied to a specific subject elsewhere in the book.

- **Troubleshooting** helps you resolve unexpected error messages in overall areas of Access.

Using the Microsoft Knowledge Base

In addition to the built-in Help screens, Microsoft provides an excellent source of answers to technical questions at no cost, if you have Internet access. The Microsoft Knowledge Base is a searchable database with solutions to problems and usage tips for all Microsoft applications. You can gain access to the Knowledge Base through the Microsoft Personal Support Center, at this address:

http://support.microsoft.com/

From the page that appears, click Search Support. This takes you to a page where you can search the entire Knowledge Base, as shown here:

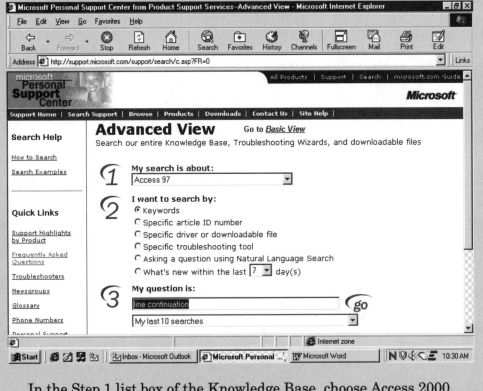

In the Step 1 list box of the Knowledge Base, choose Access 2000. You can then either select Keywords under Step 2 and enter a search term in the text box under Step 3 or select Asking a Question Using

Natural Language Search under Step 2 and enter your question in the
text box under Step 3. Click the Go button, and the Knowledge Base
will respond with one or more pages of articles that contain your
search phrase text. You can click each article name to display that
article within the Knowledge Base.

GENERAL USAGE

 **How do I capitalize the first letter of each word in a
text field?**

You can create a Function procedure that capitalizes text,
and then use this function as if it were one of Access's built-in
functions. To create this procedure, type the following into a
module:

```
Function Capitalize (Word As Variant) As String
Dim Temp As String, C As String, OldC As String, _
  X As Integer
If IsNull(Word) Then
      Exit Function
Else
      Temp = CStr(LCase(Word))
      OldC = " "
      For X = 1 to Len(Temp)
          C = Mid(Temp, X, 1)
          If C >= "a" and C <= "z" _
          and (OldC < "a" Or OldC > "z") Then
              Mid(Temp, X, 1) = UCase(C)
          End If
          OldC = C
      Next X
      Capitalize = Temp
End If
End Function
```

In the field of the query or in the Control Source property of
the text box that uses this function, change the field name to

=Capitalize([*text field name*])

For example, if an Address field of the current record contains "245 apple valley way," then =Capitalize([Address]) returns 245 Apple Valley Way.

Can I create a Function procedure that calculates a person's age?

Yes. If you know a person's date of birth, you can create a Function procedure that subtracts the person's birthday from today's date and converts into years the number of days between the two dates. You can create this procedure by typing the following into a module:

```
Function HowOld(DOB As String) As Long
Dim Birthday As Double
Birthday = CVDate(DOB)
HowOld = Fix(DateDiff("d", Birthday, Date) / 365.25)
End Function
```

With this procedure, DOB represents the date of birth. You can use this function just like you use Access's built-in functions. For example, a control in a form can have a Control Source property of HowOld([Date of Birth]). If Date Of Birth equals 7/5/66 and today is 7/14/99, this control displays 33.

How can I change the folder that Access defaults to when I choose File | Open Database?

Choose Tools | Options, and when the Options dialog box appears, click the General tab. In the Default Database Folder box, enter the full path for the new default folder, including the drive letter.

How can I speed up a report or form based on a crosstab query?

Using fixed column headings improves the performance of forms and reports that are based on crosstab queries. To create fixed column headings, display the Properties window for the query. (Open the query in Design view, right-click any blank space in the query, and choose Properties from the shortcut menu that appears.) In the Column Headings property, type the heading entries for the crosstab query, separated with commas. Supplying the column headings works only if the query has the same column headings every time you run it.

 ## How can I display the most current data while viewing data on a network?

When you're using a database that's shared with others on a network, Access automatically updates the data at regular intervals, based on the Refresh Interval setting. (Choose Tools | Options and click Advanced to change this value.) You can force Access to display the current data at any time by choosing Records | Refresh. Note, however, that this updates only the data that already exists in the datasheet or form; it doesn't display new records that have been added since you opened the query or form. To display new data, requery the records by pressing SHIFT-F9.

 ## Can I change the default font for the entire database, not just for the datasheets? I find Access's default font to be hard to read.

You can try changing your default font settings for Windows. Use these steps:

1. In the Windows taskbar, click Start and choose Settings | Control Panel.
2. In the Control Panel window that opens, double-click Display.
3. Click the Appearance tab.
4. In the Item list, click Menu.
5. Using the Font arrow, increase the font size. (For example, if the font size is 8, try a value of 10.)
6. Click OK.
7. Repeat step 5 for other items in the Item list.

Note: *The choices you make affect other Windows applications, so you should check the appearance of other software after making changes in the Control Panel.*

When I use the binoculars in any toolbar (or the equivalent Edit | Find command) to search for a record, I usually must change the Match entry in the Find dialog box to Start of Field. Can I change the default search behavior of Access?

You can do this at the Options dialog box. Choose Tools | Options and then click the Edit/Find tab in the dialog box that appears. Turn on the Start of Field Search entry under Default Find/Replace Behavior; then, click OK. (You need to exit and then restart Access before this change takes effect.)

I have two Date fields. How can I find the difference between them?

To find the difference between two dates, you simply subtract them, as in =[*first date field*] – [*second date field*]. You can enter this expression as a Calculated field in a query, as a Calculated control in a form or report, or as a calculation in a Visual Basic for Applications (VBA) procedure.

This calculation returns the difference between the dates as the number of days between the two dates. You can also use the DateDiff() function, which returns a part of the date, depending on the interval you provide for the function's first argument. The following table lists the possible interval entries. As an example of this function at work, you can enter **=DateDiff("yyyy",** [*first date field*]**,**[*second date field*]**)** as the Control Source property for an unbound control in a form or report. To display a different interval, replace "yyyy" with another entry from the following table.

Interval	Result
"yyyy"	The number of years difference between the two dates
"q"	The number of quarters difference between the two dates
"m"	The number of months difference between the two dates
"d"	The number of days difference between the two dates
"w"	The number of weekdays difference between the two dates
"ww"	The number of weeks difference between the two dates
"h"	The number of hours difference between the two dates
"n"	The number of minutes difference between the two dates
"s"	The number of seconds difference between the two dates

I regularly copy and paste the contents of Memo fields into e-mail messages, which are sent to others on our company network. Automating this process would be a real time-saver. Does an easy way exist to send the contents of a field as an e-mail message?

If you have a MAPI-compatible mail client (such as Microsoft Exchange or Microsoft Outlook) installed and configured to send mail from your workstation, you can do this from within Access, and with a minimal amount of VBA programming; a few lines of code attached to a button on a form is all it takes. You use the SendObject method, which sends data from Access in the form of an e-mail message. Figure 16-1 shows a form containing a Memo field with a command button added to send an e-mail message, along with the e-mail Message window that appears when the button is clicked.

You can use these steps to add a button that sends a field's contents in the form of an e-mail message:

1. Open the form in Design view that contains the field you want to send. Note the name of the text box containing the desired field.

2. In the Toolbox, turn off the Control Wizards, if they are turned on.

3. Use the Command Button tool in the Toolbox to add a command button to the form.

4. Right-click the button and choose Properties from the shortcut menu.

5. Click the Event tab in the Properties window that appears.

6. Click in the On Click property and then click the Build button (...) that appears at the right edge of the property.

7. Double-click Code Builder in the window that appears.

8. In the Module window that opens, enter the following code between the Private Sub and End Sub lines, which Access adds automatically. In the second line of code, substitute the name assigned to your text box for the name **Comments**. Note in the DoCmd statement that the commas represent arguments that are intentionally omitted, and that the exact number of commas shown is required.

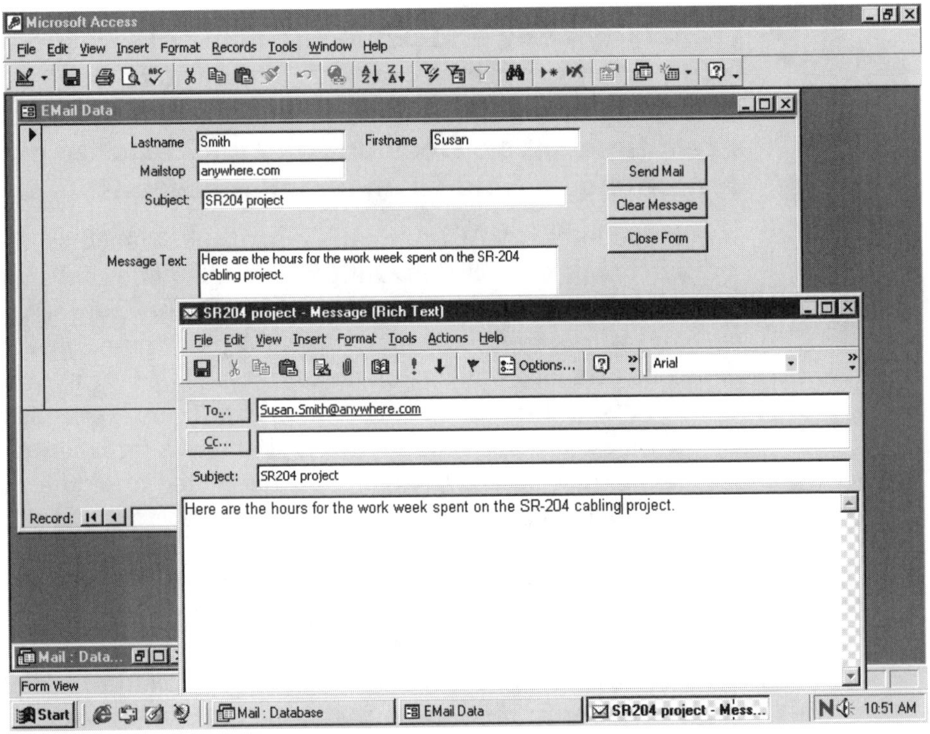

Figure 16-1 An e-mail message resulting from VBA code attached to a form's button

```
Dim MailMsg As String
MailMsg = "Comments: " & [Comments]
DoCmd.SendObject , , , , , , , MailMsg
```

9. Close the Module window and save the form.

When you open the form in Form view, locate a record, and then click the button you want to use, Access launches a Message window, using your installed e-mail package, and the contents of the field appear in the text of the e-mail message. Note that the SendObject method of VBA is successful only if either of the following is true:

● You have a MAPI-compatible e-mail application installed on your system.

● You have a VIM-compatible e-mail application and you have installed and set up Mapivim.dll, a Windows dynamic-link library (DLL) that supports the use of VIM-compatible e-mail systems with Microsoft Office applications.

For more specifics, consult the documentation for your e-mail package or talk to your network administrator.

How do I know when to use the exclamation point or the period in an expression?

Use the exclamation point before anything you can name yourself, and use a period before anything that Access names. For example, form names, report names, and control names have an exclamation point before them. Properties have a period.

How can I prevent a user from locking a record for an excessive period of time?

Access doesn't provide any table or form property to set a maximum record-lock interval, but you can simulate the effect by making your forms that are used for editing data close automatically after long periods of time. You can use the On Timer property of a form to close a form after a set time period, thus keeping users from leaving the form open. By including appropriate VBA code, you can display a message box that tells users why the form has closed. Use these steps:

1. Open the form in Design view or, if the form is already open, choose Edit | Select Form.

2. Choose Properties | View and click the Event tab in the Properties window.

3. In the Timer Interval property, enter a value, in milliseconds, for the length of time you want the form to remain open. (One second = 1,000 milliseconds, so if you want to limit to ten minutes the amount of time a form is open, you enter **600000**.)

4. Click the On Timer property and then click the Build button (...) to its right.

5. Double-click Code Builder in the dialog box that appears.

6. In the Module window that opens, enter the following code:

```
Private Sub Form_Timer()
        DoCmd.Close
        MsgBox("Maximum editing time exceeded.
Form closed.")
End Sub
```

7. Close the Module window and save the form.

When you open the form in Form view, it automatically closes after the specified time period, and the message is displayed.

One drawback to this technique is that if a user leaves a form open for a long time and then begins editing, the form may close while the user is in the midst of the editing process. If you use this approach, you need to warn your users that your forms close automatically. You also may want to provide another form without the timer event, strictly for the purpose of adding records, because the addition of multiple records might not be completed within a specific time period. In the Data tab of that form's Properties window, you can set the Allow Edits property to No, and set the Allow Additions property to Yes, so that users can use that form only for adding records.

 I've written an application in Access that I need to provide to multiple users. Can I do this without purchasing a copy of Access for each user?

You can do this with the run-time version of Access 2000, part of the Office 2000 Developer's Edition, which includes a Setup Wizard that packages your application along with an Access run-time executable (EXE) file that allows users to run your application without purchasing Access. These users can't create objects or change the design of any objects in your database, but they can run your application. You can find more specifics about the run-time version of Access 2000 in the documentation for Microsoft Office 2000, Developer's Edition.

 Can I start Microsoft Word and open a Word document from an Access application?

Yes, and it doesn't require any excessive amount of VBA programming. All you need is a macro containing a RunApp action. You can include the name of the document, including the path, as an argument for the Command line in the macro. Create a new macro and choose RunApp in the Action column. In the Command Line box under Action Arguments, type the following:

winword "c:*myfolder**docname.doc*"

where *c* represents the letter of your drive, *myfolder* is the folder name, and *docname.doc* represents the name of your Word document.

> ***Tip:*** *You can have the macro run when a button is clicked, by choosing the macro's name in the On Click property of the command button.*

How can I convert a number to its ordinal equivalent?

You can create a Function procedure that converts a number to a string with text such as "st" or "th" after it. To create this function, type the following into a module:

```
Function Ordinal(Num As Double)
Dim NumPart As String
'NumPart to contain the number's suffix
Ordinal = Num 'Assign the value of Num to Ordinal
If Num > 0 Then 'Add a cardinal suffix when Num > 0
NumPart = Right(Num, 1)
'Get the last digit from Num
Select Case Val(NumPart)
'Choose which suffix based on the last digit
Case 1
Ordinal = Num & "st"
'When Num = 1 Ordinal equals Num and "st"
Case 2
Ordinal = Num & "nd"
'When Num = 2 Ordinal equals Num and "nd"
Case 3
Ordinal = Num & "rd"
'When Num = 3 Ordinal equals Num and "rd"
Case Else
Ordinal = Num & "th"
'When Num = 4 Ordinal equals Num and "th"
End Select
```

```
End If
If Val(Right(Num, 2)) > 10 And Val(Right(Num, 2)) _
  < 14 Then
Ordinal = Num & "th"
'Replace 11st, 12nd and 13rd with 11th, 12th, & 13th
End If
End Function
```

In the Query or Control Source property, where you would usually refer to just the field, enter the following:

=Ordinal([*field name*])

This works only for numbers greater than zero. Any number less than one that is entered into the function is returned without modification. The following are examples of this procedure's output:

- =Ordinal(1) returns 1st
- =Ordinal(14) returns 14th
- =Ordinal(–23) returns –23

 How can I print a Word document from within Access?

You can handle this trick with a small amount of VBA coding. If you need to print the document in response to an event, open a new module and create the code as a Function procedure. Then, name the function in the property for the desired event. If you need to print the document as a result of clicking a command button, add the code between the Private Sub and End Sub lines that Access automatically places in the On Click property for the button. What follows is an example of the code you need. Substitute your actual filename and path for the C:\My Documents\letter1.doc example shown in this code:

```
Private Sub Command10_Click()
    Dim WordObj As Object
    Set WordObj = CreateObject("Word.Application")
    WordObj.Documents.Open "C:\My Documents\letter1.doc"
    WordObj.PrintOut Background:=False
    WordObj.Quit
    Set WordObj = Nothing
End Sub
```

 Note: *The preceding code assumes that you are using Word 2000 or Word 97. You cannot use this code with earlier versions of Word, because earlier versions use WordBasic rather than VBA as the programming language.*

How can I use a printer that's not in my list of available printers?

If the printer that you want to use doesn't appear in the Printers list box, you need to install it. Click the Start menu on the Windows taskbar and choose Settings | Printers. Double-click the Add Printer icon and then follow the instructions that appear in the Add Printer Wizard. (If you are running Access on Windows NT Workstation, see your Windows NT Workstation documentation for details on adding new printers.)

How can I round my numbers to a specific number of decimal places?

You can create a Round function that rounds a number to a set number of decimal places. If you have used rounding functions in spreadsheet applications, then you should be familiar with how to use this one. To create this function, type the following VBA code into a module:

```
Function Round(Value As Variant, Decimals As Integer)
If Decimals >= 0 Then
    Round = Int(Value * Decimals + 0.5) / Decimals
Else
    MsgBox ("Invalid amount of decimal places _
            supplied!")
    Round = Value
End If
End Function
```

You can use this procedure in a manner similar to how you use Access's built-in functions. In the query or control source where you usually refer only to the field, enter the following:

=Round([*number field name*],*x*)

where *number field name* represents the name of the number field you want to round, and *x* is a value of 10 for one decimal place, 100 for two decimal places, 1000 for three decimal places, and so on. For example, Round(123.45678,100) returns 123.46, and Round(87.654321,1000) returns 87.654.

Can I find the size of a text file in bytes?

You can create a procedure in VBA that opens text files and then uses the LOF function to return the file's size in bytes. For example, a procedure that performs this action on a text file named CONSTANT.TXT might look like this:

```
Function Size_Of_File()
Dim Filesize As Integer
Open "CONSTANT.TXT" For Input As #1
Filesize = LOF(1)
Close #1
Size_Of_File = Filesize
End Function
```

How can I speed up my Access database on my company's network?

You can take several different steps to accomplish this. Try any or all of these tips to improve the performance of your databases:

- *Run Performance Analyzer, to suggest possible improvements in the design of your various database objects.* To do this, choose Tools | Analyze | Performance. In the next dialog box that appears, use the tabs to display the various database objects, and click the check boxes to select the desired objects to analyze. Any suggestions that Performance Analyzer is able to make for improvements in design appear in dialog boxes.

- *Place only the tables on the network server.* Store the other database objects (queries, forms, reports, macros, and modules) on the users' local hard drives, and attach the objects from the local databases to the tables stored on the network server. This technique improves performance, because only the data needs to be retrieved across the network.

- *Avoid record-locking conflicts, by adjusting the Refresh Interval, Update Retry Interval, Number of Update Retries, and ODBC Refresh Interval settings.* Choose Tools | Options, click the Advanced tab, and change any settings that you want.

- *Where possible, open the database for exclusive use.* If the task you're performing with Access is being done by only one user at a time, open the database for exclusive use, even if the database file is stored on a network file server. Performance improves in such cases, because Access doesn't have to manage record-locking for the records in the tables. To open a database on a network for exclusive use, choose File | Open, click the drop-down arrow beside the Open button (in the lower-right area of the Open dialog box), and choose Open Exclusive from the menu.

- *If the workstations being used to run Access contain minimal amounts of memory (such as 16MB), consider upgrading the amount of memory.* Access will run significantly faster on a machine equipped with 32MB of RAM than on the same machine equipped with just 16MB of RAM.

Can I use a SQL statement as the record source for a form or report?

Yes, a form or report can get its data from a SQL statement. The form or report includes the same records as a query designed with the same SQL statement. You can type the SQL statement in the Record Source property of a form or report. You can also click the Build button (...) at the end of the property's field to open a Query Builder: SQL Statement window. In this window, you can use the QBE grid to create a query and view the results of its SQL statement. When the correct records are selected, close the window. Access places the SQL statement that represents the query into the Record Source property.

What's an easy way to view the query that a form or report is based on?

While in Design view for the form or report, open the Properties window and click the Data tab. If you click the

Record Source property, a Build button appears, marked only by an ellipsis (a set of three periods). If you click the Build button, the query on which the report or form is based opens in Design view.

TROUBLESHOOTING

 My computer has the Advanced Power Management (APM) feature built in. When it switches to Suspend mode after inactivity and then I restart it, Access displays the message "This program has performed an illegal operation and will be shut down." Why is this happening?

This problem occurs on hardware with the APM feature when Access has been installed by using the Run From Server option of the Setup program. A Run From Server installation of Access results in most program files used by Access being stored on the network file server. When the APM feature puts a computer into Suspend mode, network server connections are lost. When you bring the computer out of Suspend mode, Access crashes, because it has lost the connection with program files that are needed for normal operation.

The only way to avoid this problem is to either disable the APM Suspend feature (see your computer's operating manual for details) or install Access locally (on your hard disk) by using the Typical or Custom installation of the Setup program. Also, if you connect to the network regularly, using the APM feature of your computer isn't a wise choice, because it will cause problems with all types of Windows programs that rely on communicating with files stored on the network.

When entering data in a form, why do I get the error message "Microsoft Access can't find the macro '.'"?

Someone has inadvertently typed one or more spaces into an Event property for either a control on the form or the form itself. You have to open the form in Design view, look in the Properties window, find the property that contains one or more spaces, and delete them.

If the error occurs when you open the form, check the On Load, On Open, and On Current properties for the form, and check the On Enter property for the first control in the form that gets the focus. If the error occurs as you move into a control or change data in a control, check the On Focus, Before Update, and After Update properties for the control. If the error occurs when you try to save a record, check the Before Update and After Update properties for the form. If you still can't find any extra spaces, go to each property that is blank and press the DEL key.

I have 32MB of RAM installed. Why do I continually get "Out of memory" errors when no programs other than Office's Shortcut Bar are running while I'm using Access?

This message appears not only when you run low on overall memory, but also any time you run low on system resources. This was a far more common problem in Windows 3.x, but with complex Access applications, you still can tax the resources under newer versions of Windows. If you're sure you have no other applications open, check for a large number of graph objects that may be open due to charts present in your forms or reports. Microsoft Graph, the mini-application used to create charts within Access, is quite a resource hog. If you open multiple charts, you can quickly deplete all available resources. Also, note that under Windows 95 and Windows 98, this error can occur after you have been in and out of numerous applications throughout the day, due to fragmentation of system resources. If this is the case, the solution is to shut down and restart Windows.

Index

NOTE: Page numbers in *italics* refer to illustrations or charts.

To **speak to the support experts** who handle more than one million technical issues every month, call **Stream's** Microsoft® Access® answer line! Trained specialists will answer your Microsoft® Access® questions including setup, queries, forms, reports, printing and Wizards.

Have all your questions been answered?

1-800-866-7166 $34.95 per problem (Charge to a major credit card.)

1-900-555-2008 $34.95 per problem (Charge to your phone bill.)

Visit our web site at www.stream.com.

We help people use technology!